MW00416332

at the corner of

MUSIC ROW and Memory Lane

50 years of music memories and the stars who made them

by Stan Hitchcock

(Music up, stage lights down, single spot on singer, big finish. . . stage black)

ISBN — 10: 0-615-27020-4
ISBN — 13:978-0-615-27020-3
Library of Congress Control Number: 2009923121

SPECIAL COLLECTORS' EDITION

AT THE CORNER OF MUSIC ROW. . . And Memory Lane
by Stan Hitchcock
www.hitchcockcountry.com

Art Direction by McClearen Design Studios, Nashville, TN
www.mcclearendesign.com

10 9 8 7 6 5 4 3 2 1

INTRODUCTION -

IF I HAVE WOUNDED ANY SOUL TODAY, IF I HAVE CAUSED SOME FOOT TO GO ASTRAY, IF I HAVE WALKED IN MY OWN WILLFUL WAY. . .

An Evening Prayer. . . C.M Battersby/C.H.Gabriel 1939

Dear Friends and Neighbors,

Let me explain what it is you are about to read, (an important point when trying to suck up to the readers, so they will think you really know what you are talking about.) so you will know where I am coming from,

I know that there are a lot of books out there that tell the stories of the music business and that they are written by professional writers. But you know, we all see it through different eyes, and the way that it affects our lives and how we interact with events is unique. This is what encouraged me to tell my story.

This book is just a bunch of my memories, some good, some bad, but they all mean a lot to me. Because I have spent most of my life trying to share my innermost feelings with folks like you, from a stage, a radio or a television set, I figured, shoot, why stop now? Go on and spill your guts, hillbilly. So I did.

This journal does not try to exaggerate or paint a pretty picture of the entertainment business of which I have been a part of for forty- six years, since plain reality sometimes seems bigger than life.

I have often thought that I would like to tell it like it is. But you don't want to portray your friends or yourself in a bad light. And it's hard to be objective when you reach into memory and try to pull events out for the retelling.

The stories about these people are true as I see them, but certainly could be different from their point of view. With this in mind, I have tried my best to write without judgment, but rather to portray the colors, the smells, and the sounds that are still so sharp in my memory. I want to share what it was like to be there in the early days, to experience our musical history, and to tell it in the language of the music business.

I have made no effort to talk any differently than if you and I were sitting in my living room, in front of a slow burning fire, with a good glass of wine to share and a few old stories to tell. The language is a mixture of Ozark, Tennessean and show biz, and sometimes it comes out odd. But so be it. That's just the way I speak.

It is my hope that as you read this account, you will feel the love that I hold for these people, and the love I still hold for the music that has been such a part of me.

You'll notice song titles and phrases at the beginning of chapters: they bob up as I search my memory. My brain is so saturated with music that it is sometimes hard to put the pieces of the puzzle together. But finding a favorite line recalls a cherished incident or thought.

So many of the trailbreakers of our music are gone: Red, Ernest, Bill, Roy, Minnie, and Webb. Just today I have been remembering the life of Owen Bradley. While attending his memorial services, a few years ago, I listened to the orchestra playing the hits of Ernest Tubb, Webb Pierce, Patsy Cline, Conway Twitty, Loretta Lynn, Jack Greene, and Brenda Lee, and I recalled the work of this great record producer, musician, arranger, studio builder and businessman. It made me proud just to be in the same industry that this fine man helped to pioneer.

Owen once said, "When you find yourself going to more funerals than weddings, you know you are getting old." Well, I've been going to too many funerals lately, and it tends to make me hearken to the days of my youth.

Let me take you back to another time, another age, back to the people that really set the foundation for this music we all love, and let me share some of the inside stories, the insights and outa-sights that happened to one man, in hot pursuit of a dream.

Stan Hitchcock
Desha Creek Farm
Gallatin, Tennessee

FOR THE LOVE OF THE MUSIC

THE PEACH FESTIVAL. . . Gaffney, Carolina. . . August 1990

The crowd was going wild as I watched the young Oklahoma singer working the crowd in front of the stage. He had jumped down and was walking among them singing his new hit, squeezing the hands of young women reaching out for him, kissing one on the cheek as he launched into the chorus of his new song: "Yes, I've got friends in low places. . ." I told my Beta Cam shooter to get in close. . . this was good stuff. "Get a close- up of the girls in the front row!" Man, this kid was turning them on. The barber boom operator swung his camera high over the crowd and got a good shot of Garth Brooks as he worked his magic. Yeah, this kid might just make it big, all right. He's got a fair voice, and he's kinda chunky, but he's got something that the folks seem to love.

I let my mind drift back to the seven years leading up to this night of producing the series "CMT Roadshow". Boy, it had been quite a chore bringing the network to the point where we could go out and actually produce original programming, but by golly we were doing it and I was having a ball. I had brought my production crew, along with Shenandoah, The Reno Brothers and the new kid, Garth Brooks, over to Gaffney to work the Peach Festival, an annual event that was really a lot of fun for the entertainers and drew a crowd of several thousand people each year.

I had headed up the creative side of CMT since its startup in 1984, working hard to get the recording industry behind the channel and grow the business into the international force that I knew it could be. We were finally turning the corner to profitability and I had started expanding the programming to include concerts, a weekly count-down show, world premiere videos, viewer promotion contests and my own weekly show "Heart to Heart," which featured my artist friends gathering on the front porch of an old log cabin and picking a little, telling a few stories and swapping a few songs. It looked like this network was going to work, after years of scraping by, operating with very little money and only the love of the music to keep us going.

The artists had been the first ones to get it. They realized that I was providing a window for them, and they were busy kicking out the window and making it into a door to reach a younger audience than country music had ever been able to reach before. Just like the boys in Shenandoah and Garth Brooks, CMT was their springboard, and they were loving it.

I was jerked out of my day-dreaming by a security guard from back stage grabbing my arm and shouting in my ear over the music: "Phone call back behind stage. . . they say it's real important!" I turned the production over to my assistant and followed the guard to the backstage phone. I stuck the phone up to my ear and tried to hear through the roar of the crowd what the person on the other end was saying. Finally I realized it was one of the investors and board members of Country music Television, CMT, James William Guercio, and he was saying "Gotta come on back to Nashville - - we're selling the network".

I stood there with the phone dangling from my hand. . . kinda numb all over. It had been a heck of a night. I had experienced the birth of the next super-star in American music, Garth Brooks, and I had just been sold out by a couple of big money guys that had a whole different agenda for investing in my dream network. While I was out chasing the music, they took the money and quietly walked away. I hearkened back to the Kenny Rogers song. . . "You got to know when to hold them, know when to fold them, know when to walk away, know when to run." Man, I didn't feel much like walking or running away. I just felt empty. So close we were, so close to what I had been working for in the music business most of my life, so close I could almost touch it. . . as Garth hit the closing line. . . "I got friends, in lo-o-o-w places!" Ain't it the truth though?

It seemed so far back to those years, growing up in the Ozark Mountains, when life was sweet and innocent. You were surrounded by people you could trust, no matter what, and music was simply your way of communicating joy, love, worship, heartache and loneliness. . . not something you used to leverage yourself into a position to make a few more millions, no matter who you had to step on to do it.

As the crowd screamed out. . . "Garth. . . Garth. . . Garth!" I slowly hung up the phone and turned to go back out in the middle of the storm of emotion that was radiating from these happy fans. Once more I was reminded that no matter what happened, for me, it would always be for the love of the music.

Stan & Garth Brooks
Heart to Heart Shoot CMT 1990

SPECIAL COLLECTORS' EDITION
Stan Hitchcock

SECTION I

SECTION II
The Early Years

SECTION III
WELCOME TO THE SEVENTIES

SECTION IV
1980'S THE LATER NASHVILLE YEARS
THE CROSSROADS

EPILOGUE

SECTION V

Ruby (Mom), Stan, Big Stan (Dad)
1938

chapter 1

My Ozark Mountain Valley Home

Hillbilly singers are just born that'a way. . . they's got the love of the music in 'em. . . they can't hep it. . . hit's just the way they are.

Ozark Native explanation

Memories of a life, that used to be
Those boyhood days are calling out to me. . .

Stan Hitchcock

Lord knows I didn't ever intend to be a guitar pickin', nasal singin', road hoggin', honky-tonkin' sorry old hillbilly singer. . . no sir, not me. . . I was gonna grow up and be somebody.

I had the greatest childhood that anyone could ask for, growing up on the farm near Pleasant Hope, Missouri, just fourteen miles from Springfield, and right in the heart of the Ozark Mountains. We had 400 acres, lots of woods to hunt in, a creek that run right through our property, a bunch of cows and horses and I reckon it was just about right for raising up boys. I was the oldest of three boys, five years older than my next brother Danny, and fourteen years older than my youngest brother Sammy.

My folks, Big Stan and Ruby Ann were just the best, giving lots of love and attention. But they didn't cut much slack in the way of foolishness. However, by trying real hard I was able to bring a level of foolishness into the family and somehow get away with it, at least some of the time.

My Dad was a powerful man, both physically and spiritually, and I never saw him react in anger, except once. I was about ten years old and Dad had done some custom farm work for a man who had a farm close to us, and a reputation as a guy who would get to you if he could. Well, Dad went to collect his money and took me with him, and when we got to the man's house he came to the door, about half drunk and belligerent to boot. He started wrangling with Dad, and was not going to pay him what he owed him, and cussing and carrying on. Dad was taking it pretty calm, until the man reached down and picked up a piece of firewood, and made like he was going to strike Dad with it. My Dad looked him in the eye, and I'll never forget his words, "Mr. Witt, if you hit me with that, God is gonna whip you, and He may use me as the weapon." Mr. Witt saw the wisdom in paying the bill, in full.

I started singing around Mom's old piano when I was about nine years old. I don't know why, maybe a birth defect or something, but I've been doing it, in some form or fashion ever since. Next came PTA meetings, the New Salem Methodist Church, and the New Hope Baptist Church, singing on Sunday nights (we attended both, just to be sure). On the fateful day when I turned twelve years old, I decided to learn to play the guitar (as if singing wasn't bad enough).

When Dad bought me my first guitar at Ike Martin's Music Store, a youth model Gretsch flattop with a neck that felt like a two by four to my young hands, it just kinda set the stage for the rest of my life.

Throwed in with the purchase of the guitar was a couple of month's worth of guitar lessons upstairs in the old storeroom of the music store. I remember the nice man who taught guitar, Efton Allen, asking me Did I want to learn to pick lead guitar, note for note, or did I want to learn chords to accompany myself when I sang? Without hesitation: "Teach me the chords so I can play while I sing." Efton was the son of Chick Allen, a legendary Ozark character who made music down in the hills on an instrument he created out of the jawbone of an ass (donkey), and he had a gentle spirit and a lot of natural guitar ability.

From the first day that guitar became my best friend. I slept with it, drug it around everywhere I went, and within three weeks I could play "Wildwood Flower" and play a couple of Roy Acuff songs and sing just like him (I thought).

I came from folks who both loved music, Dad had a great singing voice and Mom sang and played the piano and taught me my first songs. I also had an uncle Bud who played guitar and sang, an aunt Betty who played piano and sang and a great-aunt Dot, who lived in Arkansas and could wear a piano out and sing great old folk songs. There was always music in our home, so it was just a natural part of my life.

Religion and music was always a part of my life, and even today I have a hard time separating the two. I still get a special feeling singing a good old gospel song.

At twelve years old, I not only learned to play guitar, but I also accepted The Lord Jesus as my savior, the single most important decision I will ever make.

We were having a revival at New Hope Baptist Church, and I knew that I wanted Jesus to come into my life, just like He promised in John 3:16 of Mom's Old King James. I went home with the folks from church, got into my bed and lay there thinking it all out. I crawled out of bed, knelt down on the floor and ask God to save me. And, of course, He did. One thing you can be sure of: God don't lie. When He promises you something, you can book it.

I wish I could say that from then on out I served Jesus, obeyed His commandments and lived a sin-free life. Yeah, I wish. No, like most people, I have slipped and slid a lot during my adult life. But I never have doubted that Jesus loved me, and that even with all my faults and weaknesses, I am a child of the King.

You see, God never asks for perfection, He takes us, warts and all, and is ever willing to forgive us our mistakes if we'll only ask Him. And friends, I've had to ask Him a lot.

- Old Homeplace, in the Ozarks -
painting by Stan Hitchcock

chapter 2

The Ozarks Mountains is not Just a Place, it's a way of Life. . .

Stan Hitchcock

"...going so fast I can't stop. . . just a stones throw from Little Rock, heading for that Missouri line."
"Ozark Mountain Jubilee"
- written by Roger Murrah

To understand the meaning of the above statement, let me take you back to the 30's and 40's and explain a little of the history of the Ozarks. First of all, the Ozarks was a wild land that even the Indians only visited for hunting, fishing and other necessities of life. You would need to go back to the cave-man days to find people who actually lived here for long periods of time. Isolated would be a good description of the terrain, and that very character of the Ozarks Mountains drew a particular class of settler, adventurer, pioneer. . . or outlaw. The phrase "You can't hardly get there from here" was coined about the Ozarks.

In the early 1800's, deep in the Ozarks in that area bridging Southern Missouri and Northern Arkansas, all you would find would be some renegade Indians who had slipped off from the Trail Of Tears and settled temporarily along some of the waterways of the White River, a few ragged old trappers and hunters, and some outcasts who were too mean to live anywhere else.

What started the influx of real settlers was the feeling, back in Appalachia, that "By golly things are just getting too settled and close in these mountains. I just saw the smoke of another's chimney on the far mountain and I reckon it's time to move on." The Scotch-Irish settlers who had populated Tennessee, Kentucky, North and South Carolina, Georgia and parts of Alabama started looking for just what the Ozarks had a lot of: Isolation. As the wagons started moving west, and they happened to pass through the edge of the Ozarks, a certain class of pioneer was drawn to the deep hollers, clear streams, and the uninhabited space that was in great abundance.

My mother's people, the Wallis Family, came to the Ozarks from Tennessee and settled on Boat Mountain, near Valley Springs, Arkansas, in the mid-1800's. The Wallis clan is an interesting study, made up of equal parts Baptist preacher and hard whiskey moonshiner. I don't find that particularly confusing, since both professions are dealing in the same subject, sin: one side preaching against it and the other side eggin' it on.

The Ozarks, up until about the 1960's, was the last frontier of living off the land: a "I don't need no government help, mind your own business," "Iffen I cain't make hit my own self, I prolly didn't need hit anyway" attitude. In other words: just good old American individualism. Electricity came to the Ozarks decades after it was commonplace in other areas, and in the area where I grew up around Pleasant Hope, Missouri. We still didn't have access to telephone lines when I left for the Navy in 1954. The very notion of isolation gave a great importance to being neighbors. Sharing work in the harvest time, coming to call when someone was sick, looking out for each other and a genuine love for your neighbor was a way of life.

I get a kick out of the tourists that started coming to the Ozarks in the 40's, 50's and 60's. They would drive by one of the native Ozarks home places and see what they considered trash all around the house and barns. They would laugh and joke about the Ozarks hillbillies with all the old cars up on concrete blocks around the yard and pasture. What they do not understand is that to the native Ozarkian, who has had to "make do" for generation after generation, the old worn out hulk of a car is not trash; it's a spare parts resource. I know old-timers who had every vehicle that they had ever owned, still somewhere on their property, maybe 50 years worth of driving history, and every one full of memories and usable parts. Nope, that stuff is not trash, that is 'Ozarks net worth.'

Church doin's, front porch pickin' and singin', bidding on the neighbor girl's cake at the cake and pie sale, skinny-dippin' in the clean creek water, the threshing crew sitting down at your mama's table after a hard morning's work in the field, squirrel hunting up on the ridge, getting old enough to drive the tractor for the first time, families all sitting down for supper and saying grace and really being thankful. . . all a way of life that you can build a manhood with.

A good place to grow up, move away from and miss for the rest of your life.

Stan, age 13
Pleasant Hope Grade School Picture

chapter 3

I Could Have Been a Child Prodigy But Ma Wouldn't Let Me

MAMAS DON'T LET YOUR BABIES GROW UP TO BE COWBOYS
. . .JESUS LOVES ME THIS I KNOW,
and other songs, I didn't write.
Ed Bruce. . . Anna B. Warner

This was the late 40's and early 50's, I was just reaching puberty and radio was king. I don't know if there was any connection or not, but those love songs were starting to have new meaning, particularly local radio which always had great live shows in the early morning, at noon and then in late afternoon. I was very fortunate to grow up near Springfield, Missouri which had one of America's great radio stations KWTO, 560 on the dial, and an ever-changing stable of nationally known entertainers to expose a gawky, bucktooth country kid like me to the world of show biz.

Country entertainers all across the United States were traveling from radio station to radio station, working the broadcasts for free, or nearly so, to have the opportunity to book out at the school houses and just about any other building that would hold a crowd, charge 25 to 50 cents admission and sell song books, picture books, baby chicks, patent medicines and other assorted items on the radio shows, scratching out a living; then moving on to the next station in a different part of the country. Little Jimmy Dickens was moving from a West Virginia station to a station in Topeka, Kansas; Hank Thompson was on the air in Waco, Texas; Bob Wills was on KVOO in Tulsa; Hank Williams was doing a morning show on WSM in Nashville; Carl Smith was working a station in Knoxville; Red Foley was leaving WLS in Chicago and moving to Nashville to join the Opry and head up the NBC radio network show sponsored by Prince Albert Smoking Tobacco. And down in Shreveport on KWKH you could hear Webb Pierce, Faron Young and Johnny Horton on the Louisiana Hayride. Disc jockeys had not risen to prominence yet. It was live radio, and it was great.

Springfield's KWTO radio had live shows with the Carter Family (Mother Maybelle, June, Anita and Helen); Chet Atkins was playing guitar with them and starting to make a name for himself. Then you had The Browns, Porter Wagoner, Bobby Lord, Jimmy Gateley and Harold Morrison, The Goodwill Family, Slim Wilson, Speedy Haworth, Tommy Sosbee, Hawkshaw Hawkins, Shorty Thompson and a host of local talent that was almost as good. On top of that, KWTO started a transcription radio service and syndicated shows all across the country and brought in Tennessee Ernie Ford, Eddy Arnold, George Morgan, Smiley Burnette and just about every other big country star that was working radio at that time.

Well, I'd been playing guitar and singing for about a year when I entered a talent contest, at Ike Martin's Music Store, which was broadcast on KWTO radio and hosted by the top star in the area, Porter Wagoner. I won first place and got to appear on a couple of other shows on the air. Slim Wilson, the bandleader and host of several shows, called me over and asked if my folks would let me travel with his show and do personal appearances. I was thirteen years old, and boy, was I excited! I couldn't wait to tell the folks! Uh-oh, bad mistake. Well, you would have thought I had asked to go to the moon. Mom threw a hissy fit and stated in no uncertain terms that I wasn't about to go off with a bunch of musicians and sing around. If I wanted to sing, I could sing in church like decent folks, and that was that. So, at a very tender age, my show biz career came to a screeching halt.

Well, my early career might have been short lived, but my love of the music just kept getting stronger. My room, on the farm, was upstairs in the converted attic, and I was permanently attached to the little radio that set on the table next to my bed. Every night I would climb under the mountain of covers on my bed, necessary because the upstairs was unheated, turn the radio to WSM and listen to Eddie Hill on the All Night Show. "Squall and bawl, and run up the wall, and holler good morning everybody!" Eddie had the dangedest line of radio lingo and entertainment business savvy of anyone I had ever heard of. He was the father of the all night country music radio shows, and as far as I'm concerned no one has ever come close to reaching his level of radio entertainment.

Eddie was an East Tennessee native and had started in radio in Knoxville, doing live shows with Johnny and Jack and Kitty Wells, Johnny's wife, and a young guitar player named Chester Atkins. Eddie was a fine singer, and great rhythm guitar player, but his greatest talent was on that mike, just talking to the folks and playing that great country music that he loved.

I look back on those years in the late forties and early fifties as my country music higher education, with Eddie Hill as my teacher. He was on six nights a week, coming on at ten o'clock during the week, and then following the Grand Ole Opry and the Ernest Tubb Record Shop on Saturday night. While I didn't know it then, Eddie would play a large part in my life for years to come.

When I was sixteen I met a boy by the name of David Wilhite, the son of dairy farmers in Strafford, Missouri. He had a steel guitar that he could do pretty good on, so along with my old flat top and singing voice, we became pretty hot at private parties, cake walks, revivals, back yard cookouts, snake killings and possum roasts. By the way, if you have never tried roast possum, well, don't bother; it is undoubtedly the worst tasting, greasy, stinking mess I ever took a bite of. I'd just as soon eat a cat. However, in all fairness, the lowly possum and sweet taters from the garden helped many an Ozark family get through the Great Depression of the twenties. Old timers say that the Depression 'bout wiped out the possum, rabbit, coon, and squirrel population in the hills and it took years for them to replenish.

I continued to sing in church and at all the school functions through my high school years and became accepted as the local 'voice', but it was just something I did, with no special significance and certainly no aspirations of becoming a professional singer.

However, something did happen in the high school chorus that should have given me a clue. Our chorus was competing in the regional music festival and we were doing pretty good it seemed. I was on the front row just singing my heart out, and when we finished we were all pretty excited waiting for our score. Well, the score came back and it was pretty disappointing so the music teacher, Mrs. Carver, went to the judges and asked about it. She came back, pretty steamed up, and said we lost points because the kid in the front row, (me), was singing too loud and patting his foot real strong: two of the attributes that made Hank Williams famous, but was not cool in the school chorus. Oh well, you can't make a living being a professional school chorus singer anyway, so the heck with it.

I always marvel at the folks who say they always knew what they were going to be and do in life. Me, I never had a clue. Every day was a new adventure, a new challenge and a new direction, and you know what? It still is. I start off every day with, "Good morning, Lord, what are we going to do today?" I don't necessarily think this is bad, and I can sure tell you one thing: it's never been boring.

Stan and his little
brother Sam, 1952

Stan with his '48
Chevy Fleetline
Dream Car
(photo in 1953)

Pleasant Hope High School

This Certifies That

Stanley Edward Hitchcock

has satisfactorily completed the Course of Study prescribed by the Board of Education for the High School Department and is therefore entitled to this

Diploma

Given at Pleasant Hope, Missouri, this 6th *day of* May *A.D. 19*54

SUPERINTENDENT

PRESIDENT BOARD OF EDUCATION

SECRETARY BOARD OF EDUCATION

Pleasant Hope
High School Diploma
1954

chapter 4

Memories of Growing Up In Polk County Missouri

WELL, THERE GOES CANDY APPLE RED, that's what the people said, If he doesn't slow it down a bit he's gonna wind up dead...
Stan Hitchcock - Epic Records 1964

As I said earlier, I managed to bring a certain level of foolishness to our little family, but I probably excelled in the area of foolish driving more than anything else. I saved my money from working in the hay fields one summer, and when I was 15 bought my first car, a 1936 Pontiac sedan, for the grand total of $150. Three months later I wrecked it in a head-on collision while I was playing bumper tag with another friend, Bucky Goss and his folk's car, with the lights off on a gravel road. It was kinda like hide-and-seek except it really hurt when I got found. I still have a scar cutting through my eyebrow where the wing window frame creased my skull. Loretta Noe, riding next to Bucky in the front seat of his folks' car, had a bad cut on her knee where it hit the dashboard ashtray. Denny Wright got a bloody nose and Jon Glenn got a heck of a bump on the head from hitting my windshield. My old Gretsch guitar flew all over the back seat, but survived to play again.

We were about two miles out of Pleasant Hope when we had the wreck and I ran all the way in to get help, just scared to death. We had an osteopath doctor in town that was just one step up from a witch doctor and I still remember him putting four stitches in my eyebrow, without deadening it at all.

That wreck, and us boys putting the manure spreader on the School Principals front porch on Halloween night, was the big events of that year, 1951, which tells you how exciting those Ozark hills could be.

A year later Dad bought me a '39 Ford Sedan, paying all of $300 for that one. It was a cool car, but I couldn't keep it running. When it would go on the blink, I would borrow Dad's car or truck and do equal damage to his transportation. One night, coming home from church, I took a curve on the gravel road too fast and turned the farm truck over on top of a barbed wire fence. The crash ran the fence posts through the steel body of the truck and the barbed wire wrapped around it like a spider wrapping up a grasshopper in its web. I like to have never got out of that thing since one of the fence posts came right through the cab and stopped about an inch from my head. . . I've still got barbed wire scars on my body.

Finally, when I was a senior, in 1953, I bought my dream car: a 1948 Chevy Fleetline. This was the 50's and I was hog wild over my car. I got a mechanic friend to split the manifold on the six cylinder engine, I bought a bunch of flex pipe and hangers and hooked up the darndest set of twin pipes you have ever heard. . . I'll swear you could hear those pipes backing off coming down the hill about 5 miles from our house: music to mine ears. I put two inch lowering blocks on the back springs, but that wasn't low enough, so I piled about ten concrete blocks back in the trunk and, man, it set just right. It was painted candy apple red and I still have dreams about it sometimes. It was a beautiful thing.

You baby-boomers will never know what you missed not growing up in the 50's, go on, eat your hearts out. You know this was before the free love bullcrap of the 60's, the drug-outs of the 70's, and all the craziness of the 80's.

Yeah, we just sat real low, scrunched down in the driver's seat, and circled the drive-in with the girl that looked just like Natalie Wood while we pretended we were James Dean.

That worked out OK until the night I backed up and ran over a carhop at the Corral Drive-In, and who just happened to be carrying a whole tray of root beer floats at the time. Well I didn't exactly run over her, I more or less run into her with the rear end of my car. Oh friends, it was an awful sight what a whole tray of them big root beer mugs can do to the back of a lowered, piped, moon hubcapped, candy apple red dream car. Worse yet, the ice cream melted and ran down through the cracks around the trunk, mixed with the concrete blocks and old sweat socks and a week later you have never smelled anything quite like it. Anyway, the girl was bruised and embarrassed and it flat ruined my chances of picking her up after work some night. Ah, romance, so fickle.

You know, it sounds kinda corny now, but all those high school years when I was courtin', I would carry my guitar in the back seat of my old car, go out on the back roads and up by the creek, park that car, whip out my guitar and sing to the girl. Pretty wild, huh? Deep kissing, mild petting, heavy breathing, windows steaming up: just like in the movies, and me singing the sound track.

If I could give something magic to my sons, I would give them the innocence of a boy growing up in the 50's, so they could experience that uncomplicated, sweet time that we will never see again: where dope was never heard of, sexual preference was all hetero, of course, virginity an accepted virtue. It was still all right to want to grow up and be President, you could call a waitress honey and not be slapped with a lawsuit and the skies were not cloudy all day. Does kinda sound unreal, now looking back, but that was life in the back roads. Fast lanes hadn't been invented yet.

Stan at 18 leaving for the Navy with his friend Paul Covey 1954

ARMED FORCES LIBERTY PASS	SERVICE USN	DATE ISSUED 14 FEB 56
LAST NAME—FIRST NAME—MIDDLE INITIAL HITCHCOCK, Stanley E.		CARD NO. 067 -2
SERVICE NO. 749 97 8	GRADE—RATE SN	
ORGANIZATION—INSTALLATION—BASE USS BRYCE CANYON (AD-36)		
TIME LIMITS REGULAR LIBERTY		
SIGNATURE AND GRADE OF ISSUING OFFICER J. H. SHEARER, LTJG, USNR		

DD(N)-345 1 April 1950 16—63060-1 GPO

chapter 5

Anchors Away

. . .put a capo on the third fret, G position, and hit it boys

In the middle 50's the folks at KWTO, Si Siman, Ralph Foster, John Mahaffey, Don Richardson and a whole raft of stars, lead by Red Foley, started a show that was to become a legend in country music: the "Ozark Jubilee," in Springfield, Missouri. ABC television picked the show up and broadcast it around the country, and the music boom was on in the Ozarks.

Just about the time they started this show that could have been such a great opportunity for a young singer like me, a kid who had just graduated from Pleasant Hope High School, I made a spur of the moment career move and joined the Navy.

The Korean War was just winding down and I felt so patriotic, and besides I never had been anywhere out of these hills and I wanted to see the world. See, I told you I didn't have any ideas of being a singing star. Boy, did I miss one boat and take another, or what?

Another swift move was joining the Navy in the month of September which put me going through boot camp at Great Lakes Naval Training Center just outside of Chicago, in the middle of the winter, 1954.

I'm sure that I still have scars deep inside from standing the midnight watch detail in December, it being 10 below zero, and having to guard the big Dempsey dumpster, just outside the barracks, from enemy attack. Well, as usual I did my best and sure enough I kept the enemy away from our trash, but man, it wasn't easy. If I hadn't had my guitar along during those months, I don't know how I would have made it. And, you know, that's kinda how my whole life has been, a simple piece of wood with 6 metal strings has got me through some mighty lonely times.

By this time I had upgraded to a J45 Gibson flat top, for you folks keeping score, and it was a fine piece of work, sweet sounding, yet with a full and vigorous voice.

Graduating from boot camp in January 1955, I got assigned to the ship that would be my home, and more, for the next three years. I rode a train from Chicago to San Diego, California: man, what exciting times for an 18-year-old, green, beanpole-skinny kid from the Ozarks. I really got to realize my dream of being on that old train that I used to listen to in my upstairs room on the farm: that lonesome whistle raising goose bumps on my arm. . . and now I enjoyed the thrill of actually going somewhere, warm and secure wrapped inside that steel hull speeding across the country.

When we finally got to San Diego to change trains, I took my first breath of California air, and decided I was gonna like being a world traveler. Yessir, this was the life. I loaded my sea bag aboard the new train and headed up the coast for San Francisco to meet my ship and get serious about this Navy business.

When I walked up the dock at Mare Island in San Francisco and set eyes on my first ship, the U.S.S. Bryce Canyon (AD-36), well, it was just unbelievable. The darn thing was big as our whole farm! It carried more men than we had in our entire county back home. There just isn't any way to describe those first few weeks aboard ship, after never being anywhere or around very many people. I just soaked up knowledge like a sponge; I loved it.

Not very long after coming aboard I started meeting other guys who played music, and by the time we left San Francisco for the Far East, we had put us a band together. I use the term 'band' rather loosely, but what we lacked in talent we more than made up for with enthusiasm. We had a big old boy from Kentucky playing the stand-up dog house bass by the name of Smoky, a kid from Minnesota who played a Chet Atkins electric Gretsch guitar named Roger, a guy named Pee Wee who played a fine fiddle and taught me a lot about being a man and doing the right thing, even if it was at the wrong time, another guy who played banjo and mandolin, and myself singing and playing rhythm guitar. Ladies and gentlemen, may I present: THE BRYCE CANYON TROUBADOURS.

Every night, before the movie, we would set up on the mid-hatch on the main deck and just play our butts off. Great training for a guy who didn't ever expect to do it for a living, and you talk about a captive audience, what are they gonna do, swim away? As it turned out, this time of playing music with these particular fellows probably had more impact on my later music career than anything else ever would. Those nights of playing, under that big moon shining on the Pacific Ocean, well, it was just great, and still one of my fondest memories. However, something happened that almost put an end to my picking, before I even got started.

About three weeks out at sea, we were all standing in loose formation on the main deck, going through morning roll call, when this guy standing next to me asked to see my knife. Every man in the deck force of the ship had to carry a knife, and keep it razor sharp, and I was proud of mine, so I said "Sure," and handed it to him. Well, he commenced to go crazy, just completely flipped his lid, and came at me with my own knife. I threw up my left hand to catch the knife before it cut my nose off, and it cut down through my first and second fingers almost to the middle of my hand - - just split it like splitting firewood. The other guys grabbed him and wrestled him to the deck and the last I saw of him they were dragging him off to the brig. My hand was a mess, and I was just sure I would never play again, but twenty stitches later, and a bottle of pain pills, and I was almost good as new. I never did find out what prompted the flip-out, and the subsequent cutting, but to this day I can't make bar chords on my guitar. My little keepsake from the old Navy days.

USS Bryce Canyon
the Ship Stan served on from 1954-1957

chapter 6

Picking Up Hookers, Instead of My Pen, I Let the Words of my Youth Slip Away

MY HEROES HAVE ALWAYS BEEN COWBOYS. . . and they still are it seems. . . I always loved that song. (Thanks Sharon, for writing it)

. . .Sharon Vaughn

From the time we went under the Golden Gate Bridge to when we arrived in the Philippines, I was sick as a dog. Yep, the kid had seasickness and I was pretty sure it was terminal. Even though I was a walking casualty, I still managed to sing every night. As long as I was holding that guitar I was all right. About a month later, we pulled into Subic Bay, Philippines.

Now you already know I was a green kid, very naive, raised up strict: even, you might say, the very breath of innocence (okay, maybe not that goody-two- shoes, but close) and the old salts on the ship decided it was time to break me in to the finer things in life.

The second night in port, in Subic Bay, about five of the old timers invited me to go on the "beach" with them and they'd show me around this hellhole. Now friends, if you haven't had the pleasure of visiting Subic Bay, Philippines, back in the 50's, well you just wouldn't believe the poverty these people lived in.

Seems like the Navy has a special talent for finding these places to build their bases, and you know, after a month at sea, anywhere that had dirt under your feet was mighty fine.

Well, back to the tale. The old salts took me over in town and we ended up in a little shack that served as a bar. I wouldn't have kept pigs in it back home, but it was the best there was. Being as I had never had a drink in my entire life, the good ole boys were having a fine time teaching me the basic rules of inebriation. Dang, that was awful tasting stuff! But I tried to be a tough guy and hold it down.

After a while it didn't taste quite as bad, and I had a pretty good buzz on. I kept noticing something that has amazed me to this day. The more of this stuff I drank, the better looking the little dark eyed bartender got (this is a condition that is a proven, scientific fact). She wasn't exactly pretty, but she was getting closer to it all the time. One old salt leaned over and said, "Hey man, I think I can fix you up with that gal." "Really? Man, the more of this stuff I have, the better it sounds." She was sorta short and all I could see was from her shoulders up, but I had a darn good imagination (ah, imagination, the ultimate sex tool). Finally, about an hour later, my laughing old shipmates take me to a back room and tell me to take off all my clothes and lay down on the bed. They left and I stripped down to my skivvies, but when I lay down on the bed the room kept spinning around. . . and I'm a guy that don't even like merry go-rounds.

I'm sitting on the edge of the bed with my head in my hands when I hear something coming down the hall. . . thump-thump-thump. Slowly the door swings open and there stands this right pretty girl that had been behind the bar all night. . . she pulled open her robe and there she stood, buck naked! I kinda stare through the whisky haze, and I see she's got two pretty eyes, two kinda skinny arms, two little bitty breasts, and one fine leg! Yeah, that's what the noise was, coming down the hall. Someone had made her a homemade left leg that went all the way up to the stump at her hip. Well, it wasn't really a homemade leg, it was just a smoothed off board that she used as a walking device. Well, I didn't feel amorous at all anymore; in fact, I was sick as a snake-bit dog.

I thanked her as best I could for the hospitality, just barely managed to get my uniform and shoes on, and decided my first trip to a whorehouse wasn't all it was cracked up to be. I made it all the way to the front door before I passed out, and the last thing I remember was the old salts stuffing me in my bunk, clothes, shoes and all, still green, still naive, but my breath didn't feel quite as innocent.

The best favor anyone could have done for me was get me drunk and sick the first time out, 'cause I have never been tempted to get that way again. You couldn't rope and tie me and make me drink enough to get drunk. Whew, that was no fun! The attraction of Houses Of Ill Repute surely lost their allure to this Ozark hillbilly.

And I always wondered about that poor little Filipino girl with the one leg. Man, you talk about an occupational hazard. It's gotta be rough being a one-legged whore in a Navy town. I think of her loss and the life that she was given and the sorry, lustful men that she would have to put up with most of her life. And I wonder what she thought when I said, "Thank you, ma'am, for the offer, but I got to go puke." I always did have a way with words. Mr. Smooth.

Well, for the next nine months I managed to see so much world, through a porthole, that I was kinda ready to head back to the Ozarks. The land of fish heads and rice, naked community bathing pools (yes, co-ed), Japanese taxi drivers that were all ex-kamikaze pilots in the big war, having to take your shoes off every darn time you came into the house. . . yeah, it was starting to weigh on me just a little. But hey, it just made those Hank Williams and Lefty Frizzell songs sound that much better. I was experiencing LIFE all in capitals, and getting to sing about it as it happened. What a deal.

For me, the best choice I could have made was to join the service. It gave me a level of life experience that other guys my age, who had no time in service, did not have. There was a special comradeship you shared with your shipmates, and I am thankful for my opportunity to not only serve the Navy, but to have the Navy serve me with discipline and order and a sense of purpose, and for giving me a stage on which to learn my music.

midwest tornado

south pacific typhoon

chapter 7

Hillbillies and Miracles

A TYPHOON IS 'BOUT LIKE OUR MIDWESTERN TORNADOES, except you also got to worry about drowning and getting eat up by them big fish.
(Stan Hitchcock letter home, 1955)

I come from a family that was just naturally scared to death of storms. It comes from growing up in the Midwest and having those dang twisters come out of Oklahoma, Kansas or Texas and blow heck out of poor old Missouri. You remember that dog Toto who got blowed all the way to Oz, don't you? Well, that was no bedtime story for my family; we lived it. I'll swear if the wind got over fifteen miles an hour Mom had us all in the basement, in the southwest corner, so when the house went, it wouldn't fall on us and squash us like a betsybug (that reminds me, just what is a betsybug anyway, has anyone ever seen one?).

Yes, friends and neighbors out there in radio land (that's where everyone used to live before television), I thought I knew everything there was to know about bad storms, until I experienced a TYPHOON. (You will note that it is always capitalized and printed in BIG letters, 'cause nothing else comes close to describing it right).

We were anchored in Tokyo Bay, the summer of 1955, when I learned to be a big boy around storms.

Shoot man, nothing could scare me after a TYPHOON. We heard from the Yokosuka Naval Base weather center that a TYPHOON was headed right for us, and all ships should prepare for the "big one" by lashing everything down, putting out extra ropes and cables, anchors, and anything else you could think of that might hold the great ship at anchor and keep it from washing up on shore and making a mess of somebody's front lawn.

No wonder the Japs bombed Pearl Harbor, man, these TYPHOONS came through Japan like freight trains on a regular schedule, and the home folks were looking for another island, kinda out of the way, where they could retire from this kind of action, raise pineapples and take every invention that someone else came up with, make it better - and get rich, like those round-eyed Americans.

We were ordered to keep up a good head of steam in the boilers in case we broke loose and had to fight our way out to sea. They were predicting winds in excess of 150 miles per hour (in the good old days before kilometers) and even though, by this time, I had been in the Navy almost a full year and considered myself an old salty dog, dang, this sounded serious.

I was now a full-fledged boat coxswain. That means I operated the big fifty- foot motor launch and the LCVP's and LCM's (you know, the boats you see in the war movies where the front end comes down and the soldiers all run off into the water and the music comes up real loud and the bombs start blowing them all up) that we used to haul the men ashore for liberty and to bring aboard all the produce and powdered milk that 600 men could possibly consume. Well, we got everything tied down as best we could and, sure enough, it hit like a tiger out of hell. TYPHOON!!

Well, I was doing pretty good; I mean, I was still able to function--I was coherent. Shoot man, I was proud. Then they called all the boat coxswains to the quarterdeck, on the double. The First Lieutenant informed us that a barge had broken loose from its mooring and was loose in the harbor and a danger to all the ships at anchor in the storm. He asked for volunteers to go out and secure the barge alongside a LCM and get it tied back up. Well, I waited and waited and nobody spoke up so I cleared my throat with nervousness, and the First Lieutenant just naturally thought I was fixin' to volunteer so he said, "All right, Hitchcock get your crew and get out there, boy. I'm proud of you." Well now, maybe I wasn't quite as big as I thought. "Dang, that water looks dangerous. Them waves are ten foot high. . . and the wind is awesome." That dad-blamed throat-clearing habit of mine about to get me killed.

Well, you don't back up when you've just been volunteered. So we climbed down the rope ladder into our LCM and started up those great twin Gray Marine engines. That's one thing about those landing craft, with the twin engines and twin screws, you could walk the dog with those babies. I mean, walk that boat plumb sideways and land her on a dime! That is, if you were good, and I was good. In fact, I was a little bit of a hotshot and show-off when I was operating those boats. I loved them. What I didn't love, though, was the huge waves just knocking the heck out of us, the absolutely blinding rain and the wind that was hitting a high note that would have made Bill Monroe proud.

We finally caught sight of the runaway barge, rockin' and rollin' in the waves, and we came up alongside. Trouble is, I only had a bow hook and an engineer for my crew, which left the aft part of the tie-up my responsibility. It was hell keeping that boat alongside this pitching and rolling barge, but the bow hook finally got a rope on the front of the barge and I stepped out of the enclosed pilot house and moved to get a rope around the rear cleat of the barge so we could tie it close and move it on back to the docking area. Now that rain, and the pitching and rolling waves, had made the deck of my boat mighty slick. And there was about four foot between the rear end of the barge and my boat.

You guessed it; I fell right off my boat and down between the two masses of steel that was looking an awful lot like the jaws of a vise. . . and me the vise-ee.

As I fell into the cold water, somehow I kept hold of my stern rope, and I came up to the surface coughing and sputtering. It was truly an awful sight, that barge looked to be about a mile high from my point of view, and it was a-fixin' to crash into the side of my boat and turn me into a grease spot. Now, there is no way you can reasonably expect to pull yourself three feet up out of the water onto the deck of the LCM, in the split second before the two vessels came together with a shuddering crash, but friends, that's exactly what happened.

Somehow I flew up that rope, out of the water, and back onto my own deck, just before the boat was crashed by the barge. I lay there for a moment, just incredulous that I was still alive, then got up, tied the back of the barge off and took it in to tie up at the dock.

Nobody could believe this wild event, except my crew, who witnessed it. After we got the barge tied up and motored on back to the ship, well, that old storm really hit a high key. We ended up having to untie the ship and pull up the anchor and head out to sea to ride it out. I never been so sick, losing ten pounds in three days of seasickness.

From where we were in Japan, back home to the Ozarks, mail took two weeks to arrive. Two weeks later I got a letter from my mom that still raises goose bumps. It was dated the exact date that my typhoon accident happened, at the exact time, and it said: Son, I was sleeping soundly when I was awakened by the knowledge that you were in grave danger. I fell down by my bed and cried out to God, "Lord, save my boy, protect him now in his danger." I don't know what happened, but I know God took care of it. Love, Mom.

Well, it is a sobering feeling to be a party to a miracle and all though my life I have hearkened back on that event. It is not so much the physical aspect of the lifesaving event, as much as it is the knowledge that God took time out from His busy schedule, reached down and plucked me out of the water, flung me up on the deck and let me live all these years. Thank you God, I didn't deserve it, and that's what makes it so precious.

I have been in a lot of scrapes since then, but my personal miracle has always been with me, reminding me that our God is a merciful God, and His love is beyond all understanding.

Meanwhile, the Bryce Canyon Troubadours kept playing all over the Far East, in every Enlisted Men's' Club, every Chief's Club, a few Officers' Clubs and even some hospitals. Every port the ship hit, we would swarm over on the beach and pick some music somewhere. Let me tell you folks, if you've never heard Hank Williams played by a band dressed in outlandish Hawaiian shirts and the bottom part of our uniform whites for pants, then you've missed a cultural experience. Yeah, we were cool. We got so good, in fact, that the Captain of the Bryce Canyon made us the official ship's band. Now if you are not aware of the importance of the ship's band let me tell you a little about how it works. The ship's band had always been, in the tradition of the Navy, a brass band in strict spit and polish uniform that played for special official occasions, such as when your relief ship would arrive in port to relieve your ship and you got to go stateside, or when some visiting dignitary came on board.

Thinking back on it now, it was no small thing for the Captain to have the guts to name us the ship's band and bring some dignitary aboard to the strains of "Orange Blossom Special" or "Your Cheatin' Heart". Yessir, I always wondered whatever happened to that crazy Captain, did they come and take him away with Peewee still playing "Orange Blossom Special"? That would be kinda fitting, don't you think? Well, it's easier to dance to than a military march. Anyway, bless you, Captain, wherever you are.

All in all, these were great years for a young man who used to lay in his attic bedroom, on the Ozark farm, and listen to the faraway cry of a steam locomotive as it pulled passenger cars through our country heading for everywhere, and the pull of the world was so strong it was almost physical, wanting to get out there and see it so bad. Well, I was out here now and it was every bit as exciting as I always dreamed: Manila, Hong Kong, Tokyo, Honolulu. Subic Bay! Naw, that's where I woke up, sick all over again

Marilyn and Stan on the Beach
Corpus Christi, TX
1957

chapter 8

Love Ain't Perfect, But It's All We Got

. . .and sometimes we ain't got that. . .
Stan Hitchcock, 1955

Our ship got back from our first tour of the Orient in August of 1955 and I took my first leave and went home to the Ozarks. I had thirty days to do anything I wanted, so I just got married. Yep, that does seem kinda immature and foolish. . . and sure enough, later on it proved that it was just that. Anyway, I married a neighbor girl by the name of Sandra Warren, whom I had gone to school with, but never dated. She had grown up since I had been gone, I had just gotten back from almost a year overseas, and well, dang it, it seemed like a good idea at the time.

I was 19 and she was 17 and we knew what love was, it was raging hormones and an unrealistic idea of what it took to make a marriage: just like playing house, only with real people. We got married on my 22nd day home, spent eight days trying to figure out what this was all about. . . and I went back to Long Beach, California and the old Bryce Canyon.

In August of '56, the only lasting piece of love to survive this marriage of kids was born, Marilyn Kay Hitchcock. I was back overseas on another tour of the

Far East so I missed the big event. In fact, I didn't even get to meet Marilyn until she was four months old, but through the years she and I have made up for it by being extra close, and having the same weird sense of humor. Yeah, I love you, Moose.

In 1957 I made Third Class Petty Officer and got transferred to shore duty at Chase Naval Air Station, Beeville, Texas. I never will forget the last day on board ship when I was saying goodbye to my old shipmates and band members. It was bittersweet bidding adios to those comrades who I had played music with all over the Far East, Old Smoky the dog house bass player, and Peewee the fiddle player and spark-plug of the Bryce Canyon Troubadours. As I was giving them a good ole country hug they said, "One of these days you'll be singing on the Grand Ole Opry, and we'll say we knew you when." I laughed at the absurdity of it all, gathered up my gear, and my old guitar, and headed off the ship, an old salt, at last.

Ten years later I was singing on the Grand Ole Opry one Saturday night, at the old Ryman Auditorium, the same show that we all had listened to while we were overseas on my old Philco Transoceanic radio. I looked down in about the third row and there was Old Smoky, just jumping up and down saying, " I told you so, I told you so!!"

But, dear reader, I know how you hate for the writer to jump ahead. It's almost like those people who turn to the back page of a novel to see how it ends up. I hate 'em! So now, back to the fifties,1958, to be exact: extreme south Texas in the summer. About as far away from a ship as sailor could be. As we check in with our hero. (Hey, it's my story and I can be the hero if I want to.)

After a year in Beeville, Texas, boy, was I ready to get out and go back home. It's some kind of hot down there. So I did. Get out and go back home, I mean. Yes, after three years, eleven months and twenty-nine days I was released from active duty and heading home.

After my release from active duty, in August 1958, I took a job as an inventory control person at the E. A. Martin Machinery Company, the regional Caterpillar tractor dealer in Springfield, Missouri.

That same year I met a great bunch of kids from the Ozarks that were all part of the Bilyeu family. They were early settlers in the mountains south of Springfield, and some of the best gospel singers

I have ever heard. They had formed a group called The Waymakers and were singing in all the local churches around the Ozarks.

Well, it didn't take me long to break out the old Gibson and start singing with them. I mean, I just made myself a part of that family, and I still feel a kinship today. My uncle Bob Johnson, my mother's brother, was the pastor of Seminole Baptist Church in Springfield and we sort of made that our singing headquarters.

Stan's first recording
Boys Ranch Album by Stan Hitchcock & The Waymakers
Boys Ranch founded in 1959

chapter 9

Heathens, Hillbillies and Good Samaritans

JUST A CLOSER WALK WITH THEE

. . .Grant it Jesus, is my plea

John T. Benson

My uncle Bob, "Brother Bob" as we all called him, asked me to join him in a ministry to help young, homeless boys. We had been studying the problem in our region for some time and found that the state of Missouri had many boys locked up for being homeless. There was no state facility available, and they were being held in detention homes, jails, reformatories and other places of confinement, until they could be adopted out.

I made the decision to quit my job with the Caterpillar tractor dealer and go full time into this work. I was 23 years old. I had an old car, a guitar, and a young daughter to raise. . . and now I had a mission. It was 1959 and life was good.

The three years I spent working with those boys remains one of the high points in my life. We decided to buy a 110-acre farm just north of Springfield, Missouri and start taking these young boys out of the jailhouses. We called the farm The Good Samaritan Boys Ranch and used the story of the Good Samaritan as our mission statement. We literally got down off our ass (as in jack), went down into the ditch, picked up these wounded souls, and let God's love heal them and make them whole.

My family and I lived on the grounds of the Ranch. We took care of the business of promoting the work, hauling the boys to school every morning, helping with cooking their meals, running the farm operation and just doing whatever had to be done. It seems hard to believe, looking back, that we did it all for no salary, just our living expenses and the blessing of helping someone find a new life.

The Ranch was a complete work of faith. With no government money involved at all, interested people that had a burden for others would send a little money when they could, or bring in a side of beef or a bushel of potatoes when crops were good.

I went around the region, about a 250-mile radius, and got radio stations to donate time for us to have a radio show promoting the work and making known the problem of homeless children. I got about fifteen radio stations going on our show, just me singing with my guitar. Sometimes The Waymakers joined in, Brother Bob did some preaching and some of the boys told their story or testimony, just generally getting the word out.

We held rallies at churches throughout the Ozarks, inviting singing groups from around the region to come sing with us, while we continued to tell the story. We held a rally at the Shrine Mosque in Springfield and Tennessee Ernie flew in from Hollywood to sing for us along with the Blackwood Brothers, The Statesmen and The LeFevers. Man, that was tall cotton for a country boy.

Most of our boys were from small towns around southwest Missouri, northern Arkansas, Oklahoma, and Kansas. These boys had committed no crimes. For the most part, they were just alone, abandoned, and in need of love.

I remember one family of three brothers, the oldest twelve and the youngest two years old. They lived way back in the hills of the Ozarks. They had an old, drunken, abusive father, who one day, in a fit of drunken rage, beat their mother to death, in front of them. Realizing what he had done, he ran, leaving the three boys alone with the body: no food, no phone, and no one to help in this nightmare. After two days, the local sheriff was out on a routine check of the county, came by the house, discovering the boys huddled around the body of their mother. Without another family member in the world that they knew of, the sheriff called us at the Ranch and we went down and picked the boys up. We took them back home with us and tried to love away all the hurt and sorrow which was all that they knew of life. I never will forget the look in their eyes. . . little eyes aren't supposed to have that much hurt and loss in them. With the remarkable resilience of children, within a year's time these boys were just blooming in the garden of love that was the Ranch.

The Ranch had taken a young boy, just four years old, named Chuckie who had been severely abused by his half-Indian father down in Oklahoma. The Oklahoma court called us and asked us to take him, even though we usually didn't take boys quite that young.

To give Chuckie the special care he needed, we moved him into our own house on the Ranch instead of the dormitory that the other boys lived in. Chuckie soon became like my own blood son. Before long there was a level of emotional attachment that would soon tear me all to pieces.

Things rocked along on the Ranch for about a year, with the bond between Chuckie and myself growing everyday. We applied for adoption and started the process.

One evening, about sundown, an old, rusty, smoking, worn out, Chevy station wagon pulled up in front of the Ranch office where I was doing some work, and one of the meanest looking men I have ever seen to this day, got out and came to the door. There was a dog in the back of the station wagon that matched the looks of the man, in meanness. I found out later wasn't a dog at all, but a wolf. Well, I opened the door, and without preamble, he said, "I come to get my boy, Chuckie." Looking back on that moment now, all these years later, it seems like a blur, but I knew one thing. This old devil wasn't gonna get my Chuckie. It would be over my dead body!

As it turned out it wasn't over my dead body, but over my broken heart. Because he was a Native American, or at least half, he had special dispensation with the law. After I run him off, he just went to the federal courthouse, got the judge to issue an order and got two deputies to come with him. While the two deputies held me in a vise grip, he simply took Chuckie, threw him in the front seat of that old car, and drove on out of my life.

I never found Chuckie, although we searched frantically. We tried every legal way we could to save him from this man who had almost killed him before. But he was gone.

The official adoption papers that we had applied for were only two weeks from being completed. Just two more weeks and Chuckie would have been legally ours, forever, to protect.

I still loved working with all the boys, but something went out of me when I watched that old car pull out of the driveway with Chuckie's screams echoing in my ears. Somehow, I just didn't have the heart for it anymore.

So many stories I could tell of the heartbreak of young lives that we became involved in, but, suffice it to say, that God did bless the work and we survived and grew every year. I'm proud to say the Ranch is still rescuing boys today, still helping the homeless, still down in the ditch with a hand up. God said that it would be better for a millstone to be placed around the neck, than to harm one of these little ones. Many times I wished that God would let me put the millstone around the neck of some of the sorry old heathens that hurt these children so bad. May the fires of hell consume them. I know, that's not the spirit of Christian forgiveness, but man, I can't stand to see those babies hurt. Maybe that's why I ended up being a hillbilly singer, instead of an old country preacher like Mama wanted me to be.

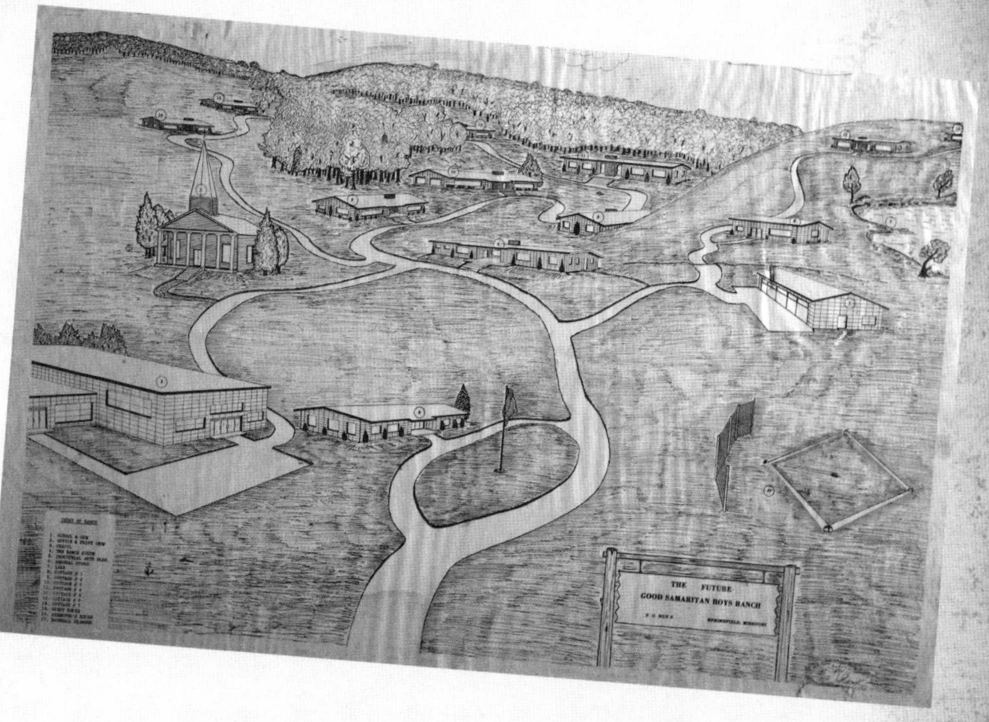

Original Plans for Boys Ranch
Drawn by Stan in 1959

Lester Roloff

chapter 10

I'll Fly Away

I'LL FLY AWAY, OH GLORY, I'LL FLY AWAY...
Albert E. Brumley, Powell, Missouri-1930's

One of my fondest memories of the years at the Boys Ranch was meeting, and getting to be friends with, a great radio evangelist by the name of Lester Roloff of Corpus Christi, Texas.

Brother Roloff called me at the Ranch, one day late in 1960, and asked me to come down to Corpus and sing for one of his revivals. I had sung for him several times when he had revivals around the Ozarks and we had grown real close. Well, of course I accepted the invitation, loaded up the car and headed for Texas. When I got to Corpus, and pulled up at Brother Roloff's church, he gave me a bear hug and said, "Come on, we got to head out."

We drove out into the country to a little grass landing field with a small quonset hut at one end. He told me he had just bought him a plane so he could get to all his revival meetings around the country, and was I scared of flying? Well, I said, I didn't know, I never had tried it. I was feeling a little nervous but I was game for most anything in those days, so I threw my guitar into the plane and got ready for the big event.

Brother Roloff had a book open in his lap, and he kept looking down at it and flipping all kind of switches. All of a sudden the engine started up and the good brother looked over at me and kinda grinned, like he was proud. He pulled the plane out into the middle of the runway and stopped, and I expected to hear something kinda with a professional pilot sound to it. . . you know how pilots like to talk pilot talk. That was not exactly what the good brother had in mind.

Now, Brother Roloff, when he prayed it was just like he was talking to God, in a conversational tone. He said, "Lord, you know I don't know how to fly this thing, so we just be trusting you to get us to Uvalde, Texas in time for the services."

Brother Roloff had a lot of faith; I had an upset stomach. My heart went into overdrive. Visions of my life passed before my eyes, just like a dying man. But we bounced down the runway, lifted off real shaky, got up about 500 feet, found the highway to Uvalde and followed it all the way. Just like driving a car.

It turns out Brother Roloff had bought the plane two weeks before and taken three lessons. Just enough to learn how to take off and land, and bingo. . . he was a pilot. We got there and back OK, but this old son has not enjoyed flying since.

Lester Roloff was a great preacher and a real man of God. I loved him: but I never flew with him again.

To show you how powerful a preacher Brother Roloff was, I remember one time in 1959 when he came to Seminole Baptist Church in Springfield and held a weeklong revival. I was leading the singing then and working with Brother Bob in the church and I was witness to a funny happening. About half way into the week's revival Brother Roloff preached a sermon on the evils of television, and its sinful influence on the Christian home. It was a powerful sermon and I could see it starting to have an effect on Brother Bob, who had just purchased a brand new console television set the week before. As the sermon progressed, and Brother Roloff got deeper and deeper into his subject, sweat started to pop out on Brother Bob's forehead. He was looking more and more like a man heavily under conviction. As soon as the service ended, I noticed Brother Bob heading out the back door of the church and to the parsonage next door.

Thinking he might be sick or something, I slipped out the back door to follow and see if he needed help. As I stepped into the back porch of the parsonage I heard this loud crashing sound coming from inside. I quickly stepped inside realizing the sound of loud crashing was coming from the living room. I followed the sound into the living room where a strange sight greeted me. . . Brother Bob had gone to his son's bedroom, brought back his baseball bat, and was pounding his new Zenith console television set to death with it. He was bringing that bat all the way over his head and smashing it, with all his force, into the glass screen. I mean, if it had been a baseball, it would have been over the fence! Meanwhile, his wife, Aunt Mary, was screaming and trying to grab his arm to stop him, thinking that he had lost his mind.

It took us awhile to get control of Brother Bob: too late to save the poor television set. It was years before he would watch one again. When I told Brother Roloff what had happened, he just kinda chuckled and said, "The Spirit leads us in strange ways sometimes."

Seeing some of the trash that is today's television fare, Brother Roloff just may have been right, y'know?

A few years later, Brother Lester was flying to one of his revivals when his plane exploded in midair, and this good man went to be with Jesus.

You can still hear Brother Roloff on the radio even today because his family continues to service the stations with his old transcriptions. It's a real treat when I can catch one of the stations on some of my late night driving trips, and it sure brings back the memories.

It seems it was just yesterday when I heard Brother Lester say, "Lord, you know I don't know how to fly this thing. . ."

ALL NEW
3rd EDITION
SOUVENIR
PICTURE ALBUM
ABC TELEVISION'S
JUBILEE USA
starring
RED
FOLEY
OUTSTANDING
COLLECTION
OF CANDIDS

Peace in the Valley

OH LORD I'M TIRED AND SO WEARY. . .

Red Foley, Decca Records

One day, in 1960, I was in the studio of radio station KWTO, in Springfield, where we taped our radio shows. As I was singing one or two of the good old gospel songs, I noticed a man standing outside the studio window watching and listening. After we had finished the taping, I stepped out into the hall and came face to face with Red Foley, the man that I respected most in music.

Red had on a full-length, white leather topcoat, and looked every inch the "star" that he was. He looked at me with kinda damp eyes, put his arm around my shoulder, and said, "Your singing touched my heart - you've got a special talent, son." Well, stick me with a fork 'cause I'm done. Whew, that's heavy when it comes from your singing idol.

We talked a little while longer, and started a friendship that would continue until Red's death a few years later.

Red was a special man and I loved him for what he was: a man with a heart as big as all outdoors, always ready to help another artist, a mentor, and a loyal friend. So many artists can list Red Foley as the man who gave them a lift up: Brenda Lee, Porter Wagoner, Bobby Lord, Chet Atkins, Billy Walker and so many more, including Stan Hitchcock.

Red was such an influence on the singing voice I always wanted to have. He was the kind of entertainer that could touch people's hearts, like I always wanted to do. Nobody could sing a gospel song like Red because he really loved those songs. There was nothing fake about Red Foley. When he sat in that old armchair, on stage at the Jewell Theater at the Ozark Jubilee, looked the folks in the eye and sang about there being "Peace in the Valley," you knew he meant it. And you just wanted to head for that valley, right now.

What many folks did not know was that Red Foley was a torn, tortured soul, who was hopelessly destroying himself with alcohol. He was not a recreational drunk: rather he was a pitiful binge drinker, one who only sought oblivion in the bottle.

Red had married early in life, his first wife dying in childbirth; his second wife, Eva, mother of his children, committed suicide while they were living in Nashville and Red was starring on the Grand Ole Opry. It is a sad story that haunted Red the rest of his life and although he did marry again, I don't believe he ever got over Eva's death. He just grieved for her. In the years following Eva's death, Red developed a drinking problem.

Red had an illustrious career for many years: starring on the Renfro Valley Barn Dance in Kentucky, the WLS Barn Dance in Chicago, and the NBC network portion of the Grand Ole Opry. In 1953 he landed in my hometown of Springfield, Missouri to host the ABC television show, Ozark Jubilee.

When he arrived in Springfield, the drinking became pretty much public knowledge. When the liquor was on him, he and his third wife, Sally, would have knock-down drag-outs on the public square, and you could read about it in the newspapers the next morning.

In addition to his other demons, at the height of popularity of the Ozark Jubilee, the IRS came after Red with a vengeance, They tried every dirty trick they could come up with to destroy him. They almost did it too. But in the end Red was exonerated. The fiendish IRS investigators, famous for their dirty tricks in those years, slunk away in defeat. That was the life he was suffering through when I knew him. And yet, I am convinced he was one of the finest men I will ever meet, and for sure, the greatest singer.

I remember, back when I was just a kid on the farm, listening in total awe, as he hosted the Prince Albert portion of the Grand Ole Opry. It was hard for me to reconcile his alcoholism with the memories I carried from my childhood of idolizing his singing and entertaining.

I suppose that the national television exposure that he received on the Jubilee was his career highlight, it was a great show and had fantastic ratings, and he was absolutely the best that ever was, on that new medium of television, and country music had its best ambassador.

I never got to appear on the Ozark Jubilee ; it was on the way down by the time I got out of the Navy. However, I did get to travel with Red and do concerts with him. There couldn't have been a more potent, advanced school of professional entertainment. There were some funny times, too.

The first fair that I was booked on was with the Red Foley Show in 1961. I was scheduled to ride with the band in the station wagon, pulling the trailer and hauling six musicians. Now, this was my first road trip, and the boys sure took advantage of that fact. Slim Wilson, the leader of the band, looked over at me after we had loaded all the instruments in the trailer, and said, "Stan, why don't you take the first shift of driving?" The Fair was in Flint Michigan, a fur piece from Springfield, Missouri, where we were starting. Well, I said OK, and headed out, while all the other guys in the band promptly went to sleep.

About sixteen hours later, I pulled us in to Flint, found the fairgrounds, and went to waking up all the other guys, who had just had the sleep of their lives. We had two hours 'till show time. I was already whipped, after that drive, but sure didn't want these guys to know it.

We unloaded the trailer, set up the stage, did the show, loaded the trailer back up, and got ready to head back to Springfield. Slim walked up, handed me a cup of coffee, and said, " Stan, why don't you take the first shift of driving?" I crawled behind the wheel, gritted my teeth and started out. Dang, this show biz is hard work. I drove all night and up into the middle of the next day. We were just going through Fair Grove, a town about 20 miles from Springfield, when Slim, who had been sleeping like a baby since we left Flint, Michigan, fifteen hours before, raised up out of the back seat and said, "Pull her on over Stan, I'll dog 'er on in!"

Bless you Slim Wilson, you were one of a kind. You did love to pull one over on the kid, but it was great learning from you, the old master show bizzer.

And about here, dear friends, I experienced the first taste of "entertainer rejection syndrome": a condition that I would experience, in one form or another, many times in the years to come. This condition is when regular folks, civilians if you will, look down on us poor entertainer types, and put us in the same category that they reserve for gypsies, carnival workers and IRS auditors. I mean, they might enjoy hearing you sing a song and entertaining them at the local Moose Lodge, but dang, they wouldn't want their kid to marry one. And they might ask you to autograph your latest album and sign it to their wife, but don't come down to the bank and try to sign your autograph on a loan application, 'cause man, that guitar is just not enough collateral. That is how it was in 1961.

You see, I had gotten very involved, not only in the Boys Ranch, but also as the young people's leader, and a song leader in the Victory Baptist Church, a new church that I had helped to found just a year earlier.

It happened like this: As I have already told you, Red Foley had asked me to travel with him on some state fair dates the summer of '61, and of course I was thrilled at the opportunity to not only work with him, but the chance to sing before those size audiences. It was just an incredible treat.

Well, I did the tour, but I lost the church. When I came back to town from the Flint, Michigan trip and went to church the next Sunday, the head of the deacons committee asked to meet with me. I went into the meeting room and there set all the church officials, looking mighty grim. "Well, we understand you been doing shows with Red Foley," the head deacon started out. . . "Yes sir, sure have. Been having some really good shows and great crowds, " I answered.

"You've got to make a decision right now between the church and Mr. Foley. . . can't do both." "Why not?" I replied. "Because everyone knows that Mr. Red Foley is a drunk, and we can't have one of our staff members running with a man that does that." I made the shortest resignation speech in history: "OK." I shook the dust of that bunch off my shoes, and have had a very low tolerance for hypocrites ever since.

Red Foley was my friend. He was a great man who had a mighty big hurt inside, and I only wish I could have helped him more; took some of his burden. But in the end, every man has to tote his own. It's a load that we put on ourselves and only God can ease it off our back and carry it for us.

One day, about seven years later, I met Red in the Nashville airport as he was flying in from a gig and I was flying off to do one. He put his arm around me and said, "Stan, the doctor told me if I drank anymore it would kill me, so I have quit completely, and I'm feeling great." I was so glad to hear he had it under control, and told him so, and we promised to get together, soon.

Six months later, Red was doing a state fair tour. He came out on stage, walked up to the mic and said, "Friends, this song kinda describes how the old Red Head is feeling tonight," and he started singing, "Well, I'm tired and so weary, but I must go along, 'till the Lord comes to call me away." He sang "Peace In the Valley"', funny thing, 'cause this was always his closing song, until tonight. Red went back to his hotel room after the show, lay down across the bed, and died. Peace at last.

First epic LP 1963

State of Missouri
County of Greene

AGREEMENT

THE FOLLOWING AGREEMENT, entered into this 1st day of August 1962, between E. E. Siman, Jr., party of the first part, and Stan Hitchcock, party of the second part, of the State of Missouri.

WITNESSETH WHEREAS the above-named parties have on the above date set forth, entered into a mutual agreement and understanding and the same is hereby set forth as follows:

-1-

It is hereby understood and agreed that for and in consideration of a commission of twenty per cent (20%) of all monies derived from and as a result of the efforts of the party of the second part in making phonograph records, personal appearances, motion pictures, television, radio, and/or any other form of entertainment, and/or advertising involving the talent of the said party of the second part, more specifically known as Stan Hitchcock; the said party of the first part, namely E.E. Siman, Jr., does hereby and hereon accept employment as the personal manager of the said Stan Hitchcock, and that for and in consideration of his services as said manager the said Stan Hitchcock does hereby and hereon employe the said E.E. Siman, Jr. as his personal and business manager to supervise, direct, and aid him in any and all business ventures pertaining to the within and foregoing designated ventures regarding entertainment, public appearances, and-the-like.

First management contract 1962

chapter 12

My Big Break Arrives in the Mail, Postage Due

WELL, GUITAR, HERE I AM OLD FRIEND, back to sing some blues again. . . ain't it funny I always come right back to you.
Stan Hitchcock and Ronnie Reno 1982

I continued doing the radio shows with the Waymakers. We even recorded, and paid for, a couple of custom albums for the Boys Ranch to help raise funds to carry on the work.

One day, in the early part of 1962, I was in the studio of radio station KWTO recording some of our radio shows, when the recording engineer, Wan Hope, asked me if I knew any country music songs. I said sure, (thinking about the old Bryce Canyon Troubadours). He said he was setting up the controls and how about singing a couple, maybe three, songs for him. You must realize that I was a total gospel singer up to this point, without a thought of being a hillbilly singer.

Well, Wan taped those songs I sang, and he sent them to Bob Tubert, who was running a publishing company for Si Siman, in Nashville, at the time. Bob had gone to school in Springfield, and later was part of the creative crew of the Ozark Jubilee, but I had never met him. Bob took the demo of just me and my guitar, and those old country songs, to the grand old man of Columbia Records in Nashville; Don Law.

Don was an Englishman who was responsible for most of the great stars of the country music roster of Columbia, and one of the nicest gentlemen this music biz will ever know. Of course, I had never heard of Don Law in my life. So, when the phone rang at the Boys Ranch, and the man on the other end said, "Stan, this is Don Law of Columbia Records, " it didn't really ring any chimes in my head. . . but I was polite, just like Mama raised me to be. Don Law asked me to come to Nashville and talk to him, and, of course, I thought he wanted to talk about the Boys' Ranch. I said, sure, I would be glad to come see him. I got the directions, and hung up.

The next day I went into the radio station and asked Si about Don Law. He proceeded to fill me in on just who this man was and told me that he had asked Bob Tubert to set up the meeting with him. Well, I don't mean to sound dumb, but I was so consumed with what I was doing at the Boys' Ranch that all I wanted to talk to him about was the work we were doing with the boys. By this time we had about thirty boys. We had put on house parents and set up a board of directors of some of the leading business people in the area. The Ranch was doing well.

Anyway, I went on down to Nashville for the first time around June of '62. I somehow found my way to Bob Tubert's office, who then took me to Don Law's office where we met with him. Don was the very epitome of kindness and warmth and I began to open up to him about the lives of these boys we were working with. He stopped me and said, "Sing me a song." Well, he had a guitar over in the corner, so I picked it up and sang him a couple of good old gospel songs. Then, back to the story of the boys. Again, very quietly, he said, "Sing me another song." A couple of hours later he finally pushed back from his desk, reached in the drawer for his checkbook and wrote me a check for five hundred dollars for a donation to the Boys' Ranch. He shook my hand and said, "You'll be hearing from me soon."

I was elated with the gift of the check and went on back to the ranch feeling like it had been a good trip and a wonderful opportunity to spread the word about homeless boys.

Three weeks later the postmaster up at the little country post office just a mile from the Ranch called and told me I had a big package from New York City. Shoot, I didn't know anyone in New York City, but I went on up to the store, post office and gas station that served as the closest tie to outside civilization, and sure enough, there was a big manila envelope with my name on it postmarked New York City. Opening it up, I found a long-term recording contract with Columbia Records and a new life that was just starting to peek around the corner, dumb luck or the fickle finger of fate? Beats me, but ain't that a weird way to get into show biz?

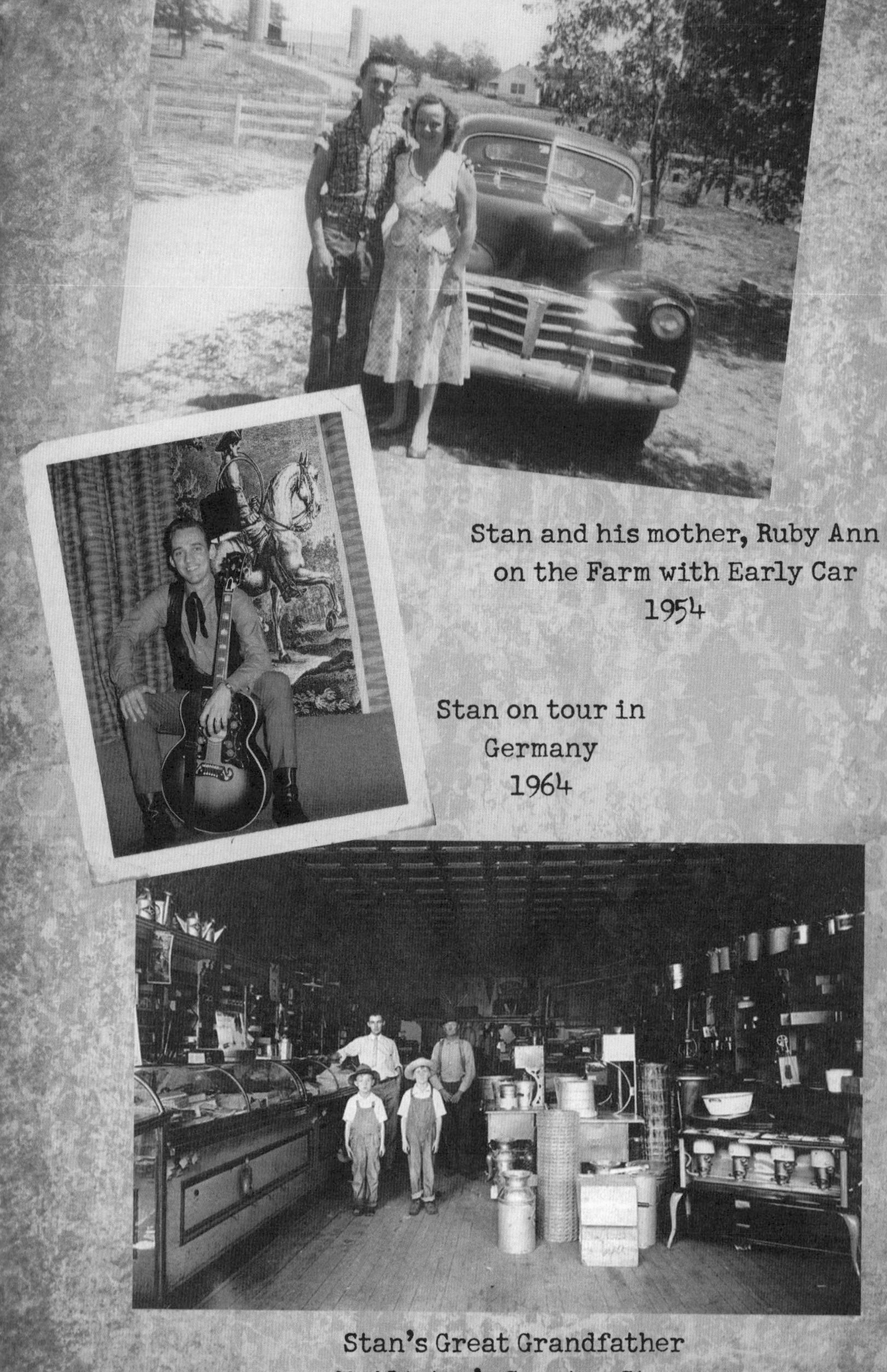

Stan and his mother, Ruby Ann
on the Farm with Early Car
1954

Stan on tour in
Germany
1964

Stan's Great Grandfather
McAlister's Country Store
- 1900, Linneus, MO -

SECTION II

The Early Nashville Years

Painting by Stan Hitchcock

Stan and Wayne Carson on Heart to Heart
1994

chapter 13

Chicken One Day, Feathers the Next

SHOW BUSINESS IS MY LIFE. . . or,
when you gonna get a real job?
(Every Hillbilly singer hears this sometime in his life)

In August of '62, Si Siman signed me to a management contract to handle the transformation of a green kid into a seasoned entertainer/recording artist. I don't know how butterflies do their transformation from a grub worm, but man, my transformation was a real challenge.

In October, Si scheduled a trip to Nashville for my first Columbia Records recording session. He wanted to let me get used to working in a Nashville recording studio and to let Don Law hear me in a professional setting, working with studio musicians.

On this Nashville trip there was a young man, just eighteen years old, who would later become one of the greatest songwriters of all time. He would write, "The Letter", "Who's Julie", "Soul Deep", "Slide Off Of Your Satin Sheets", "Barstool Mountain" and finally, the topper of them all, "You Were Always On My Mind." His name is Wayne Carson. He was another protégée of Red Foley. Wayne had more talent in that eighteen-year-old body than anyone I have ever met. We were buddies - working in and around Springfield at KWTO radio and playing a few road dates with Red. Wayne's folks, Shorty and Sue Thompson, along with Sue's sister Sally, were fine entertainers who pioneered live entertainment for radio during the 40's, 50's and 60's. So, he got his talent honest. Si was his manager too and his music publisher.

Wayne was wild as a buck then, and still is today. He just does his wild stuff a little slower. So full of talent: a great singer, writer and guitar player, and such a nice guy, you just gotta love him. Well, we were both riding high and bouncing off the sides of the car when we came up over the hill on highway 41. We looked down in the Cumberland River valley and there lay Nashville just waiting for us. Wayne said, "I'll take that half over there and Stan, you take the other half." Sounded like a deal to me, so we agreed on it and that's the way it's been ever since. Trouble is, Wayne's half made him a lot of money and I'm still trying to make the payments on my half. Oh well, that's life I reckon. Chicken one day and feathers the next, as Ray Pillow would always tell me.

Si checked us into the Allen Hotel, an old music gathering place, long gone, but pieces of it should have been put in the Country music Hall of Fame. Every picker, or would-be picker, stayed there at one time or another. Wayne and I shared a room, (Si did know how to save a dollar). The minute we got to the room he stripped down to his underwear, lit the incessant, never ending cigarette, grabbed his old beat up gut-string guitar and started writing songs. Man, he was so full of them, they just poured out. It was like raw, untamed and uncontrolled talent in action - something at that time, I had never seen before.

In years since, I have seen this manifestation of creativity in other artists, such as: Roger Miller, Mickey Newbury, Jerry Reed, Kris Kristofferson, Willie Nelson (in the 60's), Jimmy Buffett (late 60's, early 70's), Jerry Jeff Walker, Guy Clark, Billy Joe Shaver and later, Keith Whitley. The creative energy was so strong, so powerful, that you could actually physically feel the current coming off of them. It was awesome to be around them and feel the charge until you realized how volatile, how powerfully driven these geniuses of American music were. Those who knew Hank Williams best say that he had the same kind of constant, creative energy. I never met Hank. He died before I came to Nashville. But like a car engine revved up past the red line, something is gonna burn up eventually. It is tragic that those who possess this incredible gift, this overabundance of talent, so often are unable to handle the terrific strain that having such a gift carries with it. However, Wayne would just barely survive those years of candle burning, and is still today one of our greatest song writing treasures. However, I still suspect he got the best of me when he chose his half of Nashville.

Lacy J. Dalton

Heart to Heart, 1994

chapter 14

Show Biz is My Life

GOD BLESS THE BOYS, THAT MAKE THE NOISE, ON 16TH AVENUE. . . (and the girls that keep quiet about it.). . . 16th Avenue. . . written by Tom Schuyler. . . Recorded by Lacy J. Dalton

Well, from that first moment in front of the mic at the little basement studio in the old quonset hut that Owen Bradley and his brothers had built (that would later become Columbia Records studio on 16th Avenue, Music Row, Nashville, Tennessee), I knew I had found my home. Now I knew what I had been all along: a singer of songs, a picker, a professional musician, a person who entertains other folks and does it seriously - for a living. Ruby, my mother, was definitely not going to be overjoyed that I had discovered my true calling, my destiny, if you will, and it had entertainer written all over it.

That first session we put down two or three old standards including the old Foley hit, "Just A Closer Walk With Thee", and a couple of new, original songs that Bob Tubert had found, including one, "Somebody Had To Lose" - a song that was written by my old school buddy, Jimmy Gateley, and another new song, "I Had Heaven In My Hands", which was written by Sonny James. What a thrill it was. . . standing there at the mic with some of the greatest musicians in the world all around me: Fred Carter, Jr., (father of Deana Carter), on lead guitar, Harold

Bradley on tic tac bass guitar, Pig Robbins on piano, Buddy Harman on drums, Bob Moore on bass, Pete Drake on steel, Ray Edenton just eating that rhythm guitar up, and the Anita Kerr Singers on background vocals. Can you imagine how I felt? To this point the only musicians I had played with were the Bryce Canyon Troubadours and Slim Wilson's Band. Other than that, it had always been just me and my guitar.

Don Law and his associate producer, Frank Jones, were two of the finest men I ever met and they took me through the session just like the consummate professionals they were. It was quite an experience. I have been comfortable in the recording studio since that time, thanks to this great group of talented people, their kindness and understanding.

These were the days of actually having everyone in the studio playing at one time, no over-dubbing, no digital "fixing" if you sang off key - just the raw, pure joy of making music together. Not like today, where the new artists record with perfect, sterile, digital technology. The musicians come into the studio separately, put down their parts and leave, never seeing the other pickers. After the tracks are laid down the singer finally comes in, puts the headphones on, and sings along. . . yeah, Karaoke style recording. And if they sing a little off, hey, don't worry about it, we can fix it in the mix. Now, I know, it gets a perfect sound, it's great to dance to, and the public eats it up - but, man, I'm talking about a musical experience, a happening, an emotional high, a performance of excellence joined together of various musical talents, to create a piece of musical art that may not be perfect, but it has the heart and soul, and yes, the magic of the moment.

I actually feel a little sorry for the new guys of today, who will probably never experience this musical high. Then I remember, yeah, they are the ones making money and selling tons of records but you, Hitchcock, are sitting here with memories that money can't buy.

Let me tell you a little about what made Nashville so special in 1962. These were the years in country music that were dominated by Ernest Tubb, Marty Robbins, Ray Price, Bill Monroe, Little Jimmie Dickens, Flatt and Scruggs, Webb Pierce, Johnny Horton, Faron

Young, Red Foley, Roy Acuff, Ira & Charlie - The Louvin Brothers, The Wilburn Brothers, Kitty Wells, Patsy Cline, Hawkshaw Hawkins, Jim Reeves, Johnny and Jack, Stonewall Jackson, Carl Smith, Lefty Frizzell, George Jones, Sonny James, Bill Anderson, Jean Shepard, The Browns, Don Gibson and Eddy Arnold.

Mel Tillis was writing hits and starting to really sell records. Brenda Lee was a child prodigy superstar and Willie Nelson was writing some of the most progressive music the country had ever heard. Roger Miller was just a song away from his genius turning into stardom and Johnny Cash was on the way to superstar status. The rest of the Memphis gang, Jerry Lee, Roy Orbison and Carl Perkins, were carving out their niche.

Out in California, Merle Haggard was just getting his recording career started. Wynn Stewart had cut some great records and Buck Owens was establishing his Bakersfield dynasty. Glen Campbell was establishing himself as a great instrumentalist while John Hartford was writing a song called "Gentle On My Mind" that would also establish Campbell as a great vocalist. A family named Mandrell started looking toward Nashville and planning a move that would have a great impact on country music for years to come. A lot of the established stars were doing well, a few were beginning to fade and a whole new bunch was just starting to arrive.

The sixties were the great turning point in Nashville's music business: a time when it was still all controlled from the Row, before foreign ownership of record companies and publishing companies: a time when the copyrights of America's music still belonged to American's and before the influx of power from both coasts started in earnest.

Nashville's Music Row, then only 16th and a little of 17th Avenue South, was coming alive with the excitement of a resurgence in popularity of country music after a devastating decline during the birth of rock and roll in the 50's. Elvis may have still been coming to town to record at the old RCA Victor Studio B on 17th, and Conway Twitty may have been having second thoughts about whether he was rock or country, but man, Music Row was stone country and the folks who had survived the starving 50's in country music were making up for lost time. Things were happening and I wanted to be a part of it.

1962 was also the time of the Bradley Quonset Hut, Columbia Records Studio, which was the first music business built on 16th. RCA had the little Studio B one block over on 17th, Decca Records had an office building on 16th but they had no studio, (they used Bradley's as Owen was the head of A&R for Decca). Several music publishers had settled on 16th and spilled over onto 17th. There were at least five big management and booking agencies and a whole bunch of hillbillies, or would-be hillbilly singers like me, wandering the street - just eat up with the excitement of it all. Sessions were happening at all hours of the day. There has never been a bunch of pickers to rival the almost nonstop-working "A team."

Country music, which had just come from near starvation during the 50's rock years, was moving and shaking once again; attracting a new, younger bunch of singers and pickers like myself. It was the start of a new era - good, bad, but not indifferent - in the world of American music

Today, we have created a music industry that isolates and insulates the artists, singers, pickers and songwriters. I fear that a lot of the old camaraderie is gone, perhaps forever: but there was a time when it was real. You could touch it, feel it, smell it and taste it. Yep, country music, raw and unabridged.

Stan and son, Scott fishing on
the upper Mississippi River
2006

Stan's First Record

Somebody Had to Lose / Heaven in My Hands

1962

chapter 15

You're Moving Where?

Ruby Hitchcock 1962

RUBY ANN TOOK THE HAND OF THIS POOR,
POOR MAN, AIN'T TRUE LOVE A FUNNY THING...
(ain't it the truth)
Marty Robbins, Columbia Records

When I got back home to Springfield, Missouri after my recording debut my whole life had changed. I had discovered who I really was: but that's a hard thing to explain to others, particularly when they think they know who you really are - and - they have your whole life all laid out for you in a neat package.

I understand how hard it must be for civilians to understand about the music inside that won't let you stop; you just have to throw everything down and say: this is mine, it's part of me, it's what I do and I gotta go do it no matter what; sink or swim, win or lose. I don't really understand it myself, so how could I expect anyone else to have a clue?

Since our marriage in 1955, my wife Sandra and I had done a lot of growing up and now we were just going through the motions, with absolutely nothing of common interest anymore, other than our beautiful daughter, Marilyn. It's not that we fought – shoot, I don't even remember us arguing - we had just grown in different directions. Sandra was a very nice person and I take all the responsibility for our failed marriage, but ya know, when it ain't right and it ain't there, there's just not much fixing it.

When I explained that I was going to move to Nashville to do music she pretty much understood. She agreed to stay in Springfield and continue working and I agreed to go off and do hillbilly singer kinds of things. I started making my plans and talking it over with Si and my friends who all seemed to think it was a pretty neat idea.

A few months had gone by since my recording trip to Nashville and I had put off talking to Mom about it for a darn good reason: I still remember her hissy-fit when I wanted to be a singer at age thirteen. There was no reason to believe she had changed her mind about the music biz since then, and sure enough, Ruby hadn't. I went out to visit with Dad and Mom and told them of my decision to move to Nashville. It was pretty bad.

Mom cried a lot, made her dire predictions, preached to me for a couple of hours and just would not see the reason of it all. Dad was pretty pragmatic about it - him being a good singer and all maybe he understood, I don't know. I do know it seemed to break my Mother's heart and that was a hard thing to accept. Music is a tough act to fight when it is upon you - so I kissed Mom, told her I would think about it and left.

When I got home I had a message to call the Grand Ole Opry. Columbia Records had released my first record that week in May 1963 on their Epic Record label and the radio stations were just now getting the copies. The A side was "Heaven In My Hands" and the B Side was "Somebody Had To Lose". Columbia's promotion department had gotten me a guest spot on the Opry the very next Saturday night.

That night I was tuned in to WSM and Ralph Emery on the all-night show, along with his guest, Marty Robbins. Ralph said, "Marty we got a new record here from a new fella by the name of Stan Hitchcock, let's listen." He played the record, and after it was over, Marty said, "Well I like his singing and his name sounds like a gunfighter to me. I think he'll do good."

Well, that put the topping on the cake. I was heading for the big time son - hold on! Jump back and look out, 'cause I'm a'comin' through. A few days ago I couldn't hardly spell entertainer. . . and now I was one.

Stan and Ronnie Reno singing in an old country church in the Ozarks 1993

First appearance on The Grand Ole Opry in 1961.
Stan's First Stage Outfit while still living at The Boys Ranch
Light Brothers singing backup

chapter 16

Pickers and Pimps Have Been Doing it for Years

SHE'S LOOKIN' GOOD, and I'm afraid she'll find, what she's looking for. . .
Stan Hitchcock, Epic Records 1966

The trip back to Nashville seemed a lot more natural now: old highway 60 across the Ozarks, into the boot heel of Missouri, crossing the Mississippi at Cairo, Illinois, then cutting across the Mississippi and Ohio River, into Wickliff, Kentucky, Highway 121 down to Mayfield, Kentucky, then on over to Murray, New Concord, finally crossing into Tennessee at Paris Landing, turning over the bridge across Kentucky Lake, then over Lake Barkley, into Dover and Clarksville and finally topping that hill and looking down at Nashville. . . starting to feel a lot like home.

First thing I did when I got in town, after checking in at the Allen Hotel, was to head downtown to the Arcade to get some show biz threads. In the 60's, the Arcade was the place where the pickers would go to buy those cool clothes. The pimps from Jefferson Street would go there to buy their clothes too, trying to look just like us. Later, I found out that the pimps had been going there first. Oh well, you have to emulate someone, and pimps and pickers have been doing it for years.

Anyway, I bought a good looking, sorta silky sport

jacket, a real tight fitting pair of pants, a shirt with about a 4 inch collar, a real thin tie and a pair of black, English boots with a zipper on the side. It was sorta mod looking, but man, I had already decided I wasn't going to go with the cowboy suits and rhinestones - no sir, classic pimp was good enough for me. I didn't want anyone to think this was my first time in the big city.

I pretty much walked the floor of the old Allen Hotel most of that Saturday afternoon just eat up with excitement and nervous energy. Man oh man, the Grand Ole Opry! As long as I could remember I'd been listening to that radio show. All my heroes had stood on that stage: Hank, Red, Lefty, Roy. . . you could just name all the greats, and this was their stage. I never had even been inside the Ryman but in a couple of hours I was gonna be on that stage.

I put on those new clothes, pretty sharp, if I do say so, and slicked that hair down just right, shined those new boots till you could see your face in them, made sure I had extra guitar picks in my pocket, and reckoned as how I was 'bout as ready as one man could get for his first appearance on the world famous Grand Ole Opry. I grabbed my guitar and headed out the door . .

photo by Les Leverett

The Grand Ole Opry
Ryman Auditorium 1960

photo by Les Leverett

Roy Acuff

c h a p t e r 17

Entertainment School

FROM NASHVILLE, TENNESSEE AND THE RYMAN AUDITORIUM, IT'S THE GRAND OLE OPRY. . . let her go boys! (Fiddle swells, lights come up, square dancers swirl, Minnie Pearl adjusts the price tag on her hat, Stringbean stands at the edge of the stage with his long shirt, and pants that start at the knee, absolute chaos on, and around, and back of the stage, as the announcer, Mr. Grant Turner says, "And now ladies and gentlemen, here's the star of the Martha White portion of the Grand Ole Opry, Roy Acuff and the Smoky Mountain Boys!". . .)

It's just like standing in the center ring of the Ringling Brothers Circus. That's what I was thinking as I stood in the wings, looking out at the stage and the crowded auditorium. People that were stars and heroes of mine bumping and pushing past me, Roy Acuff balancing the fiddle bow on his chin while the Smoky Mountain Boys played the turn around on Great Speckled Bird. I had never been so scared in my life.

I had come to the back door of the Ryman Auditorium, stage entrance of the stars, climbed those twisting stairs, timidly pushed open the door and explained to the guard, sitting there in his steel folding chair, that I was Stan Hitchcock (except it came out sounding like Tan Itchock 'cause my throat was so dry - my tongue was sticking to the roof of my mouth) and that I was on the eight o'clock portion of the show. He looked at me right kindly, like he had seen them all come and go, and told me to come on in, I could put my guitar back in the community dressing room and to make myself at home.

I had been told to ask for Vito, the old, white haired father figure, confessor, confidant and stage manager, who somehow made sense out of this entire unbelievable, jumble. I found him, or rather he found me, standing there with my mouth open, taking it all in and looking like the country bumpkin that I was. He came up behind me, put his hand on my shoulder and calmed me just like a great horse trainer can calm a nervous horse. After we talked for a few minutes, and I started feeling a part of this circus, he sent me over to the corner to talk to the staff band's bass player, Junior Husky.

Junior's name was really Roy, although nobody called him that, but he was an old salt at this business of country music and he could make that doghouse bass of his talk. He had a note pad and took down the chord changes to my new record, made copies for the other musicians and that was the extent of rehearsal.

I stood there with my Gibson tuned up, a sick smile plastered on my show biz face, my new shirt and tie choking me and them tight pants had crawled so far up my butt that I could hardly breathe (a condition known as Entertainers Butt Breathing Syndrome). I listened to Roy Acuff say, "Well now neighbors, we've got a new boy from the Ozark Mountains of Missouri on the show with us tonight, he's gonna sing his brand new record for you . . let's give him a nice round of applause. . . Mister Tan Itchok (that's what it sounded like. I swear that's what the guard must have told him). I moved stiffly out to center stage, had the presence of mind to thank Mr. Acuff and did the only thing I knew for sure how to do. . . I reached down inside myself and pulled out a song.

All the time I'm singing, my mind keeps saying, you're standing right in the spot where Hank Williams stood when you listened on the radio as he sang "Lovesick Blues". How one part of my mind could do that, all the time remembering the words to my new record, I'll never know, but in about three minutes the song ended, the crowd applauded politely and I somehow navigated off stage.

The other entertainers were all friendly and welcomed me to their midst. But one, Dave Akeman, also known as Stringbean, sorta took me under his wing, took me over to the corner out of the way, lit up his old pipe and started telling me stories and just generally making me feel at ease. So, by the time of my next show at ten o'clock, again with Mr. Roy Acuff and the Smoky Mountain Boys, I was feeling much better and actually looking forward to getting back out on that stage. To my great relief, Mr. Acuff even got my name right this time.

I had picked a favorite gospel song that I loved, "Where No One Stands Alone", for my second number. Well, I don't know if it was because the crowd was more mellow or whether I was just in better form, but I went out there and hooked that song, I mean I wrung it plumb out. . . and half-way into it I knew that I had that crowd with me all the way. It was a powerful feeling.

As the last note was ringing out, the crowd just exploded and I stepped back from the mic with my heart just busting with emotion. I turned to leave the stage but Roy put his arm around me, turned me back to the mic and said, "They want more - do it for 'em."

With my heart about to burst with pride, I stepped back up to the mic to deliver my grand finale, when the dangdest sound I ever heard rolled across the stage. It sounded about like a baby calf that's caught in the briars, hollering for his mama, "WAAAAAOOOOOOOOOOOO!!!!!" Everything just froze on stage, especially me, as I caught sight of a figure out of the corner of my eye, just a-running for the edge of the stage.

Now, as most of you know, the man who was a mainstay with the Smoky Mountain Boys for longer than he cares to remember, the comedy relief, the Dobro player and harmony singer, was Bashful Brother Oswald.

Part of BBO's act was putting on these huge clown shoes, at least three feet long, running out to the very edge of the stage from the wings and whopping those shoes real loud on the wooden floor of the stage. This created a sound much like a watermelon hitting concrete after being tossed off the tenth story of a high-rise.

What none of us knew, however, was that between shows, Bashful Brother had slipped over through the alley in back of the Opry House and through the back door of that famous watering hole of the stars, Tootsie's Orchard Lounge. He had partaken of adult beverages to a degree not suitable for coherent and careful planning, of good, old fashioned family entertainment - a condition, as it turned out, most unusual of this fine gentleman, who was usually a credit to his race.

Well, the only race Bashful was interested in at this particular moment in time was the race to the end of the stage. Trouble is, when he ran past me and hit the end of the stage his big old shoes caught on the edge of a footlight and he just kept going. It looked like one of those news reel films where the airplane is taking off from the carrier deck, ya know the one where you see he ain't gonna make it, and he falls off the end of the deck and into the sea. Well, the only difference was, Bashful Brother fell off the end of the stage and right on top of a rather plump lady in the first row of those old wooden church pews. Pandemonium broke out in the crowd. They just roared - laughing, hollering, clapping and whatever - while I stood there just embarrassed to death.

As Oswald was being picked up and the woman being fluffed up, like a overstuffed couch, I kinda slumped off stage and headed back to the dressing room to put away my guitar, get those darn pants out of my butt and think about the encore. . . that almost was.

I was sitting in the dressing room kinda thinking it all over, when the door opened and Mr. Acuff came in. He evidently had come looking for me because he came right over, put his hand on my shoulder, and said, "Son, Oswald hadn't ought to have done that to you, messing up your encore and all, and I know he'll probably want to apologize for it later, but ya' know, the only reason any of us is here tonight is to entertain those good folks and I guarantee you they'll never forget this night of Oswald flying off stage. . . and son, you were part of it, so be proud. You did your job good tonight."

I've often thought of that night since then and the good advice that Mr. Acuff gave me: put aside ego, put aside pride and just go out there and do your job. . . whatever it takes, entertain those folks. Thank you Mr. Acuff, and thank you Bashful Brother Oswald for breaking me in right on my very first night on the Grand Ole Opry. I've never suffered from stage fright or taken myself too seriously since then. Man, how could you, when you have witnessed the world's greatest swan dive. It makes you realize that no matter how good you have just been, someone else can come running by you and do it better. Bravo Bashful Brother!

photo by Les Leverett

Bashful Brother Oswald

Dr. Humphrey Bate and the Possum Hunters
circa 1920's

chapter 18

Captain Ryman's Mother Church

THE GRAND OLE OPRY. . . that's where it all started. . .
Keith Whitley and Stan Hitchcock at the Ryman in 1987

The Grand Ole Opry was the creation of George D. Hay, known to millions of radio listeners as The Solemn Old Judge, and a man who came to the new medium of radio as a reporter for the Memphis newspaper, Commercial Appeal. He had a good bit of experience in radio by the time he made it to Nashville as the director of the new station WSM. George Hay had been with the station WLS in Chicago and was responsible for the start up of the WLS Barn Dance. Mr. Hay saw the opportunities in the Tennessee hills with the abundance of talent and folk music material and adopted the name The Solemn Old Judge. He started a show called the WSM Barn Dance at 8 O'clock, Saturday night, November 28, 1925.

The first performer was Uncle Jimmy Thompson, an old time fiddle player from Sumner County, just north of Nashville. A few weeks later the first of the old-time string bands, Dr. Humphrey Bate and the Possum Hunters, also from Sumner County, joined the show. The location of Sumner County as the home of the first performers on the country music radio show is not insignificant. This county is full of historic firsts: the first crop of corn planted by a white settler was planted right at Bledsoe Lick, now known as Castalian Springs; there's one of the first pioneer forts built, one of the major mound builder Indian sites, one of the largest log structures built west of the Appalachian Mountains - Wynnewood, and with its location on the banks of the great pioneer traveled Cumberland river, it was a hot bed of old time music. Dr. Bates and his musical neighbors would gather on the big front porch of the Wynnewood mansion and entertain the folks for miles around with the great folk music. A short time later came the Crook Brothers, the Gully Jumpers and the Fruit Jar Drinkers as the word spread about this outlet for folk music.

The WSM Barn Dance followed an NBC network show featuring classical and opera music. Toward the end of the network show the conductor of the orchestra said something like this, "Most artists realize that there is no place in the classics for realism, nevertheless I am going to break one of my rules and present a composition by a young composer from "Ioway" who sent us his latest number depicting the onrush of a locomotive. . ."

After this announcement the good doctor directed his symphony orchestra through the number, which carried many "shoooses" depicting an engine trying to come to a full stop. Then he closed his program with his usual sign-off. The engineer at WSM gave George Hay the signal that he was on the air and he introduced the program like this, "Friends, the programme which just came to a close was devoted to the classics. Dr. Damrosh told us that it was generally agreed that there is no place in the classics for realism. However, from here on out for the next three hours we will present nothing but realism. It will be down to earth for the "earthy". In respectful contrast to Dr. Damrosh's presentation of the number which depicts the onrush of the locomotive we will call on one of our performers, Deford Bailey with his harmonica, to give us the country version of his 'Pan American Blues.'" whereupon Deford Bailey, a wizard with the harmonica, played the number. At the close of it George Hay said, "For the past hour we have been listening to music taken largely from Grand Opera, but from now on we will present "The Grand Ole Opry."

The name stuck and the rest is history. The show went on to be the longest running radio show of all time. So, a black musician was involved with the naming of the show and the whole idea for the radio show came, not from the metropolitan area of Nashville, but rather from the Ozark Mountains. George D. Hay tells the story this way: "While working as a reporter for the Memphis Commercial Appeal, another reporter and I were sent on assignment to a little town on the Missouri-Arkansas border called Mammoth Spring. We were sent to cover the funeral of one of America's World War One heroes. After the funeral and after we had filed the story we spent the day roaming the region. In the afternoon we sauntered around the town, at the edge of which there lived a truck farmer in an old railroad car. He had seven or eight children and his wife seemed to be very tired with the tremendous job of caring for them. We chatted with the farmer for a few minutes and the man went into the railroad car house and brought out a fiddle and a bow. The farmer/fiddler invited us to come with him to a "hoe down" the neighbors were going to put on that night until the "crack o' dawn" in a log cabin about a mile up a muddy road. He and the two other old time musicians furnished the music. About twenty people came. No one ever had more fun than those Ozark mountaineers did that night." That experience stuck with George D. Hay until the idea became the Grand Ole Opry seven or eight years later.

This narrative of the foundation of the Opry comes from a first person account that George D. Hay wrote in 1945 describing the start up years of the great show. I believe it demonstrates the purity of purpose that was the driving force and the ultimate reason for its success for all these years.

Stan's First Publicity photo, 1959
Still living at the Boys Ranch

chapter 19

Moving to Nashville (Stan and the Flying Pigs)

LISTEN FRIENDS, I'M GOING TO NASHVILLE, IF IT HARELIPS HELL AND HALF OF GEORGIA. . . ain't nothing gonna stop me. . . uh, how bout loaning me five dollars for gas?

(Stan Hitchcock 1962)

I got back to Springfield, with my new found knowledge of entertainment, my one set of stage clothes and a burning desire to get on with it.

I went over to the radio station to talked to Si Siman and we both agreed that I, sure enough, needed to move on over to Nashville. It just so happened that Bob Tubert had quit the publishing rep job that he was doing for Si and Si asked if I would be interested in running the publishing company in my spare time - when I wasn't being a world famous singing star? After all, it would pay me fifty dollars a week.

Well, I carefully thought it all out, ran it all over, up, down and around in my mind, considered all the possibilities, and finally, twenty seconds later said I reckon I would take that job. Shoot, fifty bucks a week. . . what's not to take?

I gathered up my few possessions: one stage suit, one J45 Gibson Guitar, about four pair of Levi's, two pair of boots, one pair tennis shoes, four pair of socks, three changes of semi-ragged underwear, four shirts and assorted toilet articles wrapped up in two bath towels.

Kinda slim pickins' for a soon-to-be singing idol, but I figured when I got rich and had doubled my income to one hundred dollars a week, I could always buy another shirt and some new underwear. Besides, the only time you needed good underwear was when you had to go to the hospital, to the emergency room or something, and I planned to be real careful and not have any accidents.

I packed all my treasures in the trunk of my 1959 DeSoto (you remember, this was the car that had the push-button transmission that hardly ever worked), kissed the family goodbye, and headed out.

I had left all the money I had with the family so I went by my old friend, Warren Stokes and borrowed fifty dollars to make the trip and live until the big bucks started coming in.

With the new career in show biz financed, I left Springfield, turned that DeSoto east on Highway 60, (I can't believe y'all don't remember DeSoto, man, it was an American icon. The only reason it is not still around is because it was so long that not many people could park it). I was a man following the beat of a distant drummer, and that sucker was playing in double time.

About four hours later, around midnight, I was eating that highway up - that big straight-eight engine just humming. I pretty much had The Road to myself: I say pretty much 'cause there was one problem, (it almost caused me to wish I had put on my one good pair of underwear), you see, this was 1962 and that part of Highway 60 ran through a real remote area of the Ozarks, between Van Buren and Poplar Bluff, and it was still open range. . . uh-huh, no fences.

Well, I was kinda letting that old DeSoto have its head, feeling good, grooving to some country music on the all-night show on WSM, doing about 75 when I topped a little hill, started down a long grade. There at the bottom, laying all over the highway, a herd of hogs had set up camp for the night.

You have to picture what a DeSoto looks like; it is one of the longest cars that was ever built and had all the handling capabilities of a Sherman Tank. I wish you could have seen me maneuvering around those hogs. . . man, it was something. Hogs and hog poop was flying everywhere. I left that two-lane road, hit the ditch, did a complete 190, hit the pavement again, then the other ditch, slid sideways for about a hundred yards, finally got it straightened out and back up on The Road, eased to a stop, shut everything down and just sit there, with visions of little pigs dancing in my head. Now, if you have never had the experience of hitting a herd of hogs at 75 miles per hour. . . let me tell you something about it. You hit a deer, a buffalo or an elephant and it's like hitting a wall for a couple of seconds, then the momentum of the car throws them away to the side of The Road. You hit a pig and it rolls up under the car - you can't get rid of it. Hit a whole herd of them and it's like going over boulders three foot wide - and the sounds of this kind of accident are even worse.

The silence was really strange after that high-pitched screaming I had been hearing. I looked around and wasn't nobody there but me and what was left of the pigs, so I guess it was me. My butt had chewed the heck out of a pretty good pair of underwear, one side of that DeSoto had cleaned out a whole row of young saplings growing next to the ditch and I had burnt about an inch of rubber off all four tires. But, all in all, could have been worse I reckon. I cleaned hog poop off that thing for two weeks and my throat was sore for a couple days from the high-pitched screaming - but no lasting damage.

Later, driving on toward Nashville, my good angel on the left shoulder kept saying: "Hey, you better slow this thing down a little," while over on my right shoulder the devil would answer: "Yeah, when pigs fly."

Mom Upchurch's Boarding House
Boscoble Street, Nashville, TN

chapter 20

The Music Mother of Nashville

LORD, BUILD ME A CABIN IN THE CORNER,
OF GLORY LAND. . .
Curtis Stewart 1944

Maybe it was that I had driven all night and had way too much coffee that accounts for my memory of that early morning arrival in Nashville: the sun just coming up over the Cumberland River and shining on the few high rise office buildings downtown. It never has looked so beautiful in all the times I have come back to it. But man, that morning it was some kind of sight.

I had no idea where I was gonna live, but I had enough sense to make a phone call to my old friend Jimmy Gateley, who had moved to Nashville with his family a couple of years before. I had known him since high school and as everyone who ever knew him would attest that he was a special man. He was very talented and had been on radio at KWTO in Springfield while I was still in school. He then went on to be featured on the Jubilee. He had moved to Nashville, was having success as a songwriter and was just starting to work as front man for the Bill Anderson Show. He wrote the very first song that I recorded and he and his wife Esther had invited me to come sleep on their couch when I decided to move to Nashville.

The Gateleys lived in the Nashville suburb of Madison. I finally located their house and got there just in time for Esther to make me a good ole country breakfast of eggs, bacon, hash browns and biscuits and gravy. I guarantee you no one has ever been welcomed to Nashville any better than that. . . yessir, I love Jimmy and Esther- my home folks welcoming committee.

Jimmy was a smart man plus being talented, and he sure helped smooth the way for me those first few days in the big city. Everyone loved and respected Jimmy, mainly 'cause you just naturally knew he was a good man: a man of principle, honest, plain spoken with a gentle, kind spirit. He was having some good luck getting his songs recorded and he freely gave of his time and connections to acquaint me with the Nashville music community.

Jimmy was recording for Decca Records and writing for Champion Music, so by tagging along on his trips to the Row I met Owen Bradley and Jerry Crutchfield. Owen, of course, being the main reason for there being a Music Row since he had built his recording studio right on 16th Avenue South, and Crutchfield, the pioneer music publisher would later make a name for himself as a record producer. Both were quiet, patient men who always seemed to find time to be friendly and helpful to a new kid just learning the ropes.

Owen was the producer of many of the hits that my heroes had recorded, including Red Foley, Patsy Cline, Ernest Tubb, The Wilburn Brothers, Bill Monroe, Webb Pierce, Brenda Lee and so many more. He has always been at the top of my music pioneer list. He was a farm boy from Westmoreland, Tennessee, moved to Nashville when he was seven, and by the time he was fifteen he was playing piano in the wide-open town's gambling houses, road houses, lodge halls and anywhere else he could get into.

During the 30's and 40's Owen put together various musical groups and had started working at WSM. In 1947 he was made musical director of the station. During the 40's, 50's and early 60's the Owen Bradley Orchestra was considered the premier Nashville dance band until he disbanded in 1964. Owen started working with Paul Cohen, the head of the Country music Division of Decca Records in 1947, and in 1958 he was made head of the Nashville

Division of Decca Records.

His genius in the recording studio is legendary. His vision and leadership gave birth to what would become Music Row: attracting the artists, songwriters, publishing companies, record companies, and artist management and booking agencies that are now so famous the world over. Owen was simply the best.

The first week in town I rented an office building on 16th Avenue, just across the street from the Decca Records building. I moved the desk, chair and couch, which along with the old typewriter and Wollensack tape player made up the complete inventory of Si's publishing company, Earl-Barton Music, Incorporated. When I say office building, what I really mean is an old, two-story house that had been converted into an office building. It was typical of that time period for Music Row, which had been a quiet, middle income neighborhood until the 'billies moved in with their music business stuff. My office was actually a small upstairs bedroom that measured nine feet deep by ten feet wide. Billboard magazine had an office about twice the size of mine across the hall, and Faron Young Enterprises shared the downstairs of the house along with Hap Wilson's Central Songs. This was the way the Row started: just entertainment entrepreneurs like Owen Bradley and Chet Atkins who were buying up the old residences and changing them into offices and studios.

I touched briefly on the layout of music row earlier, but now let me take you on a tour. In 1963 if you started at the corner of Demonbruen Street and 16th Avenue South and started walking south, you would first come to the Wilburn Brothers Wil-Helm Artists Agency building where Teddy and Doyle were busy developing the career of Loretta Lynn. Next door to that was the most modern looking building, Decca Records and Champion Music. Across the street was my office building, and a half block down was Bradley's Studio, which is now Columbia Records. Next door to that was Capitol Records office and a group of booking agencies and publishers. Across the street was Cedarwood Publishing, Mercury Records and Bob Beckham at Raleigh Music Publishing. On the other side of the street, a half block down, they were just starting to construction on an office building that would be the home of

Audrey Williams Enterprises (Hank's widow, and Jr.'s Mom), Jimmy Key's booking agency and publishing company (where Tom T. Hall was just starting), Al Gallico's publishing company with Merle Kilgore and the ever beautiful Gail Talley in attendance. . . and my record company, Epic Records.

Next door to that an old house had been changed into a dark, smoky bar and hamburger joint and bore the very descriptive name, "The Professional Club". It was the local hangout of stars, songwriters, publishers reps, starving artists, con-men, con-women, drifters, settlers, pioneers, no-counts, somebodies, nobodies, snuff-queens, snuff-dippers, groupies, television evangelists, (yes, I once saw Jimmie Swaggert there), session pickers, arrangers, dis-arrangers, straight-men, crooks, good ole boys, fine ole girls and other folks that you might, or might not, want to hang out with.

That place drew me like a magnet. You remember the bar in Star Wars, with all the weird characters and aliens? Well, the Professional Club was kinda like that only the characters were weirder. Not really of course, but I sure met some interesting people there in those years - and they had a great hamburger. I guess if I had to use one descriptive phrase to describe the Row during this period it would be "hanging out." There was an attitude of total openness: sharing, mixing and mingling of talents, personalities, songs, guitar licks, rhythm patterns, piano fills, and recording techniques. We talked about which venues were good to pick in, which were hell-holes and other good and valuable information that pickers the world over should share.

At the Professional Club you could sit at one of the old beat up tables, the oil cloth eat up with cigarette burns and listen to Hank Cochran talk up a song idea with Harlan Howard, while Wayne Walker ordered one more round for Mickey Newbury and Kris Kristofferson - having to shout over the noise that Faron Young was making in his argument with Webb Pierce, while Mel Tillis tried to get a word in edgewise. It was a surreal experience, but it seemed perfectly normal at the time. I mean there was such an abundance of talent and genius that the spectacular was the norm. I remember in 1964 sitting at one of the tables with Red Lane, (one of the great guitar pullers, singers and songwriters), when Roger Miller came in and sat down with us. He had a brand new briefcase that he set on the table with a flourish. . . and then the darn thing started ringing! He opened it up, took out a phone and proceeded to astound everyone in the room: a dang phone in a brief case, who ever heard of such? Well, Roger was always ahead of the curve and he had bought the first mobile phone in Nashville. The rest of us had never even heard of one. He couldn't wait to show it off so he hurried to the sorry old club where he knew he would find a captive audience and had someone call him just as he walked in.

I set my office up that first week in early 1963, and then started looking for a place so I could get off Gateley's couch. I will always be indebted to those good folks. Jimmy died just a few years later - way too early. I think of him often and miss him a lot.

There was another friend, Leo Taylor whom I had met at a concert at the Shrine Mosque in Springfield, Missouri, just before I moved to Nashville. He was a drummer who worked with Kitty Wells and Johnny Wright. He told me that when I decided to come to Nashville he had a good couch. I had alternated between his and Gateley's for a couple of weeks and I was now ready to leave the nest. One day, about a year later, I didn't have enough money to buy groceries and somehow Leo Taylor heard about it. When I came home there was fifty dollars laying on the kitchen table and a note from Leo saying: "Use it, and don't worry about it." You don't ever forget something like that.

I soon found a place that was the very essence of the picker's Grandmother's House. It was on Boscobal Street and it was called Mom Upchurch's boarding house. She only rented to musicians.

Mom Upchurch was an elderly widow with pure white hair, sparkling blue eyes, a no-nonsense nature and a natural love for people in the pursuit of music.

Her house was an early American two-story, turn of the century stone structure with two bathrooms, four bedrooms, a small living room, an even smaller kitchen and a screened-in back porch.

You didn't rent a room; you rented a bed and shared a dresser. It was ten dollars a week, and every once in awhile, when Mom thought you needed it, she would slip you some of her home-cooked food; always a special treat for a starving musician.

Mom had a careful screening process, and evidently she knew

what to look out for, because I do not know of anyone ever causing trouble for the good lady. Well, I passed her inspection and moved in to the upstairs bedroom to the right of the stairs, first bed on the right, third drawer in the one dresser.

"No we don't have a closet, and don't use all the hot water when you take a shower or you are in a heap of trouble."

"Yes ma'am, I sure won't."

"And by the way, don't be making noise coming in at all hours of the night like some of those music people."

"No ma'am, not me."

"And another thing, do you like fresh apple pie?"

"Yes, ma'am."

"Well, come on then, don't just stand there."

So many pickers had lived there through the forties, fifties and into the sixties, that it would sound like a who's who to list them: Faron Young, Carl Smith and musicians from all the bands traveling out of Nashville. They all shared one thing: they loved this woman called Mom.

I have always believed that there should be a special award given to Mom Upchurch, or at least her own star in the walkway in front of the Country music Hall Of Fame.

When Mom Upchurch died a few years later the funeral crowd looked like a Grand Ole Opry lineup. All those starving musicians had grown up, moved on and stood out, but they had not forgotten Mom's house on Boscobel.

"The survivor, still standing
after all these years"
Painting by Stan Hitchcock
1982

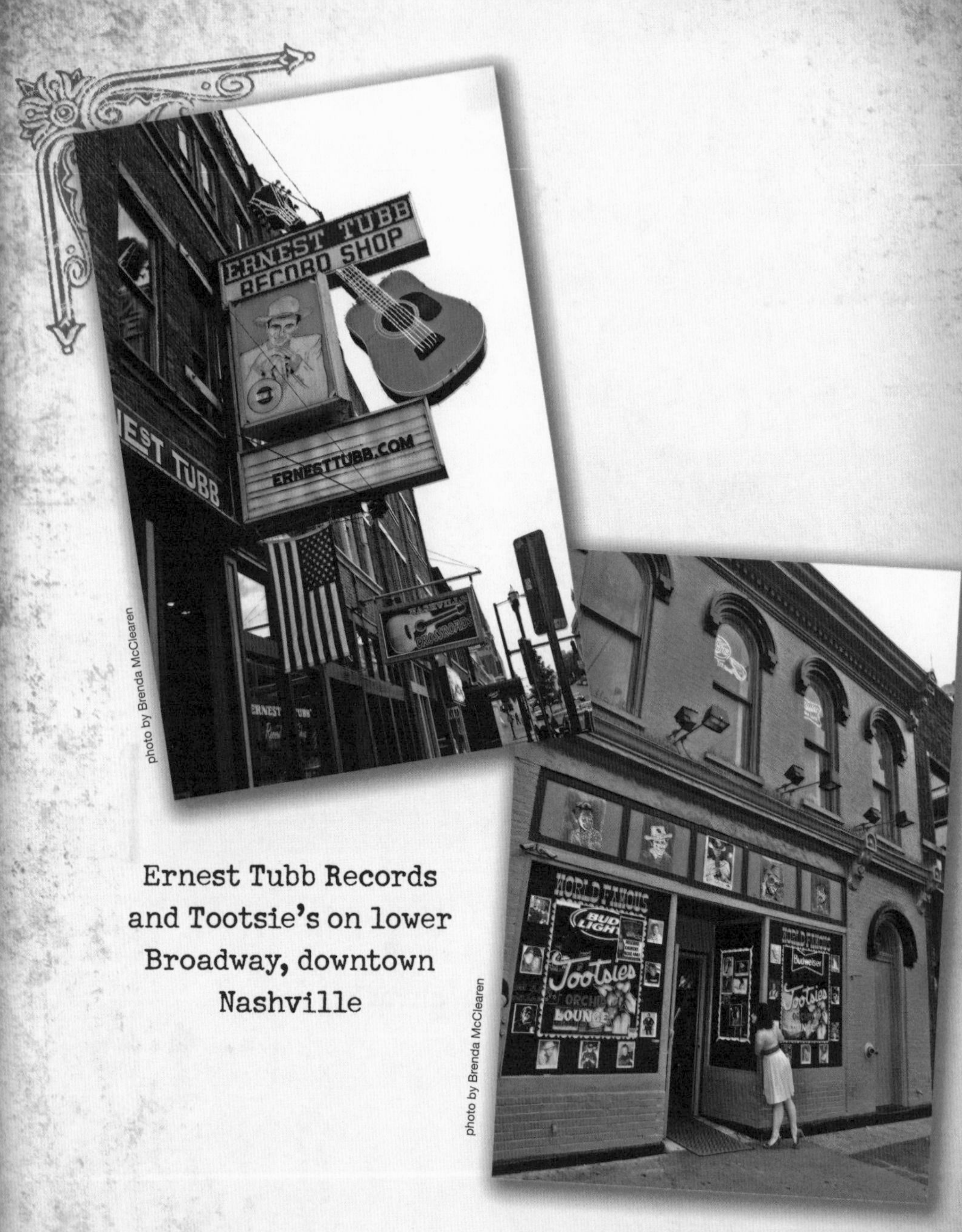

photo by Brenda McClearen

photo by Brenda McClearen

Ernest Tubb Records and Tootsie's on lower Broadway, downtown Nashville

chapter 21

Ketchup as an Entree - The 1963 Starving Musician Diet

I'M JUST AN OLD CHUNK OF COAL,
But, I'm gonna be a diamond someday. .
(Or at least a rhinestone, with a pretty good shine)
. . .Billy Joe Shaver

Now that I had an office and a bed to sleep in, I got down to the business of soaking up all I could about this music and entertainment industry. My first record had gotten quite a lot of airplay, but didn't sell diddley-squat, a condition not uncommon at that time in the business of country music. I soon realized that while the fifty dollars a week allowance I was getting from Si to run the publishing company was better than a sharp stick in the eye, it did not go very far in the big city. I was sending thirty a week home to the family, and paying ten for my bed. By my calculations that only left ten a week for food, gas and walking-around money. I realize we are talking about 1963 here, but dang, even by those standards that is 'bout as close to starvation as you can get. No wonder I can look back at pictures of myself then and say, "Boy, was I ever skinny." Malnutrition is more like it.

There was a restaurant downtown on Broadway just across from Tootsie's called Linebaugh's. It kinda took the place of a rescue mission for pickers. I mean you could order up a bowl of chili for fifty cents, eat about half of the bowl, fill it back up with ketchup and crackers, wolf that down, then top it all off with a large glass of milk, for an extra twenty cents. Man, you had a meal that would get you there. Trouble is, when you did get there you were so full of gas that people would just look at you, kinda move away and say, "Been to Linebaugh's again, huh?" To this day, chili does not taste right to me until I empty about half a bottle of ketchup in it.

Being so close to the old Ryman, the Opry crowd would always come in to Linebaugh's on Saturday night after the show. It was just kinda like going home to a family reunion every weekend. Tompall Glaser would be at the pinball machine, with Captain Midnight (a local DJ and certified character) hovering over his shoulder, driving him nuts. City View, the homeless man that lived on the roof of Tootsie's, would be cadging for drink money. Carl and Pearl Butler would be having a big plate of bacon and eggs, with Pearl's big laugh sounding out above everything. Faron Young by this time of night would be about half looped and trying to gross everyone out with his cussing. You had Johnny Cash drinking coffee, not eating anything cause he didn't want to spoil the pill buzz he was on; Roger Miller, high as a kite, traveling at the speed of sound, and just mesmerizing everyone with his genius; Ernest Tubb, dropping in for a minute for a cup of coffee, then going next door to his Record Shop; Marty Robbins setting with some of his band, laughing at some road stories; and the new kids, like me, just soaking it all up and loving it.

If it sounds like a family reunion to you too, then your family must be as funny as mine.

Courtesy Of Gusto Records, Inc.

Carl and Pearl Butler

Stan Hitchcock, 1967

chapter 22

Well, I'm a Honky Tonk Man, and I Can't Seem to Stop

. . .I love to give the girls a whirl to the music of the old jukebox. But when my money is gone, I'm on the telephone calling Hey, hey momma can your daddy comes home?

Johnny Horton, Columbia Records

Even though my first record had not exactly set the world on fire, the folks at the Opry seemed to like me and invited me to guest on the average of twice a month. It was always a joy to stand on that Ryman stage. The Opry never had paid much for its talent, and tickets were up to eight dollars a show by this time in the 60's: which always made me wonder about those early pioneer performers of years gone by. What did they do? Pay to play?

Anyway, it didn't matter, I was singing on the Opry and hanging with the big guys so I didn't care what they paid. Ott Devine was the Opry manager and he was always real good to me. He used me a lot in those early years. It was a real learning experience

I had been in town now about eight months, working the songs in Si's catalog, trying to get them recorded, and working the Opry almost every Saturday night. Still, I was just barely getting by, but having a great time, loosening up a little, knocking some of the green off, making lots of new friends, and feeling like I was ready to try The Road just a little.

I had met a singer and musician by the name of Smiley Wilson, who was half of the team of Smiley and Kitty, a fine traditional country duet. Smiley had just started a new career as a booking agent and asked me to come over to his office and talk about doing some shows. He was heading up the booking agency for the Wilburn Brothers booking them, along with Loretta Lynn, and he said he believed he could get me some dates if I was interested. I said, "Well, I believe I'm ready. Book me."

About this time, June 1964, Epic Records had released another record on me and it was getting some attention around the country. So Smiley was able to get me a few gigs down in Printer's Alley in Nashville and occasionally in other parts of the South, Midwest and Northeast.

In those days the Alley was wide open in Nashville, just like a Las Vegas gambling casino. It was really amazing. They had the private clubs, with the peek-hole in the door, and upstairs was heavy-duty gaming. Of course, gambling was illegal then, just like now, but through payoffs, crooked politicians, crooked cops and a general populace that just didn't give a rat, it was really big business in Nashville.

Red Foley loved to gamble, and one time when Si came to town we all went down to the Alley and I got to watch the big guys in action. Man, money was everywhere. The drinks were flowing, beautiful women just falling out of their dresses, people falling all over themselves to please Foley, and him laying down enough cash for me to live on for a year. Well, I did get a great steak out of it and I learned the important distinction between the haves and the have-nots. I never have cared anything about gambling, since my money is always so hard to come by, and besides, my whole business is a gamble.

Anyway, downstairs in the clubs of the Alley, they had some fine music, and some of the greatest musicians in the world: Floyd Cramer, Boots Randolph, Chet Atkins, Bob Moore. There was jazz, country, and big bands, along with some great comedians like Brother Dave Gardner and The Cut-Ups and some world-class strippers in Skull's Rainbow Room. The Alley was just another world in those days, and we are not likely to see those times again, but it sure was exciting then. For a young country boy who had led a pretty sheltered life, I was sure starting to advance my lower education.

I was spending a lot of time in the studio now, both for my own recordings, and also doing a lot of demo work for Hap Wilson the Nashville manager at Central Songs. Hap was an old music biz veteran, an ex-disc jockey, band-leader and husband of Marion Worth. He had gotten into the business end of music by running a publishing company. He had a heart as big as Texas, and throw in Rhode Island, and really was a good friend to me and everyone else that knew him.

Central Songs was a very strong publishing company that had been formed by Cliffie Stone, out in California. It was run by Joe Allison and owned a lot of copyrights. Hap had approached me to sing on his demo sessions, for his writer's new songs, and I had taken to it real quick because I have always had a knack for learning a song in a short period of time, and I soon was doing a lot of demos, at a rate of fifty dollars per song. There was an 18-year-old girl from the Smoky Mountains who had just arrived in town, and she was needing work also, so I ended up doing several demos with this girl with the big voice and the name of Dolly Parton. It is amazing to me that after all these years and all the acclaim she has attained, today's Dolly is still the same decent girl, kind, gentle and caring, as she was in those early years when none of us was sure where the next meal was coming from. I've always enjoyed her success because I know how hard she has worked for it.

Soon other publishers were calling me for demo sessions, Bob Beckham at Raleigh Music, Bob Tubert at Combine, and Merle Kilgore at Al Gallico's music publishing company. All in all, for a couple of years until my records got going good, this was a real help in fighting that old wolf, who was always just a few steps away from the door.

During this period of the demo days, I had met a young engineer by the name of Billy Sherrill who really knew how to get a great sound out of just about anybody. He was the engineer at a studio in the old Clarkston Hotel, next door to the building that housed WSM, and National Life Insurance Company. At the time my label, Epic Records, was using outside producers, and the president of

Epic, Len Levy, came in from New York and we went out to dinner to talk about producers because they wanted to pick someone to run the label in Nashville. I mentioned the great ear for music that this engineer Billy Sherrill had, and said he ought to talk to him about the job. Later that week Len Levy and Billy Sherrill met, hit it off, and the rest is history. Billy Sherrill was the new head of Epic Records, Nashville, and my producer.

Billy Sherrill is a certified genius in the business of music, and a great writer, and he was to make history on Music Row in the next few years, but, to me he was just my friend, and I was proud to share some life, and some music with him. In fact, I even sold him that 1959 DeSoto that I came to town in, just before the push button transmission went out. Hmm, not a good career move for a recording artist. We ran together during the lean years, and kinda went different directions later. But no matter, he's still a hero of mine.

Even though I now had two records out, was running the publishing company, doing demo sessions and starting to pick up a few gigs, I still needed to get some more money to live on. I had to get real work!

Dad's Old Workshop

Painting by Stan Hitchcock

1982

photo by Les Leverett

Gordon Stoker and The Jordanaires

chapter 23

The Fire in my Belly Turns to Acid Indigestion

I KNOW YOU'RE TIRED OF FOLLOWING My Elusive Dreams. . .

I had moved out of Mom Upchurch's, so I could bring Sandra and my daughter Marilyn to town by the fall of 1964. Sandra took a job at a wholesale electric company, while I landed a job as night manager of the Albert Pick Motel on Murfreesboro Road, in Nashville. Just up the street was a record distributing company owned by Hutch Carlock, Music City Record Distributing, and Hutch used to come to the Albert Pick to grab a bite or have a drink, and he recognized me as one of the hillbilly singers whose records he was selling. We got to talking and he said he needed a record promotion guy to promote the records to the radio stations, and to the retail outlets. So, I said I believe I would take that job, and I did, 'cause I have found that hunger will inspire you to take about any job that is offered to you, and a few that aren't.

Let's see now, from eight o'clock in the morning until two in the afternoon I pitched songs for Si Siman, then I rushed out to Music City Record Distributing to work the phones and pull orders and try to promote records, then at eight o'clock at night I went home to have a bite, then caught a couple of hours sleep, then worked at the Motel from midnight until six, then home for a quick shower and off to Music Row to start all over again. I did that from Monday through Friday.

On the weekends I would either work the Opry or else go do a gig somewhere on The Road. A busy schedule, but hey, I was young and full of vinegar. I had the fire in the belly and I could still hear that old train whistle blow in my mind. I still wanted to see where it was going in the dark of the night.

Meanwhile, of course, my marriage was totally gone, and for all practical purposes had been mercifully put to sleep. I had gotten used to the solitary life that I had been living in the months I had been in Nashville alone, and I wasn't taking well to domestic life. . . at all. In 1965, Sandra agreed to a divorce, and her and Marilyn moved back to Springfield. The mistakes made when you are young, you pay for as an adult. Fortunately for Sandra, this freed her up to meet a nice man, get on with her life, and find happiness in another marriage. In a couple of years Marilyn would make the decision to come back to Nashville and live with me, so all in all we made the best of a bad situation.

I remember one day I was walking down Music Row when a car slowed down and Gordon Stoker, of the Jordanaires singing group, told me to get in: he wanted to talk to me. I guess I had been in town about six months and the Jordanaires had backed me up on some of my recording sessions, so I knew Gordon pretty well. He said, "Stan, I been watching you pretty close, and I believe you're a good guy, but I want to warn you about all the temptation that this business holds for people like us. There's going to be women offering you pleasure that you have probably not even heard of. You're going to be right in the middle of drinking and partying all the time, and there are so many things that can just wipe a man and his career out. I really hope that doesn't happen to you. I just want you to know that I am pulling for you and I hope you make it."

Well, Gordon, no one has ever offered me better advice, and those words have echoed in my mind on many a long-driving night, coming or going to a gig in some honky-tonk in some town somewhere. You've always held a special place in my heart. You cared enough to try to give some good words of advice to a kid who didn't even suspect. I know that you and the other members of the Jordanaires have seen so many of us come and go, the good, the bad and the ugly, but you have stayed true, and proved that even though this business has a lot of temptation, it is possible to survive, and keep the faith. Thanks.

With me it took many years and lots of mistakes before I finally found the peace and happiness in a God-blessed marriage of love and commitment, and as I write this I almost wish I could fast-forward to the good love years. But be patient, my friends, we will get there.

Bill Anderson, Heart to Heart 1994

chapter 24

It All Starts with a Song

But Where Does it End?

MORNING COMES, AND LORD, MY MIND IS ACHING, and Sunshine standing quietly at my door. . . Just like the dawn, my heart is silently breaking. . . with my tears they go tumbling to the floor.

Mickey Newbury, 1960's.

Nothing tells it like a country song. Man, it just talks to you. It moves you and wrings you out, and after you get through singing it, if you do it right, you just feel emptied out inside. A Mickey Newbury song always has done that to me.

I have always been attracted to the creators of the music, the songwriters; Hank was one, Lefty was too. Don Gibson, Marty Robbins and Mel Tillis all had it, so did Hank Thompson and Bill Monroe. There is just something special about a person singing the songs that come out of his or her own mind and heart: Loretta had it, Haggard was full of it, and what about that Whispering Bill Anderson? Sorta got a funny voice, but who cares, he communicates the emotion of his songs, and he can sure write. And Bob Wills: he might only say "Ah-ha" and play some fiddle, but look at the songs.

Yeah, the saga of the singer-songwriter has always been an integral part of country music, but the real unsung heroes of this business, as far as I'm concerned (and after all it is my book, ya know), are the great song-crafters that kinda stay behind the scenes, pouring out their hearts in every song they create, letting that spotlight shine on someone else, singing their songs.

Now, it's not that these songwriters aren't good singers. On the contrary, some that you probably never heard of are the best singers I've ever heard. No, it's just that the songwriting gift is so strong in some people they don't have the desire to chase the entertainer/star elusive dream.

I've noticed there are two distinctive categories these people fall into, the singer/songwriter and the songwriter/singer. Marty Robbins, for instance, I would call a singer-songwriter because he lived to perform; it was his passion. He was a great songwriter also, but there was no way you could hide his talent under a bushel. He just had to shine. Newbury is to me the perfect songwriter/singer - even though he has one of the best singing voices I've ever heard. His passion is songwriting. He could have probably been another superstar if he had wanted it bad enough, because he could always mesmerize a crowd, but one thing is for sure, he is super to anyone that appreciates great writing.

In the 60's a migration of unusually talented songwriters started settling in and around the Nashville area, drawn by the changing musical climate and the ever-evolving sound of modern country music. There were new artists coming in with new influences and new ideas of how they wanted to do their particular brand of this music. The folk music boom, starting in the late fifties and on into the sixties, certainly had its impact, along with political and social unrest and the gradual change in the world we were living in. Songwriters and singers felt a new restlessness and experienced a new freedom; they were unafraid to say things just a little different and to use subject matter that had been taboo just a decade before.

The epitome of this new breed of songwriter was, and is, Mickey Newbury. Part of the time he lived in Hendersonville Tennessee, just a few miles north of Nashville, on a houseboat out on Old Hickory Lake. At other times he lived in a log cabin at the edge of this lake. Mickey is a Houston, Texas boy with music born in the Texas honky-tonks. There never has been another like him - probably never will again.

I first became aware of Mickey and the change that was creeping into our music when I listened to a Mercury album that Bob Beckham had given me one day in his office. It was Mickey's, and it was titled, "Looks Like Rain." It forever changed my musical tastes and preferences and made all three-chord songs, which was the norm at the time, sound real thin. Mickey has a way of poetically describing normal, everyday happenings, and turning them into something beautiful. His one big commercial hit, the compilation of "Dixie", "All My Trials", and "Battle Hymn of Republic", which he called "American Trilogy", has been recorded by just about everyone including myself. It stands as a monumental recording event. His "San Francisco Mable Joy" should be required listening for anyone even thinking about getting into this business. It's been a joy to be able to sit in a room with Mickey and just listen.

Mickey Newbury is the most talented person I have ever met, and I love him, but he has had his devils to conquer, just like so many others with the extra helping of talent. It's almost like they bare their souls, minds, and spirits so much, and reveal so much of what's inside them in their music, that they have to resort to a deadening substance just to stand this constant emptying out. Hank was that way, Lefty Frizzell, Red Foley, Don Gibson and so many others of their like. Addictive personalities were running free in Music City, and how most of us survived is still a mystery to me. Mickey Newbury passed away a short time ago, but what a legacy in song he left the world! And what memories they left for those who called him friend.

The people who were writing these new country songs, through the 60's and up into the early 70's and changing our whole country music culture, were; Newbury, Kris Kristofferson, Red Lane, Wayne Carson, Bobby Braddock, Harlan Howard, Willie Nelson, Hank Cochran, Mel Tillis, Wayne Walker, John D. Laudermilk, Bobby Russell, Curly Putman, Roger Miller, Bill Rice, Jerry Foster, Billy Joe Shaver, Guy and Susanna Clark, Whitey Shaffer, Bob McDill, Allen Reynolds, Jerry Jeff Walker, Tom T. Hall, Don Wayne, John Hartford, Billy Edd Wheeler, Glenn Martin, Wayland Holyfield, Glenn Sutton and Billy Sherrill and a host of others that were just arriving on the scene with their new ideas. I don't believe there will ever be another period of music and creativity, with so much done by so few, that will compare to the period of 1959 through 1974; peaking in the mid 60's. Every period of music has its peaks and hot spots, and there is argument galore for your favorite. But, man, this period was incredible for what it was proving could be achieved in American music!

Grandmother's Old Piano

Painting by Stan Hitchcock

1982

Stan in front of Decca
on Music Row 1963

chapter 25

Speed Bumps

I'M TAKIN' LITTLE WHITE PILLS, AND MY EYES ARE OPEN WIDE . . .Six days on The Road, and I'm gonna make it home tonight.

Dave Dudley, Mercury Records.

Dave Dudley recorded that song while he was working at the Flame Club in Minneapolis, had a giant record, and moved to Nashville in the 1960's. It was very descriptive, not only of the life of the cross-country truck driver, but also the pickers and grinners that were making the music on Music Row.

I don't intend to devote a lot of time to the dope subject, because it has been beat to death by so many others, but it is an important cog in the wheel that turned the mill that ground out the music in those strange years.

I want to be real careful not to glamorize what was happening, and yet give you an honest view of what it was like. So, with that in mind, come on, let's search it out and try to understand it.

Just about the time I was hitting Nashville, a new substance had arrived called "speed". Speed is an amphetamine. The choices were varied, but the favorites were; white Crosses; little white pills, with about five mils of speed, also called Bennies. LA Turnarounds; big ole black capsules that had thirty to fifty mils of speed and would let you drive non-stop to LA, turn around and drive back, and when you got back home you still wanted to drive around the block a while 'cause you didn't want to stop. Old Yellars; five to ten mils of speed in a small yellow pill, Speckle Birds; a pill that was half pink and half white, had about thirty mils of speed and a certain amount of downer, or tranquilizer, that was supposed to keep you from getting so hyper, and went by the medical term of Obedrine LA.

By the mid 60's there were many more combinations, all guaranteed to blow your mind, keep you going for days, and if you got hooked: ruin your life.

Johnny Cash is probably the most known for his use, and abuse, of speed during the 60's and 70's because of his open admission and his public battles to lick this addiction, but believe me, his experience is just the tip of the iceberg. Music Row was fueled by this stuff, and it was only going to get worse. It like to have killed Waylon before he beat it. Don Gibson beat it while Roger Miller made substance abuse a fine art: using it to write some of the finest songs that's ever been, then kicked it and lived clean and straight as an arrow. Ralph Emery talks about his battle with speed in his book. . . almost everyone, from musician to star, had at least tried it.

I was booked on a show in Loretto, Tennessee, at Gordon Terry's Terrytown. Johnny Cash was the headliner, along with the Statlers and Carl Perkins. I was standing in the wings, sorta talking to Cash, or trying to, which was not easy in those years 'cause he was kinda out there. It was just a few minutes before he was to take the stage, and his band was already on stage. He had someone hand him his little black bag. He took out a big prescription bottle of fifty mils speed pills, emptied out about eight of them into the palm of his hand, put them in his mouth and crunched them up like M & M's, then picked up a bottle of booze and chugged a big drink to swallow them. Then he strolled on stage, did that shoulder shake and throat clearing and just tore that crowd up.

Now, the mystery is how in the world did it keep from killing him when all that rush hit his heart? He must have a constitution like a draft horse. The good part of the story is, of course, his victory over drugs through the help of his good wife, June Carter Cash, and his faith in God. Johnny was a man, larger than the legend and strong enough to survive.

As far as I can determine, speed, or uppers as they were called, came from government sources and were developed for fighter pilots; to heighten their senses, give quick reflexes and sharpen their awareness in the heat of battle. Anyway, that is the romantic legend that all musicians wanted to believe. They activated your adrenaline gland, raised you blood pressure, took away inhibitions, made your mind go at breakneck speed and had the same effect of continually racing a car engine way up in the red line. Well, anything that would do all that is a natural for a musician who had the same needs and senses to sharpen in order to survive the wars and battles of the music business.

Recreational dope would come later, in the mid-seventies, in the form of cocaine, but at this early time the pills were not considered dope. They were survival tools in an exhausting, debilitating business. There were doctors who would prescribe them as diet pills for any picker who wanted them. President Kennedy was getting his "vitamin" shots of speed in the White House. It wasn't wildness as much as it was just plain ignorance of the substances we were putting in our bodies.

As I said, the sixties was payback time for country music and the starving fifties. Music Row was running wide open, at all hours of the day and night churning out the hits. For all the records that were being produced, there was really a very small core of the first team pickers: they were in constant demand. It was easier to get an appointment to West Point than it was to break in to the elite club, the "A Team," in the 1960's.

There were several "B Teams" that worked what the "A Team" couldn't get to. A session might be made up of one of the following guitar players: Grady Martin, Pete Wade, Jimmy Capps, Jerry Reed, Harold Bradley, Leon Rhodes, Jerry Shook, Wayne Moss, Fred Carter, Jr., Jerry Kennedy, or Hank Garland before he had his car wreck, with rhythm guitar handled by Ray Edenton. On steel guitar you'd have Buddy Emmons, Pete Drake, Hal Rugg, Lloyd Greene, Walter Haynes or Jimmy Day. On Piano would be Floyd Cramer, Pig Robbins, Jerry Smith or David Briggs and sometimes, a new guy named Ray Stevens. On fiddle would usually be Tommy Jackson, Shorty

Lavender, Buddy Spicher or Johnny Gimble. On drums, Buddy Harman, Larry London or Willie Ackerman. Bass was Junior Husky, Bob Moore, Henry Strezlecki or Lightning Chance with the utility position filled by Boots Randolph, who could play about anything, and the harmonica wizard Charlie McCoy. Now, there were other great musicians in this rare group also, but this is just an example of the hot players who, along with the background vocalists, The Anita Kerr Singers, The Jordanaires, The Leah Jane Singers and various combinations of each group, were on most of the records coming out of Nashville in the 60's.

A regular session usually ran three hours, and you tried to get four songs in during that time. The first sessions started at ten in the morning and would go to one in the afternoon. Then you had a two o'clock that ran to five, a six o'clock that ran to nine, a ten o'clock that ran till one in the morning. . . and then of course, there was overtime when a session might go two or three hours over to finish a particular project.

When you think of the pressure that was on these people to constantly come up with the hit sounds, the licks, the beats, the fills, the intros and endings, the harmony background, and do it all while keeping your sense of humor and pleasant personality. . . well, it's just amazing, that's all. And behind it all for a lot of the folks, to keep it going - speed.

Now, I don't want to give the impression that this was doping, running wild, party time, no; on the contrary, most of these pickers didn't have time to party; they were just trying to keep up, keep on going, be creative, get through the session and make the music special. But, of course, the result was damage to a person's health that in years to come would come back to haunt them. But these were the history makers, and man, could they play.

They had their fun, of course. . . like the time Pig Robbins, the blind piano player, got his first new Cadillac for his wife to drive him to all the sessions he was working. Well, being blind, Pig had never gotten to drive a car and this bothered the other pickers, so a bunch of them got Pig in his new Cadillac about three o'clock in the morning, after grueling, all-day sessions, and set him behind the wheel. They, being his eyes, were telling him, "Pig, turn it a little to the right, no, no, not that much. . . OK. . . push on the gas a little more. . . easy. . . hell we ain't in a race. . . OK, OK. . ." For about two hours Pig had the time of his life driving his new Cadillac up and down Music Row enjoying, for the first time, what we all take for granted in our everyday lives.

Certainly, everyone was not doing speed. There were a bunch of straight guys and gals that refused to give into it, but it was all around us: in the studios, on the street, in the clubs, on the tours, out of town and in the little writing rooms where the wired up, strung-out songwriter was churning out the hit songs that this mill required.

I was talking to Billy Joe Shaver, a survivor of those times, just the other day on my television show "Heart to Heart" and he told me, "Stan, I was just running wild, taking all kind of substances into my body, smoking so many unfiltered Camel cigarettes that my fingers had turned yellow; staying up for days writing songs and then crashing so hard that I didn't care if I lived or died. I had lost my wife and family, and I just didn't care anymore. I was at the end of my rope. One night I woke up in a cold sweat. Jesus was standing at the foot of my bed - you can believe it or not, but He was just standing there looking at me, kinda sad. Well, I got up out of that bed, went out to a big old high bluff overlooking the Harpeth River, (about twenty miles southwest of Nashville), and I stood on the very edge of that cliff, ready to jump off and end it all. Instead of jumping, I fell down to my knees and asked God to help me and heal me from all my bad habits. God saved me up there on that cliff. Then He gave me a song. I came down off that hill singing, 'I'm Just An Old Chunk Of Coal, But I'm Gonna Be A Diamond Someday.'" Yessir, Billy Joe found Jesus, whipped addiction, and came up with a hit song - all with one mountain climbing. I'm proud to be his friend and know that he survives.

Although I had never even heard of speed when I came to Nashville, it didn't take me long to get acquainted.

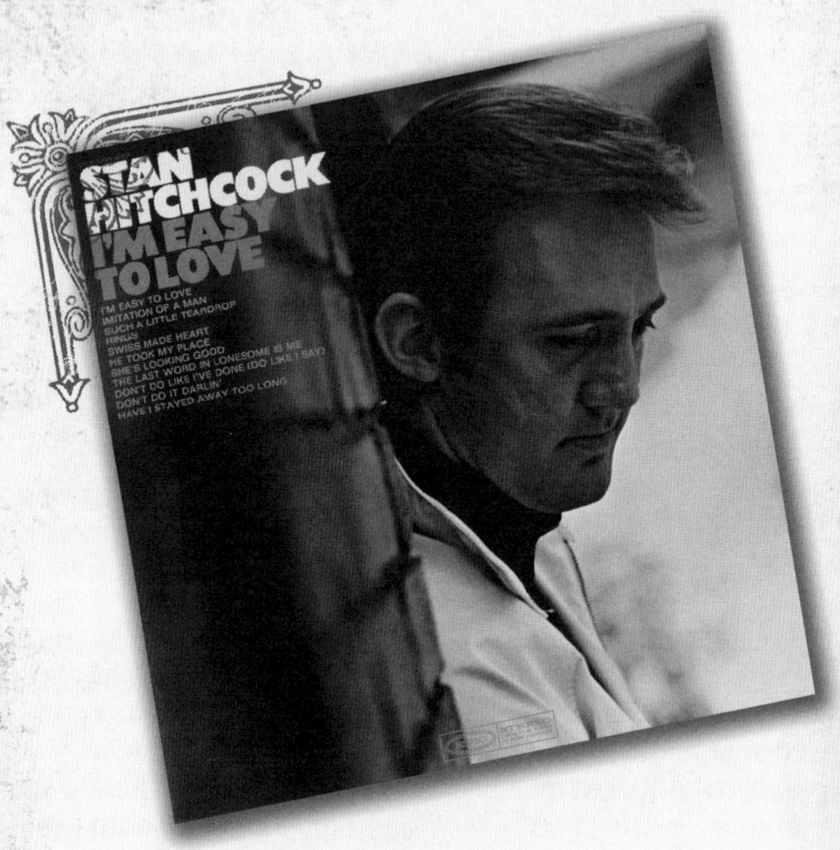

Easy to Love LP
1969

chapter 26

GodTalk on Clear Channel 650

I'M BACK IN BABY'S ARMS, how I miss those loving arms (written by Bob Montgomery)...

Stan Hitchcock, Epic Records 1966

Soon after arriving and settling in Nashville, I met and became friends with Ralph Emery. He was the all night DJ on WSM and also had a 6:00am morning television show featuring news, weather and country music. Television, the medium that I would be involved with for the next thirty years, was brand new to me, since, when I grew up in the Ozarks, we didn't have one. Ralph's show was my entry into the world of television. He, and later, Eddie Hill, taught me to communicate with a camera just as if it were a person.

I became a regular guest, and the chief stand-by when someone else would cancel at the last minute, for Ralph's show. Ralph was a natural on the tube and his show was really hot in the Nashville market. Trouble was, Ralph was really burning the candle at both ends; working the all night show, from 10 o'clock at night until 5:00am in the morning, then going down stairs to the television studio and signing on for the morning show. He pulled it off great, but it had to be a strain - particularly when he would have a radio transcription, voice over, or other project during the day when he should have been sleeping.

Ralph and I and spent a lot of time together and got real close. On top of his unbelievable schedule, he was going through some rough personal times, and I wanted to be his friend. We had some mighty deep, soul-searching conversations during this period, and he was good to me.

In 1965 I had been working on my first album, and doing a lot of sessions to get it all done. On one particular night, when we were all in Columbia's Studio B trying to get the project wound up, Ralph stopped by the Studio on the way to the radio station. I was worn out and in conversation with Ralph, mentioned the fact. Ralph reached into his jacket pocket, pulled out a pill bottle and shook out a couple of yellow pills. He said try 'em and see if they don't help you wake up. So I did. . . and they did; wake me up that is. In fact, thirty minutes and a couple of cups of coffee later, I felt great and was singing my heart out. That night I cut a song that was a big chart record for me and would become my theme song in later television shows; a song written by Bob Montgomery entitled, "Back In Baby's Arms." Ralph should have gotten credit on the liner notes, cause he sure saved the night.

That was my introduction to speed, although at the time I didn't think about it being dope: just something like NoDoz only better.

Two weeks later I was a guest on the Friday night Grand Ole Opry show. I was talking to my buddy Ray Pillow backstage, and telling him that I was heading out to drive to Florida after the Opry, to do shows down that way for a couple of days. Well, Ray took me back to the dressing room, dug around in his ditty bag and produced two black capsules, Black Beauties he called them, and said, "Hitch, if you get tired driving by yourself and start falling asleep, take these - man, don't have a wreck and kill your fool self." I stuck them in my pocket, grabbed my guitar and jacket and headed out the door, anxious to get on down The Road.

I had a show in Pensacola Saturday evening so I drove straight through getting there in time to clean up a little, do the show and start driving on down to South Florida for another show on Sunday afternoon. Well, it was about midnight Saturday night and I was just beat, nodding off at the wheel, jerking back awake and driving on. I stopped, got a cup of coffee to go, got back in the car and turned the radio real loud to WSM and the Grand Ole Opry. I still couldn't hardly keep my eyes open. Then I remembered the pills that Pillow had given me to keep me awake. I dug them out, and swallowed them both with the coffee: I figured if one was good, then two should be twice as good. Man, oh man, it wasn't any time till they hit me like a bomb. My eyes flipped double open, not even a blink, and stayed there. My mind was going ninety miles an hour, and so was the car. . . boy, I felt great. . . just tingling all over. I felt this way for the next hour: I was really grooving, all by myself, not even aware of the radio. Suddenly, in the middle of the music that was playing on the radio I heard this strange, disembodied voice saying, "Hitchcock, come in, Hitchcock. . . I know you're out there. . . Hitchcoooooooooock!" I'd like to had a fit: I mean, I was scared to death. It had to be God, (no one else knew where I was), talking to me just like a person - right there in the car. I pulled over, got out, just shivered and shook all over, kinda like the dog and the peach seeds, and just walked around the car for about fifteen minutes. Finally, I got back in the car and drove on, but I was one shook up hillbilly.

The next weekend after I had gotten back from Florida, I was at the Opry again and backstage in the dressing room talking to my friend, the great guitar player, Jimmy Capps. I kinda cleared my throat and said that I had something to talk to him about: a mystical spiritual experience that had happened on the way to Florida. After I got through telling my "Great Experience" story, Jimmy started laughing, and then, wiping tears of laughter from his eyes, told me what had really happened: Following the Opry show, every Saturday night, was the Ernest Tubb Record Shop. It came on about 12 Midnight or there-abouts, depending on how many encores Marty Robbins would get on the last show of the Opry. Well, that last Saturday night after the Opry, Ray Pillow was the host of the Record Shop, and Jimmy Capps was playing guitar. Seems that Ray had made several trips to Tootsies that night, and was feeling no pain. In the middle of the WSM broadcast from the Ernest Tubb Record Shop, Pillow was singing a song and turned to Capps for the turnaround. While Jimmy was picking the turnaround, Pillow went around to the edge of the stage, knelt down with his back to the audience, and got hold of the big old microphone that they used for the stand up bass. Using his hands to cup around the mic, he started sending me the message - just like it was a CB radio instead of 50,000 watts of clear channel power. The sound engineer, about half asleep by this hour of the night, like to have gone through the roof. He quickly got Pillow off that mic and back in front of the mic at center stage before anyone was any the wiser. Meanwhile down in Florida, driving through the night high as a kite, I was sure that God had called. . . and we had got cut off: "Hitchcock, come in Hitchcock. . . Hitchcoooooook. . . I know you're out there. . ."

This was just the prelude to many funny experiences that Ray Pillow and Stan Hitchcock would get into, and out of, in the years to come. Pillow, you're a hoss, old son, and you have made life much more interesting. I wouldn't take nothing for those years of our adventures. But dang, you like to have killed me with too much fun several times.

A short time later, I had my regular checkup with my doctor in Franklin, Tennessee and asked him about the diet pill every one was taking. He said, yeah, they were good things - he used them himself, and he would be glad to give me a prescription for Obedrine LA. As simple as that I had a whole bottle of fifty pills and a ticket to drive just about as long as I needed to, in any direction. Man, just grab that guitar and go. Uh huh, diet pills. . . I was six foot tall and I weighed a hundred and forty-five pounds.

There was a doctor who was the musicians' friend in Nashville, and every Monday morning his office looked like a who's who from the music community. They had all come to get their prescription for "diet pills". Sadly, he got busted, and the musicians mourned for months afterward. It was kinda unfair to single him out because doctors all over the country were prescribing speed as diet pills. . . for mighty skinny people.

I guess I am blessed with not having an addictive personality: no drinking problem, no weakness for cigarettes, I've never even been close to cocaine, and a marijuana cigarette is about the stinkiest thing I ever have smelled. I hate them. However, I could have fallen real bad for this speed: this elixir for extended romance, this song inspiring, creative juice releaser, nectar of the stars, or just dope, in plain English. No matter how you try to romanticize it, that's all those diet pills were. It didn't happen however, because shortly thereafter a big report came out about the dangers of these drugs and they were taken off the legal market. That was enough for me - and most of my friends, too. But for a lot of folks it only led to heavier duty drugs, and wasted lives.

Every time I get to thinking about those days, I feel more thankful that we made it through. Like Billy Joe Shaver says,

So, ride me down easy Lord
ride me on down
Leave word in the dust where I lay
Say, I'm easy come, easy go
and easy to love when I stay. . .

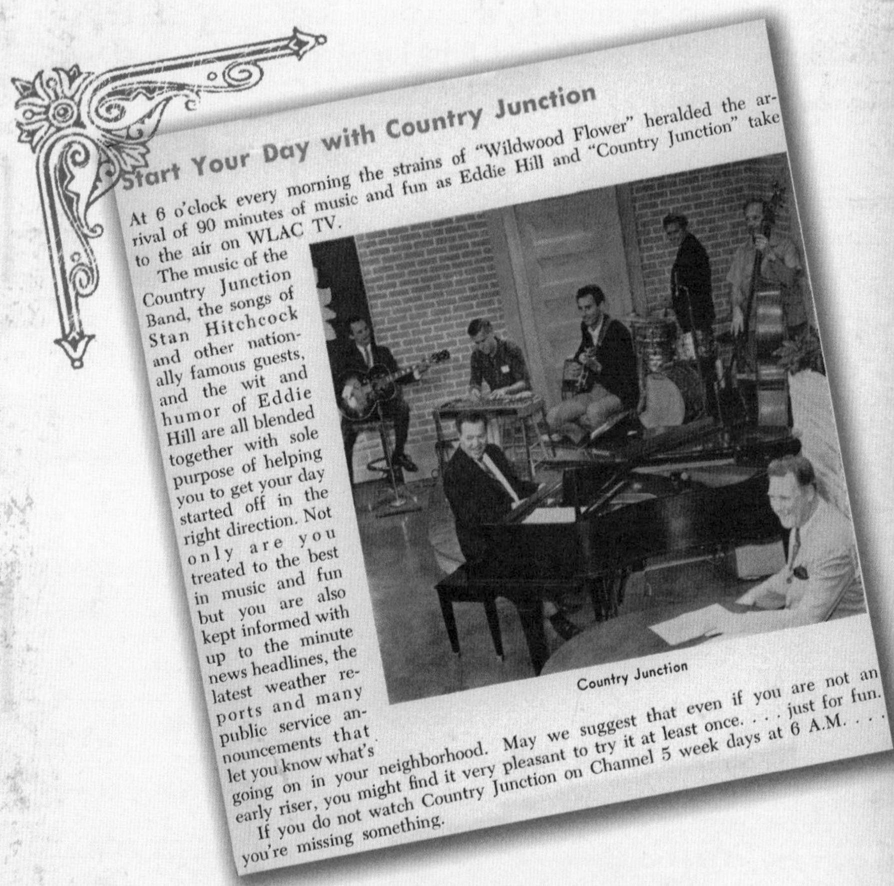

Start Your Day with Country Junction

At 6 o'clock every morning the strains of "Wildwood Flower" heralded the arrival of 90 minutes of music and fun as Eddie Hill and "Country Junction" take to the air on WLAC TV.

The music of the Country Junction Band, the songs of Stan Hitchcock and other nationally famous guests, and the wit and humor of Eddie Hill are all blended together with sole purpose of helping you to get your day started off in the right direction. Not only are you treated to the best in music and fun but you are also kept informed with up to the minute news headlines, the latest weather reports and many public service announcements that let you know what's going on in your neighborhood. May we suggest that even if you are not an early riser, you might find it very pleasant to try it at least once. . . . just for fun.

If you do not watch Country Junction on Channel 5 week days at 6 A.M. . . . you're missing something.

Country Junction

Early Morning Show
"Country Junction"
1966

chapter 27

Ain't No Insurance In the Music Business

THAT TELEVISION IS A DEVIL BOX, SON,
and I wouldn't have one in the house.
. . .Big Stan Hitchcock to his son Stanley Edward in 1950.

In 1966 I started two new things: another marriage and the beginning of a television career. Of the two, only the television career lasted. I don't know anyone who was less prepared for a successful marriage. . . or a television career, but I jumped in with both feet -- just like I usually do. Look out boy, here I come, ready or not!

I married JoAnne Roberts, and we moved out to the Franklin, Tennessee area. JoAnne had a four-year-old daughter named Jay who I later adopted, and not long after, my daughter Marilyn came back to Tennessee to live with us. Soon another daughter was born and we named her Lori. I had hopes that I could do this marriage right and live happily ever after, just like grown folks are supposed to do.

My television career came about when I got a call from Lightning Chance, the legendary bass player and true character from the Grand Ole Opry and recording studios. Light told me that my old idol from radio, Eddie Hill, was putting together a new band for his morning television show, "Country Junction", and they wanted me as the vocalist and rhythm guitar player. I didn't know it then, but this was the turning point in my show biz life.

Eddie Hill had been a legend in early country radio, first as a performer and musician, and later as show host and disc jockey. He went on to be a part of the Grand Ole Opry, both as an announcer and performer. Eddie who had written some early hits, including one recorded by Hank Williams called "Some Day You'll Call My Name", had now left the Opry and was hosting the early morning television show on WLAC-TV, the bitter rival of WSM, in both radio and television. It was pretty common knowledge, in those days, that if you wanted to work on any of the WSM properties, including the Opry, you did not work for WLAC. There was a reason for all this: for behind the scenes, what was really controlling everything, was not entertainment. . .it was insurance.

The National Life And Accident Company of Nashville, Tennessee, had entered radio with the formation of WSM. In fact the call letters stand for "We Shield Millions", their company motto. Yes, The Grand Ole Opry was formed as a radio show to sell insurance. In the late 30's and all through the 40's National Life agents gave away tickets to the Opry in order to sell policies. It was genius marketing, and they expanded into television with the formation of WSM-TV, the NBC affiliate.

The Life and Casualty Insurance Company of Nashville, Tennessee, had formed the radio station WLAC, which also identified the company in its call letters, and they too had gone into Television with WLAC-TV the CBS affiliate.

Well, it was a case of this town just is not big enough for the two of us, kind of thing - bitter rivals, and woe to the one who got caught up in the feud.

Just prior to my meeting with Lightning Chance, the rumor on the Row was that Bob Luman and myself were to be the next new members of the Opry, and that coincided with the frequency in which I was being featured as a guest. So there was some real consideration about my career choices.

I met with Eddie Hill and was just captivated by the man's warmth, charm and his vast knowledge of this new medium of television. He said he believed that I had what it took to make a success in television, and that he would help me do just that. Well, how often do we get the chance to work with our boyhood idols? I gripped his hand in a deal shake and said, well, let's do it and see where it goes. I have never regretted that handshake.

A couple of weeks later, I recorded my favorite record, "She's Looking Good", a song I found in the waste basket of Billy Sherrill's office written by Autry Inman. It did real good for me, and has been recorded by lots of other Artists since, but it was mine first, and I'm proud of it. The Jordanaires sang back up and got that high lonesome harmony that I love. It charted well, and the bookings started picking up so I was able to quit taking outside jobs, and concentrate on my music career, just like the big guys do.

Stan and Eddie with matching hats
and Eddie's two sons quail hunting in 1966

Eddie Hill

chapter 28

OK, Just Look Into the Eye of the Camera and Pretend it's a Person. . .

. . .and sing your heart out, to those folks watching, at home

. . .Eddie Hill to Stan Hitchcock. . . 1966.

Eddie Hill only knew how to do things one-way: the right way, and with all the enthusiasm you can muster. He had learned how to talk to people, through television, in such a manner that you just felt he was talking right to you, no one else.

He was a big man: robust, and fit, with a smile that came from way inside. His formula was simple. Just be yourself, and don't try to fool those people out there by pretending to be something you're not, 'cause they know better, and it's not gonna work. Because of that, he could only really sell something that he believed in, but boy, if he believed in it, watch out. . . he'd sell it to you.

The first band consisted of Lightning Chance, bass player and bandleader; Hal Rugg, steel guitar; Pete Wade, lead guitar; David Reece, vocals and comedy; Willie Ackerman on drums and myself on vocals and rhythm guitar.

This was a great show, and soon was number one in its time slot. Everyone wanted to guest on it. . . in one week you might have John Hartford, singing a new song he had written called "Gentle On My

Mind", Dolly Parton singing "Dumb Blonde", Johnny Paycheck doing "Apartment #9", and Jerry Reed with "Remembering". . . just an endless variety of talent. The quality of the musicianship was just spectacular - these guys were all "A" Team players, and it was just great picking rhythm guitar behind them.

Sammi Smith, the great singer who would later record "Help Me Make It Through The Night" and have so much success, had just arrived in town. I had heard her singing down in the Alley and invited her to guest on the show. She was so good that we all turned her into a semi-regular guest. I would pick her up coming in from my house in Franklin and give her a ride to the station. Sammi had written a song called "Sand Covered Angels", about being separated from her children in a divorce, and I always begged her to sing it 'cause it just tore me up. Well, we about worked her to death, which was fine for Sammi until her big hit record took her away from us. Those million selling records will do it every time.

We all had to get up about 3:00am and be at the station in downtown Nashville by 5:00am, not an easy thing for these musicians who were sometimes working at recording sessions until one in the morning. I would sing at least two songs per show, which ran from 6:00am to 7:30am five days a week; and we had to constantly learn new material. I was also part of the Lonesome Valley Trio, a gospel trio made up of Eddie Hill, David Reece and myself. We would stand at the mic and sing the great songs of the church out of an old hymn book.

David Reece is a gospel legend, having worked in early gospel quartets and writing some of the great songs that are in those hymn books. He is also the best baritone singer I have ever heard: and I have heard a few. In addition to being a great musician, singer and songwriter, David Reece is the most naturally funny man that I know of. He would change into another character sometime in the middle of the show: a comedy character named Uncle Willie, complete with white wig and white beard. He was hilarious. People still talk about him today: remembering the great skits we used to do. Eddie would be his straight man - it was like Abbott and Costello, gone Country. David Reece passed away after a long illness in 1999.

Hal Rugg, who passed in 2005, was one of the great steel guitar players, having experienced it all out on The Road as a traveling road hog musician for a number of years. He was part of the George Jones band when it was one of the best out there; a wilder bunch never lived. The Adams Brothers were part of the band, along with Charlie Justice and Hal. This was in Jones' heyday and Hal's experiences could fill a book, all by himself. He had quit The Road, stayed in town, and was one of the more sought after musicians for sessions and the one Owen Bradley would call for all of Loretta's sessions. Hal has the kind of personality that just makes you want to be around him: and he was always the same, even at five in the morning when he had been working most of the night.

Lightning Chance, who passed in 2005, deserves to be placed in the Country music Hall of Fame as an example of a Country musician who has seen it all, and been a vital part of most of it. He would look good standing there in the glass case, his old pipe with the alligator carved in it, that arm wrapped around that old stand up bass of his with that devil may care grin on his face that says, "come on give me your best shot, I'm ready". Light had worked with Eddie Hill for a number of years in Memphis and Nashville and they were real close, Lightning knowing what Eddie wanted even before Eddie did most times. He always had the ability to give me confidence in whatever we were doing at the time, and I learned a lot from Light: truly one of the good guys.

Pete Wade played lead guitar but only worked the show for a short while because of his busy recording session schedule. He is still one of the leading guitar players in a town that has seen the best. Jimmy Capps, who would stay with the show the rest of the course, then replaced him.

Jimmy Capps and I had become friends from working The Road and the Opry. He was working for The Louvin Brothers, Ira and Charlie, and then worked for a while with Ferlin Husky and later Margie Bowes. I remember one show that Jimmy and I traveled on together when we were all just barely getting by, up through the North Country ending up at Alpena, Michigan in the dead of the winter. Now, I wasn't making much money then, and every date counted. Boy, you wouldn't believe how it counted. Anyway, we got to the show, Jimmy Capps, Margie Bowes and myself, all traveling in Margie's Cadillac. It was snowing so hard you could barely see The

Road. The Headliner of the show that night was Slim Whitman, with Margie and myself the supporting acts. We got all set up on the little stage of the city auditorium, changed clothes in the dressing rooms and started waiting for the crowd, and waiting, and still waiting. It was snowing a dad blamed blizzard outside and these folks living up here knew better than to be out in it. However, about 50 folks managed to get to the auditorium, and we put on a heck of a show. After the show the promoter called us all together and said those dreaded words, "Folks, I don't have the money to pay you all, what with the advance sales and the few walk ups, I only took in four hundred dollars. He held the small roll of bills out to Slim Whitman, the star and the one with the most clout. Well, my heart just sank as I watched those bills disappear into Slim's big hand. And then, a funny thing happened. Slim took the bills, counted them out, divided them equal into two parts, handed Margie two hundred and then handed me the other two hundred, and said, "Here you go, I'll just get mine later. Y'all have a good trip home." Good lesson: when you have the clout to take it all and you choose to share with others who might need it even more than you do, well, that's the making of a man; and in my book, Mr. Slim Whitman is a hell of a man.

Capps and I shared many adventures in the years to come, and I consider him one of my brothers-in-arms. We have fought the wars together, and survived.

Willie Ackerman, who later went on to be featured on HeeHaw for so many years with the hand-clapping shout: "We'll be right back, we'll be right back", worked with us for a short while and then turned the drums over to Buddy Rogers who later became rich with his catfish restaurants.

So this was the bunch that spent several years together, working that old morning shift. We all loved the show. It was special because of the people involved; Eddie, the band, the guests, and the television crew - all of them eager to share talents, ideas and creativity, and nobody worried about who got the credit.

Live Television is a special event in itself, just by its very nature. It keeps you on a high level of expectation with the excitement of everything happening real time: no stopping the tape and doing it again and again, no edit points, no erasing bloopers, just the real thing. It also can be real embarrassing when you get caught off guard.

Working the show, the long hours and the traveling sometimes took a funny turn. I would work the show Monday through Friday, and then leave for road gigs on Friday morning as soon as the show was over. I had been doing the show for about a year, traveling as a single using house bands, doing all the driving by myself. Being sleepy all the time was becoming a way of life.

One particular weekend I was booked Friday night, Saturday night and a Sunday matinee, and it finally got the best of me. I left as soon as the show was over on Friday morning and drove all day to Bristol, Virginia for my show that night. When the show was over, about two o'clock in the morning, I loaded up and started driving to the Washington, D.C. area for my Saturday night show. I got checked into the motel about three o'clock that afternoon, got a shower and slept, or tried to, and after a couple of hours got up, dressed for the show and went on over to the club. I played four sets from 9:00pm to 2:00am. Sunday morning I got loaded up and headed out for Roanoke, Virginia where I had an afternoon show. I arrived at the Roanoke gig, an outdoor park, and did two shows, between 2:00pm and 6:00pm then loaded up and was on The Road again heading back to Nashville, pushing to get there in time for the 6:00am TV show.

Well, I made it back to the station, getting there just in time to clean up and change clothes. I went out to the studio, tuned up my guitar and sat down on my stool in the corner by the band. I was so tired that my eyes could barely focus, but I looked at the schedule and saw that our special guests that morning were The Happy Goodman Family, a great gospel group from Kentucky.

I made it all right for the first hour of the show, but I was only hitting on about two cylinders going into the last thirty minutes when Eddie called the Goodmans back out for another number. Now these folks are about as good as you get in Gospel music, they can flat sing and I love their music. But, right in the middle of their big number I fell sound asleep, fell off my stool, fell on top of the mic, running it through my guitar. I hit the concrete floor and rolled right out in front of the Goodmans, who were just at the high point of their big ending. Well, they saw me roll out there in the floor in front of them and being good Pentecostal folks, they just naturally thought that I was having a religious experience and holy-rollin' all over the studio. . . so, of course, they started shouting and praising the Lord. I wanted to crawl in a hole somewhere and die, but instead, I just kinda slunk back to my newly ventilated guitar, picked it up, placed the mic back in the right place, set the stool back up and meekly nodded my head that yes indeed, I had an experience all right, just not exactly the experience they had in mind. After the Goodmans left, the band just ragged me unmercifully. I never did have the heart to tell the Goodmans any different, but my little girl Jay, who was at home watching television while she was getting ready for kindergarten, calmly stated, "Mom, Daddy just fell off his stool on the television, and all those other folks are hollering about it."

Painting by Stan Hitchcock
1986

Connie Smith

Stan Hitchcock's
Heart to Heart
Guests 1994

Dan Seals

Tom T. Hall

chapter 29

"Television is My Life, If it Don't Kill Me First"

LADIES AND GENTLEMEN, FROM NASHVILLE, TENNESSEE, IT'S THE STAN HITCHCOCK SHOW brought to you by Campana's Ayds Reducing Candy. . . and now here's the star of our show. . .

Eddie Hill was good as his word about helping me do well in television, and after we had been working together on the morning show for a little over a year, he began talking to the station owners about doing a syndicated television show called "The Stan Hitchcock Show".

WLAC-TV had formed a newly syndicated television division called Twenty First Century Productions, and were interested in the booming syndication business, particularly, the country music syndication business. In the 1960's there were a number of country music television shows: Porter Wagoner, Bill Anderson, Jim Ed Brown, Del Reeves, The Wilburn Brothers, That Good Ole Nashville Music and Buck Owens, who produced his show out of Phoenix. Everybody worked everybody's show, and it was great times to be in television.

Twenty First Century Productions started producing "The Stan Hitchcock Show" in 1967 and Eddie Hill was the executive producer. Soon, Aaron Brown, the company's super-salesman was out on The Road clearing the stations and had got us on the air in about a hundred stations nation wide.

We had been in production for the first thirteen episodes of my show and it was looking pretty good on the air. Eddie and I were working to keep improving the on-air look and production value as we started laying out the next thirteen shows, which would be shot in the new studios that WLAC was building. One morning, after the Country Junction show, Eddie and I went to breakfast with some of the band and he started complaining about having a headache. Nobody could ever remember Eddie complaining about anything hurting him, so this was an unusual happening. All through breakfast his headache kept getting worse and finally it got so bad that he asked me to take him to the emergency room at St. Thomas Hospital to get something to stop the pain. We had just gotten to the emergency room and they had him on the table when the aneurysm on the blood vessel in his brain burst and the cerebral hemorrhage hit him like a freight train. Doctors and nurses worked frantically to save him, and they were successful, but Eddie would never be the same. He suffered brain damage, partial paralysis and speech impairment. His television days were over. This was a deep personal loss to me because of the love I had for this man: my hero. His wonderful family, wife Jackie and the two sons and daughter, gathered around him and loved and cherished him for many years until he died a few years ago 1994. It was one of the great privileges of my life to have worked and studied under Eddie Hill, and though it would not be the same without him, we had to pull ourselves together and move forward, just like he taught us.

The head of Twenty First Century Productions, Roy Smith, asked me to go with him to Chicago to meet with the chairman of the board of the Campana Corporation, which manufactured such products as Cuticura Soap and Ayds Reducing Candy. This company was looking for a new promotional vehicle since Arthur Godfrey, who had been their spokesman for years, had retired. Well, we must have said something right, because the sponsor bought the show, and I became the new spokesman for their products.

We had determined that to compete with the other shows featuring country music, we had to do more of a production type show and not just a stand-at-the-mic-and-sing show. So, we would open the show, after going to commercial immediately following the introduction, with a themed number that had some kind of unique twist to it. The studio at the station had just installed an effect called Chromakey that allowed you to put different backgrounds behind singers. We had a ball with it.

We were shooting a series of thirteen shows, two shows a day for a week, and we had invited the chairman of the board of Campana and his wife to visit the set and watch some shows being produced. They were seated in comfortable chairs in the studio, and we had gone out of our way to impress them with our good production.

I was scheduled to sing a song about traveling to start the show off, and the director had brought in a parachute specialist from Fort Campbell, Kentucky to strap me into a parachute harness. Now the plan was this; they would hook a block and tackle to the ceiling of the studio, tie the parachute cords to a rope, run it through the block and tackle, hook me to the cords and pull me up to the top of the ceiling: about twenty foot off the concrete floor. Then they would super-impose a picture of an airplane flying along and a parachutist jumping out. Then cut to me being slowly lowered down on the rope, holding to the parachute cords, singing my song. Everything was working fine as the crew hauled in the rope and pulled me up to the top of the studio, even though this parachute harness was a little tight, and kinda binding me where it crossed between my legs with my entire weight centered on my crotch. The music started, the film of the plane was rolling, and the director gave the signal for me to start singing and for the boys on the rope to slowly start letting me down. I don't know what happened, but somehow the rope slipped, and when they grabbed it, it jerked and one of my precious body parts got caught under the parachute straps that were between my legs. Excruciating pain, tears in my eyes and no way to get it out because my whole body weight was on it, I was singing at the top of my voice, hitting high notes that only a dog could hear with every color of the rainbow flashing before my eyes. Oh why did I choose a three-minute song? I don't care about television anymore. Am I being punished for falling asleep during that gospel song? . . .oooooooooome. . . at last I felt the concrete floor under my boots, and the hundred and fifty pounds of pressure suddenly let up. I stood there, weak in the knees, tears still in my eyes, when the director hollered: "Cut, that's a take". The chairman of the board and his wife hurried over to where I was standing, trying to get my breath, and said, "My boy, that was the most emotional performance I have ever witnessed. Our company is proud to be associated with you." I mumbled my thanks and stumbled to the dressing room, where I did a quick inventory and found that everything was still there, though black and blue and throbbing like all get out. I remembered the old show biz saying, "Break a leg", but man, this was asking too much.

Well, after that fiasco, I should have known better, but show biz folk are not known for their common sense: just their creative sense. A couple of shows later the director decided that he had a fool proof idea for the setting of my singing of "Jambalaya", and asked me to climb up into an aluminum fishing boat that they had rigged up on some three foot high saw horses. The idea was for me to sit in the boat with my fishing rod, pretending to fish, while they show a scene of the Louisiana bayous on the screen behind me. They had to elevate the boat up three foot high to get the right angle. Meanwhile, the director had told a couple of stagehands to crouch down out of sight of the cameras and gently rock the boat to give the illusion of the movement of waves. OK, everything in place. Lights, action, camera. . . start music. . . cue Stan. . . sing. . . OK, rock boat. . . easy, not that much. . . Watch it! Look out! Woooooow! I am laying flat on my back with the dang boat on top of me and I feel like every bone in my body is broken. The energetic stage hands had rocked the boat all right: right off those three foot high saw horses and crashing down on that old concrete floor that I am getting to know so well. It wasn't the fall so much as it was that sudden stop, and then the boat landing on top of me. OK, everyone take a ten minute break while we get the boat set back up. . . Stan, go back to make-up - your face looks funny.

Another time, I had chosen the song "Early Morning Rain" as the opener. At the end of the song, just as I'm singing. . . "In the Early Morning Rain, In the Early Morning Rain, Ummmmmmm", they threw a full bucket of cold water in my face. They didn't want to warn me before hand because they wanted the surprise reaction. Well, they got it all right. By the end of the song I was feeling it so much that I was singing with my eyes closed and didn't see it coming. The shock almost made my heart stop. . . and, it set my bladder free. It took an hour to get me cleaned up, made up, sopped up and scrubbed up to where we could finish the show, but boy, they sure got their reaction.

These were great days in the late sixties: working with the best and the most creative people in the entertainment industry. My guest list was just great: Jerry Reed, Mel Tillis, Stringbean, Barbara Mandrell, Tom T. Hall, Bobby Goldsboro (Singing "Honey" for the first time on TV), George Hamilton IV, Lynn Anderson, The Irish Rovers, Bob Luman, Don Gibson, Little Jimmy Dickens and so many others. I was learning just how important it could be to a performer's career to join music and television: a lesson that would prove to be very important to me a couple of decades later with the creation of music videos which would change the face of country music forever.

Tammy Wynette

chapter 30

Alligator Rasslin' at the Eden Roc Hotel

IF I CAME HOME TODAY, WOULD YOU STILL BE MY DARLING,
or Have I Stayed Away Too Long
. . .Stan Hitchcock, Epic Records, 1968

Billy Sherrill is a genius producer and was having a lot of success at Epic. I was there when he discovered Tammy Wynette. We were working on my new album, listening to hundreds of songs, planning the project and just hanging out shooting the breeze in Billy's small two- room office that was the Nashville headquarters for Epic. I had noticed, as I was coming in to meet with Billy, a pale, thin, shy looking blonde sitting in the receptionist office holding tightly to a recording tape box. I didn't pay much attention just thinking she was there visiting with Nancy, Billy's secretary. I went on in Billy's little cubby hole office, and we killed a couple of hours just messing around with the music, when I got up to go down the hall to the bathroom. As I was going out, I noticed the blonde girl was still sitting there and when I came back in I asked Billy who she was. He said he didn't know her. She had just walked in and said she needed to talk to Billy, and that she was from Alabama. We worked on the songs for another hour or so, and finally Billy said, "Hell, let's bring her in and see what she wants." She came into the office and just kind of handed the tape to Billy without much fanfare. He threaded it onto his tape machine. . . punched the button, and one of the greatest female voices of all time started singing, "Just follow the stairway. . . to apartment number nine." It was chill-bump city, friends. The look on Billy Sherrill's face was marvelous to behold: because he practiced being Mr. Poker Face and he had taken it to a high level. But not this time - no, 'fraid not. Miss Tammy, who was a hairdresser from Alabama, had just knocked the socks off of Mr. Sherrill, and blown me completely away.

Musical history was about to be made with the partnership of these two: the quiet, introspective, intense producer, and the quiet, shy, beautiful lady with the God gifted voice. It was a special moment to be witness to this meeting. Sherrill would write most of Tammy's hits, along with Glenn Sutton and Tammy herself pitching in, and he created the sound that would become the 'Wynette trademark.' The full, rich, big Nashville production that Billy became so famous for would forever change the face of country music.

After Tammy's first Epic release, she used to come over to the television station and do our morning show and later my own show. It was a joy to watch her grow as a performer and mature into the superstar that she became.

In 1968, Columbia Records decided to include country artists on the annual Columbia Records Convention and Show at the Eden Roc Hotel in Miami Beach, Florida. This was a big deal, because they had never given us the time of day before: it was always the big pop acts from New York and California that did the show, while we just read about it in the trades. Well, they chose Tammy Wynette, Charlie Walker and myself as the token hillbillies to appear at the convention that year, and we were pretty proud to be there. All the promotion people: producers, executives and artists from all over the world gathered in Miami for this one time a year affair.

We really put on the dog. I mean it was kinda like the Beverly Hillbillies coming to town: we just swarmed that place. The Eden Roc was not quite ready for country, but that's okay, Country wasn't quite ready for Eden Roc either. However, the show went off without a hitch. Tammy and Charlie just knocked them out, and I didn't do too bad myself. It was something being on the same show as Tony Bennett, Barbara Streisand and the Staple Singers.

When I finished my bit and walked off stage, a very distinguished gentleman, resplendently decked out in tux and black tie, cornered me at the side of the stage. He introduced himself to me as the president of Columbia Records, Goddard Lieberson, and I was pretty impressed because everyone in the music business knew who this gentleman was. . . he was The MAN, The Chief, The Lead Dog of the biggest record company in the world. "Yessir Mr. Lieberson, glad to meet you." He got right to the point, "Stan, I was impressed with your voice, and I want to bring you to New York and record you with a full orchestra. I believe you are a pop singer." Well, that shook me up 'cause I sure did not want to be one of those. Nonetheless, he was the MAN; I sure would not argue with him. Lieberson told me he would work out the details with Billy Sherrill when they went to dinner that night; and we parted company.

Glenn Sutton had taken over as associate producer at Epic and he and I were running mates; if there was ever a funnier guy than Glenn Sutton, I've never met him. Well, this night just about did us in; I still don't know how we got away with it, but let me set the story up. Billy and Glenn were sharing a room in the Hotel, and Glenn knew that Billy was going out with the big dogs, namely Mr. Lieberson and Len Levy, the president of Epic; we thought this would be a good opportunity to play a little joke on Billy. That afternoon we had been out exploring the Eden Roc complex, and found that this hotel was built in a sort of concave design, facing the Ocean, and that in the middle of the concave was a tropical garden with an alligator pit. We decided this would be our joke on Billy; we would put a live alligator in his bed to surprise him when he came in from his party.

Around 1:00am, we went out to the beach and found a piece of driftwood, about the size of a baseball bat. I took the driftwood and climbed over the chain link fence into the alligator pit while Glenn held a flashlight on one of the alligators that was about four foot long, and just kinda laying there giving me the fish eye. I whopped him between the eyes with the driftwood, and he went out like a light. I lifted him up over the fence to Sutton; then climbed over myself. The darn thing was pretty heavy, and starting to come around a little so we wrapped him up like a mummy in three beach towels, and carrying him between us, sneaked back in the lobby of the Eden

Roc and up the service elevator to the twenty-first floor, where Billy and Glenn's room was located.

We let ourselves into the room, pulled the covers back on Billy's bed, lay the Alligator under the sheets with it's head on the pillow, and covered it up. It was still wrapped up tight in the towels, but it was awake. . . and it was pissed off. Just as we got him all settled in, we heard Billy Sherrill coming up the hall singing a Tammy Wynette song at the top of his voice, heading for his room. We hid in the bathroom with all the lights out; the bathroom door cracked just enough for us to see into the room. Billy had been to a heck of a party, and was having a little trouble navigating; but he finally got the door unlocked, turned the light on and saw what he thought was Glenn Sutton sleeping in his bed. Being in a boisterous mood, he hollered, "Sutton, you bastard, get out of my bed! Then Sherrill jumped right in the middle of what he thought was Sutton.

It wasn't Sutton, he realized, when he jerked the covers back, and in so doing pulled one of the towels off the head of the alligator. The alligator opened his mouth wide open and hissed, 'bout like a snake, and Billy, who was astraddle that thing, just levitated: I mean he went straight up. I've never seen anything like it--before, or since. He went up, and then, somehow did a flip and landed on the floor about five foot from the bed. He was instantly stone-cold sober, and I don't know who was the madder, him or the alligator. We finally got Billy calmed down; after all it was just a joke. "Come on Billy, where is your sense of humor?"

We transported the alligator back to what we thought was his abode, (anyway, it was a handy piece of water), without losing an arm or leg; it being darker than all get out. It had been an extremely tiring day. After all, I had been a country singer, then been mistaken for a pop singer, and then changed into an alligator wrestler all in one night. That's enough for this 'billie, I'm going to bed.

My room overlooked the pool area and I had been asleep just a couple of hours when I heard the hollering and yelling coming from the pool; "Alligator in the pool !!! Alligator in the pool !!!" I didn't know what was happening, but it kinda sounded like maybe someone had mistaken the swimming pool for the wild alligator pool, and had stocked it during the night. I put the pillow over my head and went back to sleep.

About this time, Glenn Sutton started producing my recording sessions for Epic; our friendship has lasted all these many years over some real bumpy roads. Sutton is the type of guy that funny things happen to, and when he tells them, they get even funnier. Glenn arrived in Nashville in the early 60's, a starving songwriter, and landed a writing gig with Al Gallico Music. He was just barely getting by, sleeping on friends' couches, in his car or just anywhere he could find a spot. He warmed my couch quite a lot, and would stay up all hours of the night writing songs.

To illustrate how hungry it could get on Music Row, he tells the story of the time he was staying in a house with a bunch of other starving writers, singers and musicians; including Mel Tillis, and between them they didn't have enough money to buy food. Mel was standing at the window looking out at the back yard, when he spotted the neighbors pet rabbit hopping through their yard. Mel ran out the back door, picked up a rock; and with one throw, got the rabbit. He took it in the house, cleaned it, added an onion and a couple of potatoes, and the boys all had rabbit stew. When Sutton told me this story, I was aghast. . . "Y'all killed the little pet rabbit? Don't you feel guilt?" Sutton replied, "Hell, don't blame me. I didn't kill it; Mel did. I just ate it. I was hungry." Makes me wonder what would have happened if the neighbor's cat had run across their yard instead of the rabbit. . .well, a hungry stomach knows no shame.

I had gotten a booking at a club in Kansas City, and I asked Sutton to ride along with me, play a little rhythm guitar, see how us road hog musicians made our living, and have some fun. Well, the magic word for Sutton was "fun"; something that he could not get enough of. We left Nashville, drove all night to Kansas City, checked into a hotel near the club, and headed on over to check out the bandstand and set up our guitars.

It was a pretty nice club, and we drew a right good crowd; including a nice young couple that came over and struck up a conversation with me during the break. Now, they seemed the very essence of the happy, straight, Midwestern, young marrieds and I enjoyed talking to them. During the conversation, I mentioned how tired we were from the trip over and that we couldn't wait to get back to the hotel and get some sleep. All night long they would dance by, while I was singing, and she would smile real big, while he seemed to be getting progressively sullen and just a little drunk. I ended the last set, packed up my guitar, and Sutton and I headed back to the hotel for some much needed sleep. We had just got in our beds and were fixing to drop off, when somebody knocked on our door like they were trying to knock it off the hinges. I slipped into my Levi's and went to the door. When I unlocked and opened it, there stood the lovely young couple from the club, except they weren't lovely anymore. She was crying and shaking, and he was drunk as a skunk. He pushed his way into the room and pulled her in after him. He turned to her and said, " OK Bitch, you wanted to screw him? Now here's your chance." This was one scary situation. Over the drunk's shoulder, I saw Sutton pull the covers up over his head, just shaking; huh, a lot of help he was going to be. I maneuvered the couple out on to the balcony, got them quieted down and started getting the picture. The man was obviously consumed with jealousy, and in a dangerous frame of mind under the influence of all that alcohol. I spent about thirty minutes getting them calmed down, and finally got them out the door and into the hall.

When I shut the room door and locked it, Sutton came out from under the covers and breathed a sigh of relief. I finally got the story out of him explaining his nervous reaction to the guy busting into our room. Seems that a few years ago, back in Mississippi, Sutton had fallen head over heels in love with a pretty girl. He was having a real hot affair with her, when she broke it off. Well, Sutton was heartbroken, and willing to do about anything to get back together; even though she had started going with this big, tough redneck that would have torn Glenn's head off for even looking at her. Glenn decided to go over to her apartment and try to mend the relationship; maybe talk her into some romance. Later, in her room, things were going pretty good between the old lovers when all of a sudden someone knocked on the door. The girl jumped up, straightened up her clothes and peeked out the window, only to jump back and whisper to Glenn: "Oh my gosh, it's my boyfriend!" The apartment was on the third floor, with no other exit except the front door, and Glenn, knowing he was about to get beat to death, quickly crawled under the bed. The girl opened the door to her new lover, who had come over for a quickie during his lunch hour, and the clothes began to fly. The room exploded in passion, right on the bed under which our hero was hiding. Glenn said it was the longest fifteen minutes he ever spent; with the sagging springs of the mattress hitting him in the head with every wild bounce. When at last it was over, and the red necked lover had gone back to work, Glenn crawled out from under the love nest; his pride gone, his heart broken and his body criss-crossed with spring bruises. As he was slumping out the door, he made his exit with as much dignity as he could muster: "Well, that's it for us babe. . .we are through. . . besides you got dust balls under your bed bigger than I am - that's it. I'm gone." So, he explained to me back in Kansas City, "When that goon knocked on the door and started raising so much hell, I just flashed back on my Mississippi darling; I really miss her"--Sutton, the eternal romantic.

A few years later, Sutton married another one of my friends, Lynn Anderson, and produced her giant record of "Rose Garden". They have a beautiful daughter together and are finally friends again, after divorce kinda messed things up for a little while. Anyway, good folks and powerful talent sometimes creates real explosive situations.

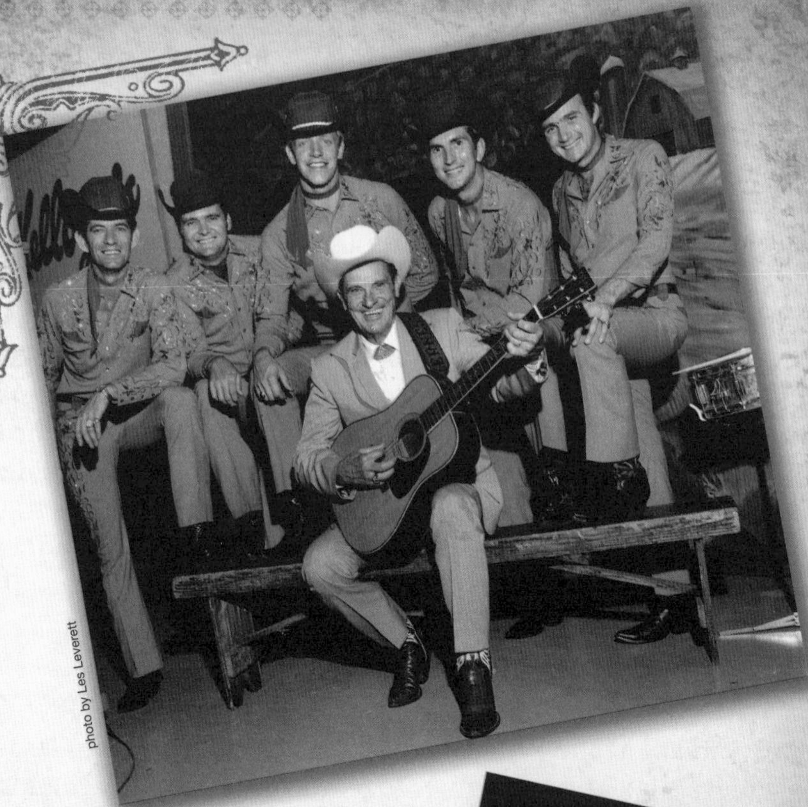
photo by Les Leverett

Ernest Tubb and the Texas Troubadours

photo by Les Leverett

Hank Snow

photo by Les Leverett
Dickens

Little Jimmy Dickens

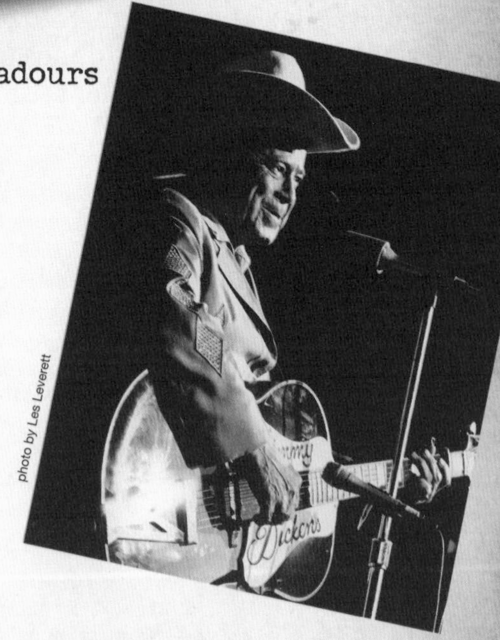

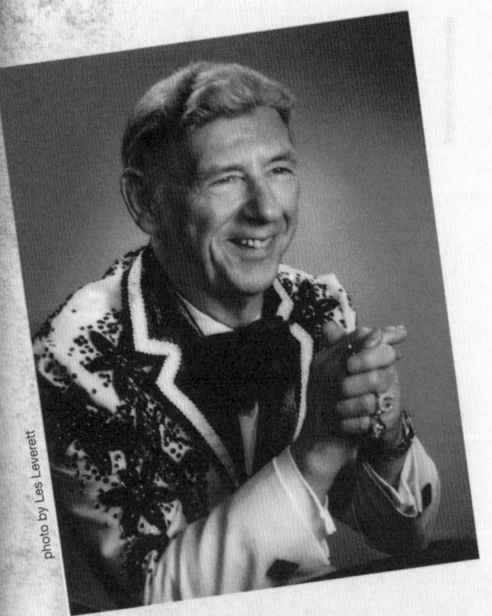

chapter 31

The Family of Country Music

SOMEDAY YOU'LL CALL MY NAME, AND I WON'T ANSWER...
Someday you'll look for me, I won't be there
...Stan Hitchcock, Epic Records, 1968

The Fugitive and the Hillbilly

With the morning show on Channel 5 every day, and my own show on Saturday afternoon playing all around the country, my visibility factor had gone up considerably; but the fact hadn't sunk in to me yet. One weekend when I had time off, I learned the hard way that my fame had spread; and proved to me what a hard core of fans I was making.

That Saturday Afternoon, we were having a backyard barbecue. In the mid-sixties, I had become friends with some of the men in blue that protected the good citizens of Nashville, The Nashville Metropolitan Police Department. When you think about it, the police and the pickers have a lot in common: they both run on a high degree of adrenaline, they deal with the public, they lead a dangerous lifestyle, and they love staying up all night. I was fascinated with the police, loved to ride with them at night, and had made close friends with a few of them.

One of my Nashville Police Department friends, a homicide detective named Dave, asked me to ride with him to the store to pick up some more supplies for the party. He was off duty and driving his personal car as we came up Dickerson Road, heading for the market. We stopped at a stoplight and another car pulled up alongside us. Dave glanced over at the car full of tough looking men, and exclaimed, "Dang, that's a murder suspect that I have been looking for!" At the same time, the hood that was driving the car looked over and recognized Dave. He immediately took off, running the stoplight; the race was on. We were screaming down Dickerson road at a hundred miles an hour, lights flashing, horn honking, and my heart just pounding. I was transformed into Dick Tracy; I mean this was it. . . I was living it. The fugitives slowed down just enough to make a turn; up on two wheels, down a side street, and into a residential area. They were going flat out when they ran out of road. The street was coming to a dead end, and at the very center of that dead end was the biggest oak tree you ever saw. Well, they slammed into that tree: smoke, oil and car parts flying everywhere, with us sliding to a stop right behind them. The doors flew open and the hoods started jumping out to make their escape. Dave reached over, slapped open the glove compartment, reached in, brought out a gun and handed it to me. Reaching behind him he pulled out another gun from his belt, shouting to me to get the one that was getting away on my side. He leapt out of the car and started running after the ones on his side, while I did the same thing on the passenger side. You cannot imagine the mind frame that I was in; I was totally engrossed in capturing these hoods, no matter what it took. My hood was running up an alley, and I took off in hot pursuit. At the end of the alley, someone had constructed a chain link fence; my hood hit it going full speed, and started climbing it like a squirrel up a tree. Just as he got to the top and was fixing to throw his leg over and drop to the other side, I reached the fence, took the standard police stance with legs spread, both hands on the gun, fire in my eye, and with a sense of command in my voice, I said, "STOP RIGHT THERE OR I WILL BLOW YOUR HEAD OFF!" Well, the hood was hanging on the top of the chain link fence, and as he swiveled his head around to look at me, an expression of total amazement came over his evil, crooked-life face, and he uttered the words that I can still hear ringing in my memory today, "Oh God, don't shoot. . . I watch you on television!"

Yes friends and neighbors, I was holding a gun on a fan. He might not look like much, hanging up there on the fence, and yeah, he was kinda ugly with that scar running across his face, but by golly, he was my fan, and I was proud of him. Every bit of adrenaline just ran out of me, and I felt like a deflated balloon standing there with a gun in my hand, pointing it at this good ole boy who was probably just misunderstood, had had a rotten childhood, and didn't really mean to kill that guy. Well, I was saved from myself and my changed feelings toward my prisoner, because someone had called the cops, and a patrol car screeched to a halt just behind me. A patrol-man jumped out, relieved me of my gun, and took control of the felon. I was standing there, wanting to say something nice to the guy, like; thanks for watching, be kind to your neighbors and you'll have better neighbors, or maybe, may the Good Lord take a likin' to you, but as it turned out, he got the last word as they were leading him away in handcuffs; he turned to me and said, "Sumbitch, I sure won't watch you no more."

We're Talking About Money Just Flyin' Out the Window

Lest I slip into egomania for having such dedicated fans, an incident about two weeks later brought me back to reality. I was working a tour with Ernest Tubb up in Ohio; it was after the show and Ernest and the Texas Troubadours were stage left, all lined up, signing autographs on pictures and albums. Ernest had a line of about two hundred people waiting for that all important autograph while I was sitting there, stage right, with five people lined up to meet me. Well, I thought, as I signed the first four autographs; it could be worse, at least I had these five fans. As I reached out to take what I thought was my picture to autograph from the last lady in line, she handed me a picture of Ernest Tubb and said, "Just sign this 'To Linda, From Ernest Tubb', his line is too long." Yeah buddy, that will grow an ego for you.

This particular tour, with Ernest and the Troubadours, was to be quite a treat, and one I will never forget. I had been invited by my friend Don Mills, the drummer in the group, to ride along on Tubb's bus for the duration of the tour. Now, everyone knew that Tubb's tour bus was the home of an endless poker game when they were out on tour, and the guys in the band loved to get fresh meat; new players like me that they could strip a few dollars off of, and who would help to pass the endless miles of highway that were the life of the traveling picker. Well, they had the perfect victim for their poker cleaning in me, 'cause as I told y'all earlier, I can't gamble worth a darn.

One night, after a show in Findlay, Ohio, we were motoring down the interstate, hitting about 78 miles per hour and had a hot game going, with Ernest being the big winner. We were sitting around the table; Ernest on my left, the bulkhead and the window of the bus on my right, and there was about three hundred dollars in the pot, lying in the center of the table. Ernest was raising and looking like he was going to take it all again. It came around to me; I folded, and it passed to Ernest to make his bet. Well, I noticed it was getting kinda warm on the bus, and losing my little dab of money was making it even warmer; so I reached over, sorta slid that big window open about six inches and learned a very important lesson; you don't open the window on a big tour bus when it is barreling down the highway at 78 mph, because the window immediately becomes a vacuum cleaner and sucks whatever is loose right out; in this case, the three hundred dollars in the pot that Ernest had just won. It is a moment frozen in time in my memory; the tens and twenties sailing right by my nose and out the window, like butterflies heading for sweet nectar on a warm spring morning. After the last bill had zipped by, I sat, paralyzed by the horror of what had occurred. Ernest said, in that deep, quiet voice and without even looking up from his cards, "Son, you want to close that window?"

That is a good example as to the character of Ernest Tubb; he had a kindness and patience that is legendary, and a love for this country music business that knew no bounds. He was happiest when he was on tour, in touch with his fans, traveling and living with his band, and doing three hundred shows a year; year after year. Yes, he was patient, and he loved those boys in the band, but sometimes he had to crack down with tough love.

Ernest Tubb's Tough Love

Cal Smith, one of the legendary graduates of the Ernest Tubb School of entertainment, tells of the time when he was the front man for the Texas Troubadours. He and Ernest had a disagreement, and Ernest fired him and kicked him off the bus. Cal was low on cash so he had to borrow enough money off of Ernest's bus driver to get him a Greyhound ticket back to Nashville. He had been up for a couple of days partying and was plumb wore out, so he stretched out in the back seat of the bus and went to sleep.

About forty miles down The Road, the bus stopped to pick up some more passengers, and Cal, who was still stretched across the back seats heard a familiar voice say, "Move over Cal, and let me in". Looking up he saw his buddy Jack Greene, the drummer in the Ernest Tubb band, looking down at him with an embarrassed grin. "Yeah, that's right, Ernest fired me too, about thirty minutes after you left." Of course, when they got back to Nashville, Ernest was waiting to hire them back on, but they didn't ever want to ride no Greyhound bus ever again; shoot, there wasn't even a poker game on one of them buses.

Steppin' Off the Cadillac

I love the story that Little Jimmy Dickens tells about the time in the 1940's, when, after his first hit record, he couldn't wait to travel back to the hills of West Virginia to show his Grandma and Pap his new Cadillac Limousine. He got the car down the gravel road, through the woods, and pulled up in front of the old house. Ma was in the kitchen fixin' up some eggs and ham; Jimmy was talking to her when he glanced outside the window and saw Pap steppin' off the Cadillac to see how long it was. Jimmy went outside and Pap said, "Jim, what kind of car is she?" Well, Jimmy knew that Pap thought the only good car ever made was a Buick, so he replied, "She's a Buick, Pap". Pap just smiled, shifted the chaw of tobacco around in his mouth and said: "Wouldn't you know." Later, Jimmy took Pap for a ride to town, and Pap sat in the back seat while Jimmy drove. Jimmy was watching Pap in the rear view mirror and noticed that Pap's chaw of tobacco was getting mighty moist, in fact, it was starting to run out the corner of his mouth as he was trying to figure out how to roll down the back windows; after all electric windows had not made it into that part of West Virginia yet. Finally, Pap hollered, "Jimmy, how you get this window to roll down?" Jimmy answered, "Just point your finger at it," watching in the mirror as Pap pointed his finger at the window, Jimmy hit the electric window button on the driver's side that controls the back seat windows. Pap spit brown tobacco juice all down the side of Jimmy's new Cadillac limousine. This went on all day as they drove around the area showing off Jimmy's new car. . . Pap pointing his finger at the window, and Jimmy rolling it down. When Jimmy finally told him, Pap made Jimmy swear he wouldn't tell anyone because he was afraid the people in the white coats would come and pick him up.

The Family Tree

Some of my fondest memories are of the times talking with Ernest and listening to the stories of the historic years in country music. In those years the groups toured the land with their doghouse bass tied to the top of the touring car. These were the glory days when Bill Monroe toured the country with his own baseball team and circus tent, bringing communities both country music and sports, all in one package. Pee Wee King toured the country with featured vocalists Eddy Arnold, Cowboy Copas and Redd Stewart, while Hank Thompson was inventing western honky-tonk music; The years when you could go to your Saturday afternoon movie matinee, watch your favorite cowboys and hear the music of Roy Acuff, PeeWee King, Bob Wills, Spade Cooley, Johnny Bond, Cliffie Stone, Tex Ritter and the Sons Of The Pioneers, Roy Rogers and Gene Autrey; When the great cavalcades of stars went on The Road from Nashville with Ernest Tubb, Roy Acuff, Patsy Cline, Red Foley, Carl Smith, Johnny and Jack, Kitty Wells, Little Jimmy Dickens, Wilma Lee and Stoney Cooper, Eddy Arnold, Johnny Horton, Bill Carlisle, Martha Carson, Jim Reeves, The Louvin Brothers, Faron Young, Billy Walker, Stringbean, The Duke of Paducah, Ray Price, Rod Brasfield, Minnie Pearl, Hawkshaw Hawkins, Slim Whitman, Hank Williams, Hank Locklin, Marty Robbins, George Morgan, Hank Snow, Webb Pierce and Lefty Frizzell.

In my generation of pickers there were the Statlers, The Oaks, Jack Greene and Jeannie Sealy, Bill Anderson, Jim Ed Brown, Porter and Dolly, Sonny James, George Jones, Tammy Wynette, Bobby

Bare, Charlie Rich, Tommy Overstreet, Cal Smith, Loretta Lynn, Conway Twitty, Johnny Paycheck, Helen Cornelius, Mel Tillis, T. G. Shepard, Ray Pillow, Barbara Mandrell, Charlie Pride, Connie Smith, Stonewall Jackson, Del Reeves, George Hamilton IV, Dave Dudley, Lynn Anderson, Ronnie Milsap, David Houston, Claude Gray, Claude King, Buck Owens, Merle Haggard, Sammi Smith, Leroy Van Dyke, Ferlin Husky, Jean Shepard, Jan Howard, Billy Grammer, Roy Drusky, Jeannie Pruett, Dottie West, Narvel Felts, Skeeter Davis, Billy Crash Craddock, The Wilburn Brothers, Johnny Russell, Don Gibson, Bobby Lord, Willie Nelson, Waylon, The Glasers, Red Sovine, Donna Fargo, Barbara Fairchild, Bob Luman, Roger Miller, Brenda Lee, Carl Perkins, Tom T. Hall, Charley Walker, Jimmy Dean, Jeannie C. Riley, Carl and Pearl Butler and Johnny Cash.

When Bluegrass Music was in its early development there was Bill Monroe, Flatt and Scruggs, Mac Wiseman, Reno and Smiley, The Stanley Brothers, The Osborne Brothers, Jim and Jesse and Jimmy Martin.

Yes, these were the heroes of entertainment, and there were a lot more that never made star status, but still played their part of working that road, singing those songs, getting through the lonely nights anyway they could; finally fading from the scene but knowing that they were only one song away from the dream coming true. All of these, and more, blazed the trail for Garth Brooks, Reba, George Strait, Brooks and Dunn and all the others who would follow.

Now, I didn't do that exercise of name dropping just to get your attention good friends, no, I simply want to celebrate the architects of country music and pay homage to these innovators of a musical heritage that has spanned these many years and touched countless lives with songs. Think about the periods of American history that Country music had a part in: The Depression, World War II, the Korean War, the Vietnam War, the turbulent 70's, the fast time 80's and on up to the present time with music video bringing a whole new audience to this most American of music. Country music has achieved its prominence with a relatively small number of participants, but what a group they have been and continue to be, the few, the proud, the creative.

When I started out, I didn't intend to enter this rare society of singers, writers and musicians, but by the mid-60's I couldn't imagine being anything else and I was proud of my little piece of turf, shoulder to shoulder with some of the most dedicated and creative people in the world.

The common thread that runs through the country music family is the simple lifestyle that most of us were raised in, and the basic goodness at the heart of most of them, and, the heartfelt love of the music. The folks we think of as "stars" are just regular people that have a unique gift of expressing what all of us have experienced some time in our lives through their music.

The Wordsmith

Tom T. Hall says that growing up in Kentucky, his family didn't even know they were poor until they read about it in the Saturday Evening Post. It was a real disappointment. He also says that he was too young to go to the Korean War like the rest of the young men in his town, so he took a job at the local radio station when he was fifteen, and one of his jobs was reading the news. The first week he ripped off the Teletype news copy and sat down in front of the mic. "In England today Winston Churchill was diagnosed with the. . . (he stared down at the copy at the word he had never heard of: Ptomaine Poisoning) with the Flu." After the newscast the station manager came in and said, "I thought Churchill had Ptomaine Poisoning." "Oh, he does," replied Tom T., "but he's also got a small case of the flu." No wonder he turned out to be a wordsmith.

Yes, those were the years when the stars traveled in sedans and station wagons, strapping the dog house bass on top of the car roof, moving it inside when it was raining, trying to catch a few minutes of sleep sitting four to the backseat and three in the front, hardly ever stopping for a motel; shoot, who could afford it. One time I was on my way down to Florida to play a gig, I stopped at a truck stop to get some coffee, and get rid of some, when I walked into the men's room, an entire road show of Nashville musicians were trying to clean up in the sinks, and change into their stage outfits for a show on down The Road. Yep, I only do this for a living 'cause it's so glamorous.

If the Hat Fits – Wear It!

Hank Snow is an old road warrior that was known to occasionally take a nip, and when he did he tried very hard to not let it show. One time, on tour, he had a touch too much and decided to call home to check on things. The conversation with his wife, Min, was going along pretty smooth, no slurred speech, until he let the cat out of the bag with, "So, Min, how's our boy Jimmy getting along?" There was silence on the line for a moment. . . then she replied, in a chilly voice, "Hank, he's with you." The Singing Ranger, not one to get discombobulated easily, signed off with, "Of course he is, Min, and he's fine."

An extremely proud man, very correct in his carriage and the image he projected, you can just imagine his discomfort when an incident happened at one of the big package shows in the 60's. Now, it's no secret to anyone but Hank that he wears a toupee, and is very sensitive about it. It's a full head toupee and he spends a lot of time getting it just right before show time. On this particular show a local DJ was Master of Ceremonies and he was about half goofy, (a common trait among radio people), and he was wearing a big cowboy hat. It was time to bring Hank on stage as star of the show. After he introduced Hank and Hank came out to the warm applause, the DJ took the hat off his own head and crammed it down tight on Hank's. . . right down to the ears. No one knew why a man would do such a fool thing, but there was one mad little Canadian on stage that night with a big old cowboy hat down on his ears. He didn't dare try to take off 'cause he knew the old toupee was solidly stuck to the inside of the hat. To Hank's credit, he did his usual fine appearance, but it was a good thing the DJ had sense enough to leave early, before Hank got back stage, 'cause Hank was ready to kick butt and take names.

Del Needs a Dime – 'Real Bad!'

And then there's the story that Del Reeves tells of traveling on tour up through Illinois. The bathroom was broken in the bus, and Del had to go real, that's real, bad, and there is only one service station open for the next hundred miles. They get there just in time, Del dashes from the bus, runs into the men's room, grabs the handle of the stall, and notices that it is one of those that takes a dime to get into. Frantically searching his pockets he realizes he doesn't have a dime, and there is no way he can make it back to the bus in time. This calls for drastic action. Del drops to his knees on the old, wet, dirty tile floor and starts to crawl under the door. He gets half way under when he comes slap up against the bare shins of the guy sitting on the stool and getting real upset; hollering, "WHOA NOW, FELLA!" Well there is no explaining the situation to a mad truck driver, and Del just barely makes it back to the bus in time to make a clean get away. Well, a reasonably clean getaway, under the circumstances, and live to entertain another day.

"Ozark Moon"
Painting by Stan Hitchcock
1981

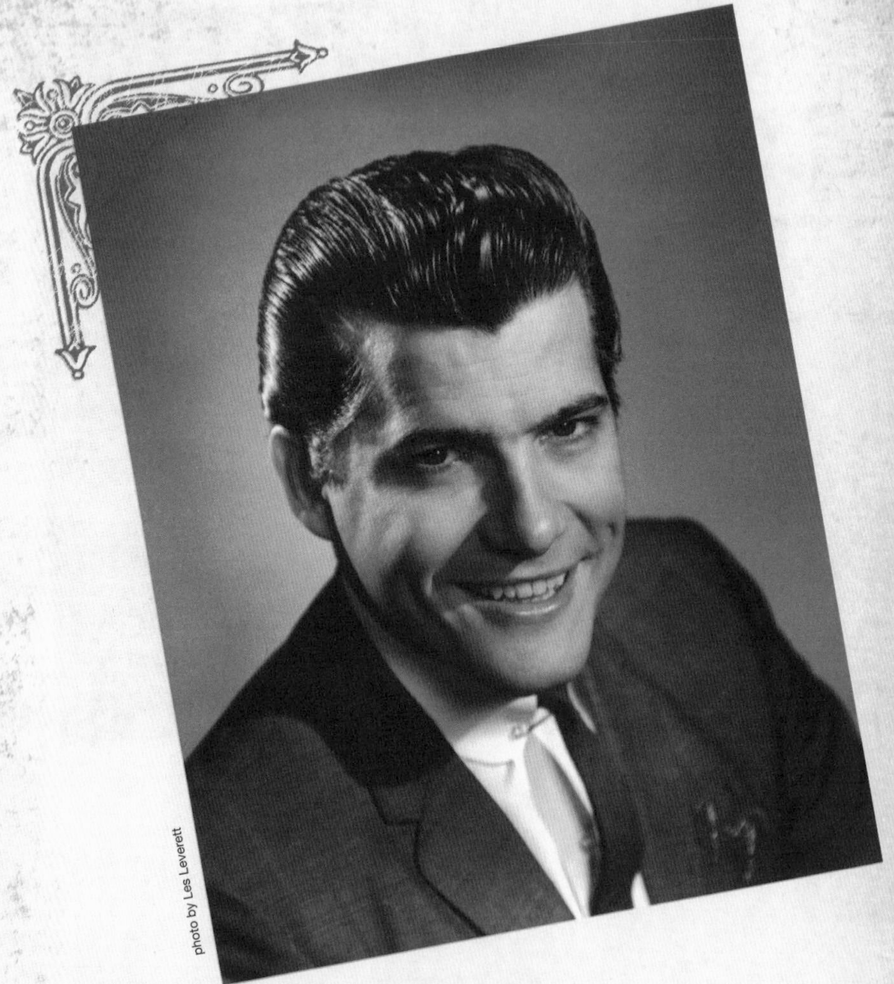

photo by Les Leverett

Ray Pillow

chapter 32

Sea Monsters On the Harpeth

Old friends. . . are the best friends.

Ray Pillow and I used to do a lot of shows together and we are friends on and off the stage. We kept noticing, as we would travel up Interstate 40 out of Nashville, heading east, that we crossed this beautiful river about 40 miles out of town called the Caney Fork. We kept saying, "Hey, we ought to buy a boat and float that thing, catch a lot of fish." Well, that is exactly what we did. We went to WalMart, bought this aluminum john- boat for a couple of hundred dollars, a couple of paddles and we were in business.

We were ready all right, but we didn't take the time to research this particular river. The Caney Fork is the river that comes out of Center Hill Dam, and is used to generate power. Shoot, we didn't know that. . . it was just a pretty river; it crossed the interstate highway about 6 times in 10 miles. We figured we would put in and have a relaxing float down the stream, throw a few lures, see some pretty scenery, and maybe write a song. . . just take life easy for a day. We estimated it would probably take us about four hours to float the ten miles, then we would take the boat out, walk back up the interstate and bring the truck around to pick up the boat. Good plan, huh?

When we got to where we wanted to put in, a rest stop on the Interstate which was right on the river, we were kinda surprised at the volume of water and the speed at which the current seemed to be traveling, but hey, let's go catch some fish!

We got the boat put in and struck out. When it hit the current, it picked the boat up and just threw us down the river. . . I mean we hit top speed that this little john boat had not been designed for. We are back paddling frantically trying to slow this thing down. There goes the first bridge, here comes the second. . . look out for that rock. . . hold on, man we're taking water. . . should have brought a can, bucket or something. Here comes the third bridge; we must be doing thirty miles an hour. Man, we are half way through the float and it's only been ten minutes!

About five miles down the river we finally get the boat pulled over to the bank and quickly tie up both ends to a couple of trees on the bank. Ah man, our lunch got wet. . . shoot. Well, might as well explore that cave up there on the bluff. We climbed up to the cave and explored for about thirty minutes. Meanwhile, upriver, the dam folks have decided to shut off the water for the day.

When we got back to the boat we had the shock of our lives. It was tied to the trees all right, hanging above our heads about ten feet. The water must have dropped at least twenty feet in thirty minutes; it was now a trickle of its former self.

Pillow and I both had to climb the trees to untie our boat, and then hike up the Interstate where we got a ride back to our truck with a state trooper. I had a hard time convincing Pillow that this was just kinda like beginner's luck, and that next time would be really great, just you wait and see.

A couple of months later I called Pillow and said, "Hey son, how 'bout we go float the Harpeth River? It will be a great adventure, yeah buddy, you're gonna love it all right, uh-huh, that's right, it'll be one of those male bonding things, ya know?"

Well, I had to fast talk him, but he finally gave in and we headed for the river. It had kinda gotten cold on us, but we were bundled up pretty good, so shouldn't have been a problem.

It started out pretty well, the water was up and running pretty good so we didn't have to paddle very much. I sat in the back, for

I felt that I was the superior outdoorsman, and therefore I should steer this thing. After all, I had been in the Navy, hadn't I? And that gave me the edge to pretty much take control, a situation that did not sit well with Mr. Pillow.

Even though it was pretty cool, Pillow was still scared to death that we were going to get snake bit. Did I tell you that Pillow had this awful thing about snakes? Well, he's kinda embarrassed about it, so I told him I wouldn't tell anyone about it; keep it to yourself, OK? Anyway, we were going down river at a pretty brisk pace and Pillow was kinda crouched in the bow of the boat hanging over the front watching for rocks and logs as we hit a series of rapids. I was having to really work the oar to keep us straight in the rough water and as I took a deep dip into the water, back paddling as fast as I could, my oar must have scooped up a white sucker about fourteen inches long and weighing about three quarters of a pound; they were pretty thick in this part of the river. Anyway, when I brought my paddle up, the fish came with it; did a perfect little loop and landed in the bottom of that aluminum boat. It made a sound about like that of a rattlesnake fixin' to strike. brrrrrr. . . wham! Before I could stop myself I hollered, "SNAAAAAAKE!" Pillow just did the prettiest swan dive off the front of that boat and into that cold water, at which time the boat hit him and drug him through the rocks of the rapids. It wasn't a pretty sight.

I never could get Pillow to float the river with me again, something about the guide service not being worth a darn, but I believe he's just got a short attention span, and of course an unreasonable fear of rattlesnakes coming into the boat to get you. Shoot, I don't think rattlesnakes can even swim. And even if they could, that water was so cold it would have shriveled up his rattle. Anyway, I know it sure did shrivel up Pillow. Say, I wonder if he would be interested in Hang Gliding off of Lookout Mountain?

Stan Hitchcock, 1968

chapter 33

Sure, But Can You Play Orange Blossom Special?

HONEY, I'M HOME. . .
kiss me for it's been a trying day. . .
Stan Hitchcock, Epic Records 1968

About six months after the 1968 Columbia Records Convention, Billy Sherrill got the call from Goddard Lieberson, president of Columbia Records, to make good on his promise to take me to New York City and make a "pop" star out of me. Evidently, the alligator episode had been forgotten and it was time to see what I could do in the big city. Billy and I flew to New York City, checked into the Plaza Hotel and started going over some songs the New York Office of Columbia and Epic Records had left for us at the front desk. This was a whole new world of music and one that I was totally unprepared for, but I was up for the challenge and dug in to learn the songs. The only songs that we had brought with us from Nashville were a Roger Miller tune that I really liked called, "The Last Word In Lonesome Is Me", and a Jan Crutchfield song called, "Hush A'Bye". The rest of the songs were pure "pop" fluff.

We went into the main CBS studio for the recording session at 9:00am on a Tuesday morning. I had gotten used to the recording style of Nashville where all the musicians would come in and gather around; talk, joke, cut up a little and then start listening to the demo tapes of the songs we would record; make their number system chord charts, offer ideas on licks, intros, fills, tempos and background voice parts and then start running down the songs. Well, you could forget all that good stuff here in New York; the musicians started filing into the studio, no one said a word, no one spoke to me - or even looked in my direction. They sat down in their chairs, sorted through the music that the arranger had placed on their music stand, picked up their instruments and sat at semi-attention waiting for the music director (leader) to give them instruction. When they finally all got into the studio I counted thirty musicians - including about an acre of violins- dang, I'll bet there wasn't a one of them that could play "Orange Blossom Special" like ol' Pee Wee used to do. I started trying to catch just one of their eyes and at least make visual contact, heaven forbid I should try to touch one of them. No one would look at me. This was the coldest bunch of stuffed shirts that I had ever seen, and all I wanted to do was get the heck out of there and get back to the country pickers that I knew and loved.

We did a three hour session, cut four songs, everyone folded up their sheet music, put away their instruments, packed up and left; all without saying a word to me or each other. They had frozen out this hillbilly all right, boy, what I wouldn't have give for a good steel guitar, Ray Edenton's rhythm guitar, Pig on piano or Junior on bass.

Billy and I went on back to the Hotel and judging from his comments he wasn't all that thrilled with the New York recording scene either. Anyway, it was an experience, recording with that many musicians, and the Plaza did have a good hamburger, and besides, now I didn't have to worry about being a "pop" singer cause they could stuff it up their elite, blue blooded violin cases, I was going back to the fiddle where I belonged.

About a week after the New York trip, a booking agent friend of mine, Mike Hight, brought me a demo of a song by a couple of new writers, Jerry Foster and Bill Rice. The song was "Honey, I'm Home" and when I played the demo it just knocked me flat out. We set up a session and recorded it with Glenn Sutton producing and it came off just like a charm. I got to know Foster and Rice, and for the next few years I recorded about everything I could that had their name on it. They are phenomenal writers and set some records that still haven't been broken at ASCAP for writing hits. The single came out on Epic and was a good chart record for me. "Honey I'm Home", Foster and Rices' song, was used for the title of the new album. Thank you Mike Hight, for the help.

Jerry Foster and Bill Rice were writing for Bill Hall's publishing company; they had a new way of putting words together that just clicked. Bill Hall handled them like thoroughbred race- horses, keeping them in a writing room beside his office and churning out hits like a song factory. Foster was from the boot heel of Missouri, and Rice was from across the line in Arkansas. They arrived in town with a suitcase full of songs believing they could make it by hard work, determination and talent, and by golly, they did it. Two more diverse personalities could not be found: Foster, the outgoing, fun loving extrovert who wanted to be a singing sensation like Elvis, and Rice, the quiet, deep thinking musical genius who just wanted to write songs, and to heck with the spotlight. In the late 60's and all through the 70's these guys put together a catalog of songs that is just incredible. They are both individually creating magic in song today, having gone their separate ways, still believing that hard work, determination and talent is the secret to songwriting success. A tip of the old cowboy hat to Jerry and Bill (or baseball cap, since the cowboy hat didn't really come into general use in country music until the 70's), two who that proved it could be done.

On May 2nd, 1968 my son, Stanley Edward the 2nd, was born in Nashville, Tennessee and I was a mighty proud man. He joined the three girls, Marilyn, Jay and Lori, already at home. Soon they were to be joined by another little baby girl, whom we would name Joli. She would be born a few years later and would round out the Hitchcock gang of my youth. They were a great bunch of kids for a traveling hillbilly singer to come home to at the end of the tour.

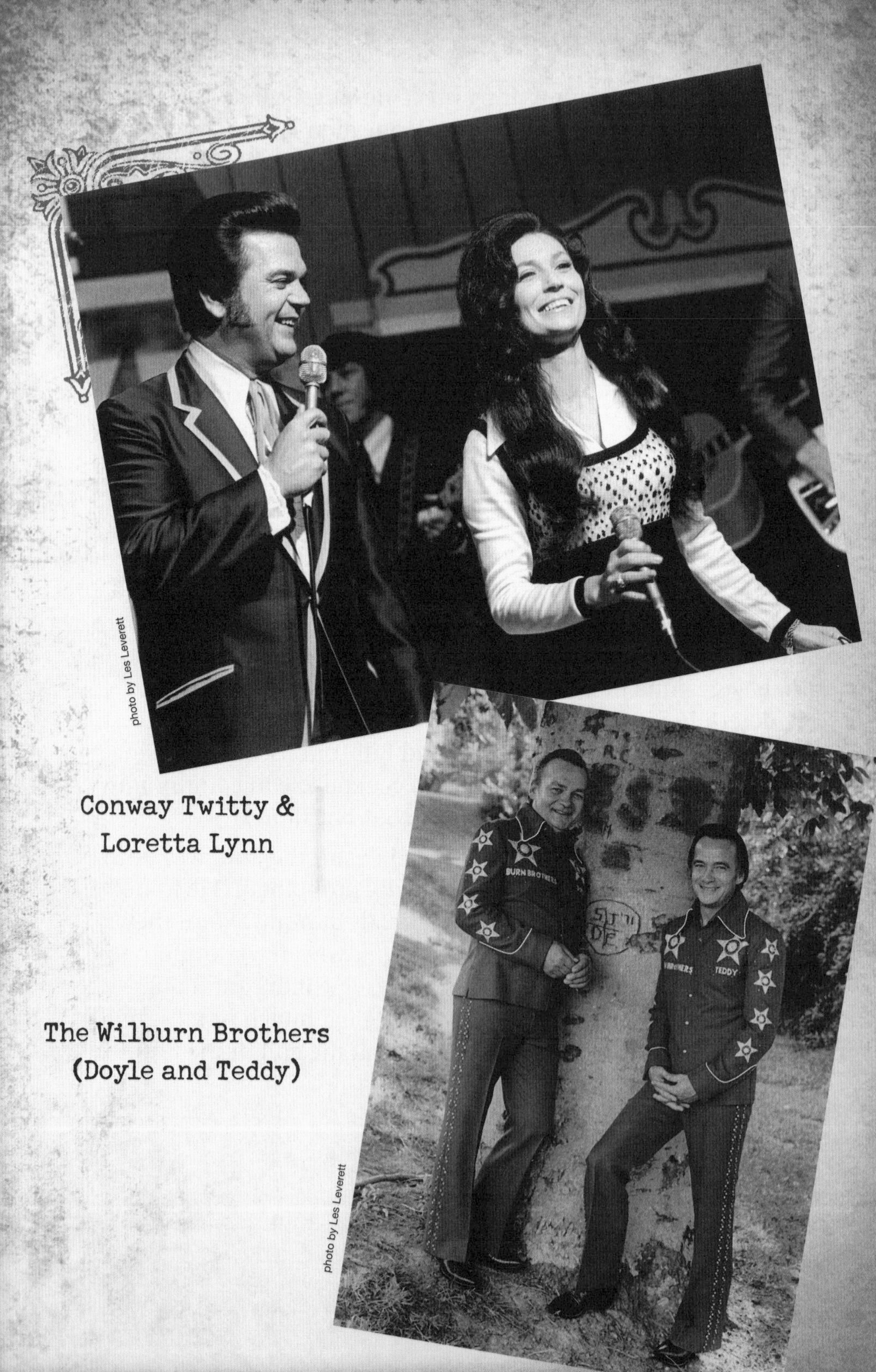

photo by Les Leverett

Conway Twitty &
Loretta Lynn

The Wilburn Brothers
(Doyle and Teddy)

photo by Les Leverett

chapter 34

"The Road"

Favorite Songs, Good Friends,
Old guitars, Special Loves,
Lonely times when the music got you through,
Applause that told you that they really cared,
Silence that told you when they didn't.
The Road that went on forever,
missing it when it finally stopped.
(some short thoughts and memories to share)

The Road becomes an integral part of the pickers life, both hated and loved, anticipated and dreaded, but always necessary for the development of a career. It was always an adventure for me, an escape from the ever-present pressures of life, a brief freedom to just follow the music and enjoy the excitement of entertainment. The Road was also where a lot of funny and strange things happen.

Most of the dates that made up a touring picker's life in the 60's involved nightclubs and dance halls, with a few fairs, auditoriums and outdoor festivals thrown in for good measure. All in all it wasn't a bad life, but you could sure end up in some strange places doing your little song and dance routine.

Personally, I found it strange to perform on the roof of the projection booth of a drive-In theater on a cold, rainy day in November with your audience snugly seated in their automobiles, motors running to keep the heater working, honking their horns at the end of each song. . . but it happened just that way while on tour with Loretta Lynn and the Wilburn Brothers in the mid-sixties. It was weird singing to that bunch of cars, not a human face in sight, colder than heck, somewhere in southern Illinois. Just imagine what we must have sounded like on those little speakers on the poles, you know, the ones with the long curly wire that would reach inside the car attaching to the inside of the window. They had the acoustic performance of a little transistor radio with the speaker the size of a quarter. For months after that concert, every time I heard a horn honk I wanted to take a bow.

Touring artists spent most of their money on the musicians that would make up their particular band. There was a darn good reason for this: traveling the country working with different local bands at each gig or house bands, was just torture. In the first place, the local musicians were mad 'cause you were coming in to their turf and stealing their thunder. A lot of them made a point to play the music so bad behind you that you just wanted to pack up and head for the house.

I remember one particular tour I made for a promoter in North Carolina. He had booked a series of seven or eight small-town, high school auditoriums with me as the headliner for the shows, and with the understanding that he would furnish the band for the whole tour. I was supposed to come in a day early to rehearse and get the show down real good. Well, I got there a day early all right. The promoter took me to the local high school gym to rehearse with the band. This was the mid-sixties and my television show was pretty hot in the area, and the local stations were all playing my records to promote the show. We got to the gym and I met the band. One rhythm guitar player (who had no rhythm and very few chords), one acoustic (dog house) bass holder, one claw hammer banjo player (who hated country music and only wanted to play real bluegrass music), and one kid about thirteen years old who owned a snare drum. The leader of the band (the un-rhythm guitar player) stared at me impassively when I asked him if the band had practiced on my songs from the tape I had mailed earlier. He kinda grunted, scratched himself a couple of times, run his finger in his ear to dig at some unknown substance, and said, "Why doan' ya run 'em fer us?" Well, I was starting to wonder what the penalty was in North Carolina for beating promoters to a bloody mess with the business end of a Gibson guitar. . . but, no, let's try to be professional here.

These guys don't look like much, but they can probably really play the fire out of these instruments. . . OK, here's the songs guys. I started singing some of my records and showing the chords on my guitar. Four pair of eyes were staring at me like a tree full of owls, and I noticed that the drummer had taken off his shoes and socks and was picking his toes, and not in tempo either! Finally, after I had exhausted myself singing and playing extra loud to try to get through the solid wall of dumb, the leader of the (alleged) band held up his hand for me to stop, and said, with the classic pick-up, local band logic: "Chief, 'yer songs are real purty and all. . . but all them chord changes are making the boys in the band nervous. Could you just do a whole show of singing Hank Williams songs? We know pert near all of his'n." For the next seven nights of little country town auditoriums, I would work solo, just me and my guitar, for an hour, singing my records. The boys in the band would stand, like statues, in a row right behind me, never playing a lick until, at the end of my show, I would close with a Hank Williams song that they would play with such enthusiasm that it sounded like we had actually planned this Grand Finale. Show Business is a beautiful thing.

You had to play some pretty tough clubs along the way, being as how country music was the music of the common workingman; and the common workingman had some pretty common ways of having fun after a hard week's worth of work. After years of painstaking research, hours of study, close examination, professional evaluation and gut feelings, I have compiled "The List Of To-Do Things" for any red blooded working man (country music club patron), and my results are as follows:

1. Get drunk as fast as possible.
2. Fight anybody and everybody, including best friends, bartenders, waitresses, bouncers, wives, mothers, girlfriends, police; or if you were really in the mood for it, all of the above, all at the same time.
3. Have carnal knowledge of a female, preferably one that is alive and reasonably ambulatory.
4. Fight anyone who you have not already fought with and who has not beaten the crap out of you in the last ten minutes.

There were clubs on the circuit that actually had chicken wire strung up around the stage to keep the band from being struck by flying beer bottles, although, I have had pickers in my band so mean that I thought the wire might be to protect the audience.

For years, from the late sixties through the mid seventies, I had a bandleader-bass player by the name of Buck Evans, a tough guy from south Texas that could whip his weight in wild cats, and who saved my bacon on several occasions. You have to realize that with the kind of audience I've described in those sixties honky-tonks, the guy up on stage, singing and smiling at their girlfriends, is a natural target for a butt-kickin', just for the sake of making a social statement; kinda like the dog hiking up his leg to pee on the shrubs, just marking his territory.

Now every picker knows that part of your job is to smile and be nice to the ladies, and I will admit sometimes you tended to be nicer than you should, but shucks, man, it's just part of the gig, uh-huh, that's right. Well, workman's comp don't cover a cowboy boot up your butt, so it was always wise to carry a guard dog musician in the band. Buck's favorite defense strategy was the long neck of that old fender bass that he played. Buck's position was always to my right on stage, working right next to me so he could sing harmony.
We had several close calls during those early years playing the skull orchards, with buckets of blood, and knock-em-down and drag-em-outs. This was the life of the country picker before the birth of the big acts in the late seventies and early eighties that moved country music into the nice venues that they play today. Heck man, we played some joints that were so bad that they stopped you at the door and asked if you were carrying a dangerous weapon. If you said "no", they would issue you one just to keep the fighting fair. Buck had a way of bringing that old fender bass neck up under an attacking drunk's chin that invariably brought peace on stage.

You know, while being center stage makes you a perfect target for the aggression of the overly saturated testosterone crowd, it is also a great vantage point to observe the behavior patterns of this cross-section of the human animal. People watching has always been a favorite sport of mine and I have had the opportunity to observe some mighty peculiar happenings from that country music stage.

For instance, The Sherman Club in Indianapolis was owned by the toughest ex-cop I ever met. In 1967 Little Jimmy Dickens and myself were booked there on a Friday and Saturday night and the first thing the owner told us was, "If a fight breaks out, stay on stage and keep the music going, don't stop no matter what." Well, that first night it was my turn on stage, and right in the middle of my set the dangedest fight broke out on the dance floor, right in front of where I was singing. . . blood, teeth and eyeballs flying, we just kept playing, trying to get them to fight in tempo; they didn't seem to have a bit of rhythm. The owner, who was behind the bar pouring drinks, reacted immediately: he vaulted clear over the bar and arrived at the fight just as one of the guys pulled a gun and was just bringing it up to shoot the other one, who was standing right in front of me, (I'm still singing. . . but it's hard to sing and keep your sphincter muscles tight at the same time). The owner had a black jack about a foot and a half long and he whopped the guy with the gun on the wrist. There went the gun, sliding across the dance floor, (keep singing fool. . . don't worry bout that dampness in your jockey's), Mr. Sherman then proceeded to beat this guy about the head and face with the black jack until his face looked like silly putty, then he stood up and knocked the other guy down, (an equal opportunity beating), and drug them both off the dance floor just as I ended the song. Never once did the crowd stop dancing, they just moved a ways away from the action and kept rubbing bellies together, all the while the massacre was going on. So, years later I was not overly impressed with the Rodney King beating; shoot, I had kept the music going for one worse than that.

In 1968 I played a country music club in Jacksonville, Florida that had a great facility for shows; big stage, big dance floor, big crowd and big rednecks. I was taking a break after my first show and this nice young man came up to talk to me about guitars. He was about nineteen and aspired to be a musician someday. We talked on and off most of the evening as I continued to do my shows. About midnight I was taking a break, before my last show, and walked outside to get out of the smoke and get some fresh air. I was strolling around the building, just kinda relaxing, when I saw this figure of a man bent over leaning up against the building. As I got closer I could see it was this young guy that I had been talking to all night.

I thought from his cramped position against the wall that he must be sick or something, so I went over to see if he needed help. As I got up to his shoulder he kinda lurched back and turned and I could see he was sick all right - someone had stuck a knife in his guts and walked around him. He was trying to hold his intestines in, but it was a losing battle. I laid him down on the grass and ran inside to get help, but by the time the ambulance arrived he was already dead. I felt terrible. This nice young man's life ended so needlessly, and no one even knew why. Life gets pretty cheap in those old honky-tonks.

Another time, in Marion, Illinois, I was playing a dance at the Moose Lodge, and there was this one guy who was the life of the party. I mean every dance, he was on that floor having a ball and leading the cheering and applause for every song. Well, he was a big fan of mine and knew all my records.

Late in the evening he requested an up tempo song and he and his wife started dancing right in front of the stage where I was singing. He was having such a good time and everyone kinda backed off and watched him dance. I was singing to him and looking him right in the eye when he suddenly stopped, stood there a beat and a half, and then fell forward like a tree that has been cut down, dead as a door nail. I do not ever want to repeat that experience, and I never again used the expression that was so common among pickers, "hey, son, knock'em dead!"

I remember the time we played a show and dance in St. Joseph, Missouri, at this club that had just opened up for country music. We had driven all the way from Texas, where we had a show the night before, and just got to the club in time to go on stage, set up our instruments and start playing. Well, we worked four long, hard sets, playing until two o'clock in the morning, and after the show, while the band was loading up the bus, I went into the manager's office to get paid. The manager was a real tough-acting hood. His bouncer and bodyguard were straight out of central casting from the Godfather. I thanked him for having us and asked him for my money. He kinda smirked at me and said: "I ain't gonna pay you nothing, you got here thirty minutes late. I don't owe you a dime." I leaned across his desk ready to get real serious, but his bodyguard pulled his coat back to casually display his shoulder holster. Well, I'm not a coward, but I'm not a fool either, so I backed away from the desk, turned and left the office. I went out to the bus where the boys were loading the equipment, and told Buck what had happened. Buck kinda grinned and said: "I'll get our money." As I said, we had been down to Texas on tour, and while we were there we had done some hunting with a few of Buck's friends, so we had a whole arsenal of hunting guns on the bus. Buck called to the Vic, the drummer, who was 'bout as bad as Buck for not cutting any slack. They went in the bus and came out with one twelve gauge shotgun and one thirty-thirty deer rifle. They walked in to the office. Vic quietly edged next to the bodyguard and eased the hammer back on the thirty-thirty. . . while Buck walked over and rested the shotgun on the manager's desk, saying very calmly, "We need to get our money--cash only, no check, and then we'll be headin' on out." Them boys came out about five minutes later, jumped on the bus, threw the money bag in my lap and said, "Let's make like Jesse James and get the hell out of Dodge!" It's the only time I ever left a show and felt like I was making a getaway at the same time. Yessir, you had to be tough to be a picker.

One time we were playing a show down in Georgia at an Air Force Officer's Club on a stage that was only about six foot by six foot; I mean, postage stamp size for a singer with a four-piece band. I had hired a guitar player named Bruce Osborn who was a great picker, but with one weakness, he was goosey. If anyone touched him from the shoulders down to his knees he had an immediate reaction: he would lash out at anything in front of him. Well, we were so crowded on this little stage that we were practically on top of each other. The drummer was clear back against the wall, the steel guitar player was to my left, the new guitar player right behind me, and Buck on bass to my right.

Because of the small stage the guitar player was only about twenty inches in back of me as I stood center stage at the mic. This crowd of officers and their wives were not really country music fans, so we were on our best behavior, but we had not considered Vic's weakness: he was an uncontrollable practical joker.

It was toward the end of the night and I was into a big ballad; eyes closed, head reared back, just singing my heart out. The crowd was mellowed out and filled the dance floor, one single spot light on me, the star, when suddenly Vic, dang his joking heart, reached out with his drum stick and stuck it in the Bruce's rear end. Bruce exploded: hit me like a jack-hammer and knocked me clear off stage and into the second row of dancers with visions of sugar plums dancing in my head. I was totally cold-cocked, sucker-punched and loose as a goose as I hit the dance floor and skidded through those dancers, flat on my back like I was sliding into home base. I was still holding my guitar when I wound up staring up at that darn revolving mirror ball that some of those dance halls thought was so cool.

I slowly picked my bruised pride up off the floor, and turned just in time to see Buck, the guard dog, start reaching for Bruce; probably to kill him or something, as I rushed back to the stage to break it up. Meanwhile, Vic was scrambling off stage, realizing how bad his joke had gone over, and just knowing he was fixing to get beat to death by Bruce, Buck, and then me, while the steel guitar player played something sad and haunting like "Danny Boy", or "Faded Love". Well, by the time I reached the stage, the humor of it all hit me and I just broke out laughing while stopping Buck from his planned attack. We went back to the dressing room to try take a break and regroup, and discovered that while we were on stage, someone had broken into the dressing room and stolen all our stuff: clothes, boots, jewelry, even my shaving kit with all my goodies. So much for the officer and gentlemen crap; give me the plain old joints where only the crowd got knocked around and they would never think of stealing from you.

Bobby Lord, star of the Grand Ole Opry, legendary story-teller and all around good guy, tells of the club he worked once, in Louisiana. The entire crowd showed up drunk, and then proceeded to do some serious drinking – It was so bad, all the while they were shouting for rock and roll while engaged in the pursuit of seeing who could hit each other the hardest. He felt lucky when he cut the show short and sneaked out of town, all in one piece.

Some pickers really loved The Road. Rumor had it in the 1960's that Bobby Bare had his bedroom in his home in Hendersonville, Tennessee, decorated just like a Holiday Inn, so he would feel at home when he was not traveling. Now, that is loving the Road!

I was on stage in a favorite club of mine down in Tampa, Florida when a whole group of professional wrestlers came in. Included in the group of wrestlers were two midgets who fought on the circuit, and were as tough as whet leather. Now let me tell you, I have seen some boisterous crowds before, but these folks take the cake. In the middle of the drinking, dancing, arm wrestling contests and general macho demonstrations, they took over the dance floor and started a midget throwing contest. Yeah, that's what I thought, kinda strange recreation: one wrestler would grab a midget and toss him about twenty feet to another wrestler, all the while betting on who could toss the farthest. Now, I've got to sing through all of this, midgets tumbling through the air, doing barrel rolls and loop-de-loops and the crowd just going crazy. I might have thought that I was an entertainer before, but now I knew - I was only bush league compared to this bunch. What a night.

It was in the late sixties that some of the clubs who had been featuring country music for many years were having a hard time making ends meet. So, a few of them started featuring country music aaaaand. . . strippers! Talk about making ends meet. Son, them old gals were rough business. We had to share dressing rooms sometimes, and many a bizarre sight would meet these old country eyes. I only worked a couple of these, and then I said, I believed that I had enjoyed about as much of that bare flesh as I cared to.

I worked a club in Kansas City that all the 'billies enjoyed, Genova's Chestnut Inn. It was owned and operated by a quaint old gentleman named Charlie Genova, who always treated me with the utmost courtesy and respect and would let me sit back in his office with him to watch old television reruns between sets.

It was rumored that Mr. Genova was connected with the Midwestern Mafia, but I sure never saw any evidence of it. The last night I worked the Chestnut Inn, in the mid 60's, I was back in Mr. Genova's office settling up after the show, when he looked at me, cleared his throat, shifted his cigar to the other side of his mouth and said, "Stan, some associates of mine are interested in this business that you are in, this country music, and they might be interested in putting some money into your career, you know, sort of investing in your talent. Give me a call when you get back home and I'll set up a meeting." Well, I never called him because of the rumors I had heard, but I always wondered what the deal was about. . .

That last night, it was right around 2:00am when I left the club. I had gotten my money, said goodbye to Mr. Genova and as I was walking to my car I noticed a car parked just up the street with his lights off and motor running. I threw my guitar in the back seat and climbed into my old road car, a Lincoln Mark III, and pulled out for home. The car that had been sitting there behind me pulled right out after me. I nervously watched in my rear view mirror as he pulled right up behind me and started flashing his lights. I moved over to let him pass and he pulled right up alongside me.

I looked over to see a car load of rough looking guys and the guy in the front passenger side had his arm out the window and holding the biggest gun I ever saw, pointed right at me. Without even thinking, I floor boarded that big, old Lincoln motor and screamed up the street; running red lights and anything else to keep ahead of them. I thought surely I would get the attention of a cop driving eighty, ninety, a hundred miles an hour right through downtown Kansas City with the another car right on my tail, but nary a blue suit was in sight. I finally just flat outrun the hoods because that old Lincoln had an engine as big as a bus, and there was no way they could keep up. Besides, I was an old hot-rodder from way back and the barrel of that gun was all the incentive I needed to blow the cobs out. I never went back to work for Mr. Genova after that; that part of town was just getting too rough. But he was a nice man and gave a lot of pickers work.

A rather strange recreation occurred at a club I worked in Wichita, Kansas. At the end of the night they cut my last show short and set up the dance floor for tricycle races. These big old rough necked Kansans took kids tricycles and would somehow get astride them and race around the dance floor like stock car racers, except these didn't have roll bars, harnesses and helmets to help survive the wrecks.

I was working a show at a supper club in North Carolina. As I got into town I noticed an advertisement for a show at another club featuring Johnny Paycheck. I hadn't seen Johnny in a while and decided to go holler at him when I got through with my own show. I finished my show, got paid, loaded my stuff up and started across town to where Johnny was playing. When I pulled into the parking lot and stopped next to Johnny's bus, I could tell something was bad wrong. Police cars were everywhere and the crowd was just kinda standing around outside the club looking dazed. I walked over to the bus and Johnny's bus driver recognized me motioning for me to come on aboard. He quietly told me that Johnny was back in the state-room of the bus, and to go on back and see him. I stood at the door of the state-room. Johnny was sitting on his bunk with his head in his hands and tears running down his face. I sat down beside him, put my arm around his shoulders and asked what was wrong. I finally got the story out of him, and it wasn't pretty. Johnny was on stage, singing one of his hits, and a very lovely young lady came down the aisle to the front of the stage and just stood there looking up at Johnny as he sang the song. She was so entranced by the music and the song that she didn't even notice the man that was coming down the aisle behind her: a man that we later found out was her estranged husband. The man stood behind her while Johnny sang, and then just as the song was ending, he pulled out a pistol, stuck it up to her head, and blew her brains all over the stage. Johnny was covered with bits of his fan and he just went all to pieces as the security men wrestled the murderer to the floor, disarming him. It is a wonder that Johnny was ever able to get past this, return to the stage and continue to entertain all these years, but he prevailed and is still one of the finest singers in all of country music.

In the mid-sixties I had a tour with Loretta Lynn. It was in the early years when neither Loretta nor myself carried a band on The Road: we would work with the house bands in the venues where we were booked to appear. Loretta asked if she could ride along with me and share expenses, and I was glad for the company because I had already learned that The Road could be a lonely place when you were traveling by yourself.

We started out with a gig in St. Louis and then worked our way across Illinois, finally heading up toward the upper edge of Wisconsin for a Saturday night show in Marquette. Our venue was a dance pavilion that jutted out into Lake Superior, and it was about as far north as you could go in mid-America. All the way up to the dance I had been listening to the radio, and they were telling stories about the sighting of unidentified flying objects in and around this part of Wisconsin. They were interviewing people and making wild speculations about the sightings. Loretta and I were just fascinated by the news and our imaginations were running wild.

Well, we got to the lake pavilion, had a good crowd and just sang ourselves plumb out. The people seemed to be having a great time. By the time we wound it up, about 2:00am, one of the thickest fogs I had ever seen had come in off the lake. Still, we didn't even consider staying overnight: the rule of the picker in those days was to do the show, load it up and move it out for home, no matter how tired or how bad the weather.

I got the car loaded up and Loretta crawled in the back seat and promptly went sound asleep as I started navigating south toward Nashville. In that part of the country the pine forests grew right up to the edge of The Road, and with that old, two lane highway so covered in fog, it was just exactly like traveling in a tunnel.

After about an hour of crawling along, my eyes were so tired that I was having to sing along with the radio at the top of my voice to just keep going. There are no towns for miles and miles; not even security lights to show that human habitation was anywhere close, nothing but pine trees and that little bit of road that I could see through the fog. I glanced up at my rear view mirror and it almost seemed like there was a blue haze behind me. I figured it was the reflection off the taillights in the fog, but it kept getting stronger.

Now it seemed to be swirling around and around, getting closer. I nervously reached over, shut the radio off and pushed the accelerator down farther, even though I was already going faster than I should for these foggy conditions. As soon as I turned the radio off I heard this strange sound: whoop. . .whoop. . .whoop. . . an undulating low pitched tone that kept going up and down, and getting louder. The blue light was ghostly, shining through the fog and just whirling round and round. By golly, I was scared to death. I'd come all this way to Wisconsin, and dang if I wasn't getting chased home by aliens.

I hollered for Loretta to wake up, 'cause I sure didn't want her to miss our being captured and maybe hauled off to some other planet. Shoot, Wisconsin was far enough for me; it almost seemed like another planet.

My heart was pounding and my mouth was so dry you could have struck a kitchen match on my tongue. I was going so fast that I was out-driving my headlights by a heck of a lot, and if The Road hadn't been so straight we would have killed ourselves with the car before the little green men got to us.

I was trying to pray my way out of this, but I was having trouble convincing God that the UFO was a real threat and just about to get Loretta Lynn. . . and many others. I could see the headlines now. . . "Country music songstress Loretta Lynn and an Unnamed Male Vocalist Abducted By Alien Airship!" Shoot, I hadn't even cut my memorial album yet. That thing was almost on me. . . the sound was piercing. . . the light was all around us. . . oooooooh boy, this is it. . . uuuuuuuhhhhhhh! As the ambulance screamed around us, I'll never know how I kept control of the car; we were plumb on the shoulder and just hanging on by sheer guts.

I pulled over and tried to catch my breath, realizing that in the north country they had gone to a blue emergency light and the European type emergency siren: a color and sound that I had never experienced before down south. Loretta thought it was funny, but you would have had a hard time pulling a laugh out of me at that time. I was as weak as water gravy, but by golly, I'll tell you what, I sure wasn't sleepy no more.

1967 Dodge Motor Home

chapter 35

Buck and the Hillbilly Drivin' School

"...boys, this here motor home will let us travel in style!"
- Stan Hitchcock 1967

When we traveled in cars, or station wagons pulling trailers for the gear, we all took turns driving. It was no big deal. In fact it helped break the boredom of sitting all scrunched up together for all those miles down the two lane highways. However, as we started making a little more money on the gigs, we wanted to move up to a better mode of transportation.

The big names were buying the Silver Eagles and the MCI busses, but down in the trenches, us regular folk who were not pulling in the big bucks yet, were happy when the 60's brought in a new wave of campers. . . yeah, motor homes. The name inspired visions of being right at home, even when you were traveling. Well, I visited an outdoor show, walked through a bunch of these camper, motor homes, and decided I just had to have one. It was about 1967 when I went to the biggest dealer in Nashville and found a Dodge Motor Home with a bedroom in the back, bunk beds, a kitchen, a shower, a dinette and all the goodies; and just had to have it. Now friends, you have to realize that the good engineers designed these things for the normal, everyday consumer; anybody that had the sense that God gave a goose. They did not have in mind a bunch of wild-eyed, long-haired, hillbilly musicians that could tear up a Caterpillar tractor if given the chance. I bought this fifty-foot long monstrosity and took it to show the band; proud as could be, announcing that from now on, The Stan Hitchcock Show was gonna travel in style. Well, that first weekend we were booked in Ft. Worth, Texas at Panther Hall, and we couldn't wait to get on The Road with our new toy.

I always took the first shift of driving, so I took us on down The Road to Texarkana, Arkansas, just smooth as glass, truckin' on like the big boys, no problem. I pulled it over at a truck stop, filled it up and woke Buck so that he could drive us on into Texas. I crawled on back into my bunk, with my head on the pillow right at the rear bulkhead, and went to sleep thinking this was a great life man, traveling in style. About four hours later, I was awakened by this horrible ripping sound. I opened my eyes and found myself staring out at the blue sky over my head. Buck had pulled into a gas station to get some coffee and when he backed up to leave. . . he backed up over this filler pipe that was sticking up out of the concrete, (the one that the gas trucks would fill up the hidden gas tanks with). This pipe stuck up about two foot; just high enough to catch the back end of the fiberglass rear end cap of our motor home, and rip it off when he pulled forward. Our brand new home on wheels looked like it had been in a tornado: the whole rear end was gone. I was speechless, sick to my stomach, just laying in my bunk with only my skivvies on for the whole world to see. Buck, how the hell could you do this to my new motor home? Buck allowed as to how it could have happened to anyone. Well, I been to two county fairs and four goat ropings and I ain't never heard of anyone doin' it! Oh dang, never mind. I don't want to hear it. Let's see what we can do to fix it. We bought all the duct tape that the station had, pushed and shoved the cap back on to the frame and taped it all the way around. It was ugly. I was mad. We made it to the show on time. Buck said it would never happen again. I forgave him.

We left Ft. Worth and headed to our next series of shows down in Florida. Two days later I was back in my bunk, sound asleep. Buck was driving and he stopped to get gas in Orlando, Florida. I was awakened by this horrible ripping sound. Buck had misjudged the height of the canopy over the gas pumps and torn off our air conditioner, which used to sit on top of our motor home roof. It was a hundred degrees in the shade as we finished our Florida tour. . .without the benefit of air conditioning. It was ugly. I was really mad. Buck was sorry. . . I forgave him.

Six months later, Buck ran all over another car that was stopped at a stop sign in Mayfield, Kentucky, slid on the ice, smashed up this poor old couple's Buick and messed up the front of the motor home. I realized that the only end of the camper that Buck hadn't torn up was the bottom. He had got the back, the top and now the front end. It was ugly. I was just tired of being mad. Buck was sorry. He didn't get to drive no more. I might have forgave him, but I ain't never gonna forget it. My beautiful home on The Road looked like a crumpled-up tin can. I had to look at a brochure the dealer had given me to remember what it used to look like.

I never did get to take it camping, like normal folks do, I thought a year later when I sold it for half of what I had paid for it. I finally gave up on the thing when the engine blew just outside of Wheeling, West Virginia. . . which was right after we put in the new transmission that had blown in Shreveport, Louisiana. . . which was right after someone broke the door window out in Poplar Bluff, Missouri and stole all my personal articles. . . which was right after the shower froze up and busted in Minneapolis, flooding the whole floor of our home away from home with about a foot of water. . . which was right before the stove caught on fire, causing massive smoke damage, as I was barreling down the highway in North Carolina, and I hit the brakes when a dog ran across The Road. Buck was frying some chicken fried steaks. Dang, that chicken fried steak grease is hard to put out when it gets on the carpet. Buck was pretty mad. I said I was sorry. Buck forgave me.

Other than those few little setbacks, I kinda enjoyed having the motor home. Think of the adventures we could have had if we had a big, old Greyhound bus like Jack and Jeannie. . . and Cal Smith. . . and Bare. . . and Porter. . . Oh well, poor folks have got poor ways and it would have just been more to tear up, I reckon.

Yessir, you got to be tough to hold up under the pressure of a traveling band of gypsy hillbillies.

Stringbean

chapter 36

Grandpa and String - Friends Do for Friends

"CHIEF, IF YOU'LL PULL 'ER OVER BY THAT TRUCK FULL OF WATERMELONS . . .I'll show you how to cure that old Asian Flu bug."

Stringbean to Stan Hitchcock 1968.

On Saturday, November 11th, 1973 at 11:00pm, backstage in the dressing room of the Ryman Auditorium, Stringbean finished snapping his coveralls over his cotton work shirt, zipped up his clothes bag, full of the famous long shirt, short pants and porkpie hat that had been his signature stage outfit for so many years; closed up his old, worn banjo case and stepped out in the hall to gather up his wife, Estelle. Then they headed out to the parking lot behind the Opry to load up and go home. Estelle got behind the wheel of the new Cadillac that String had recently bought, as he did every year by paying cash on the barrel head, and assumed her usual position as pilot for her man, who could not drive. There was sparse conversation between the two old friends and lovers, married for so many years. But then, their understanding of each other was so strong that words were not always necessary. It was a fairly short trip out to Goodlettsville where they had their little farm, and they had made that trip from the Opry House to home so many times that by now it was just automatic. When they reached the lane that led up to their rustic, old farm house, String asked Estelle to stop and let him unload his stuff in front of the house before she went on down to the garage, which was some ways from the house. String stepped up on the porch with his arms full of banjo and stage clothes, and pushed open the door, which they always left unlocked, as did all the farm folks around there. As String took a couple of steps into the dark house, he put his banjo case on the floor and was reaching for the light, when a person standing behind the door put his gun to the old entertainer's head and ended his life in a blinding flash of powder. Estelle, just getting out of the car down by the barn, heard the shot and started running across the yard in a panic, but she just wasn't fast enough to outrun the two men who chased her down, knocked her to the ground and shot her through the head as she lay there screaming for String. The two fiendish men; neighbors to String and Estelle, and cousins to each other, then entered the house where String lay dead on the floor next to his old banjo, went through his overall pockets, ransacked the house and finally left without finding the money they believed would be hidden there.

Dave Akeman, Stringbean's real life name, didn't have much faith in banks: a carry over from his raising in the hills of eastern Kentucky where all the people lost their money in the banks during the Depression, so he always carried a large roll of bills in his overall bib pocket. Because of his sweet nature and natural good will, it never occurred to him that someone would covet his hard earned money, and go to any extreme to take it from him. This horrible crime of violence against two of the finest people that ever drew a breath affected the entire music community in a way that nothing ever had before. Sure, we knew that we took a chance with our lives every time we left the house to go on The Road, whether traveling by car, bus or airplane, but we had never feared folks. . . the thought of anyone wanting to physically harm us had not even been considered. All of the sudden, the reality of this senseless crime came home to us real hard.

Grandpa Jones was String's dearest friend, and in fact, was their neighbor on the farm just up The Road. He loved String and Estelle above everyone other than his own family, and always sorta looked after String.

Not only could String not drive a car, he had other manual skills that eluded him; and Grandpa, knowing this, tried to help his friend in any way possible. Grandpa and String loved to hunt together and would go out in the woods every week during hunting season in the earlier years of their friendship. Grandpa had stopped going on the hunting trips now that he had gotten older, walking through rough terrain started bothering his legs, but he carried on a special tradition that he had started years before: Grandpa knew that even though String could play the fire out of that banjo and was one of the cleverest men he had ever known. . . he simply did not have the manual skills to take his guns apart to clean and oil them after the hunt. Even though he was no longer hunting, Grandpa would come over to String's house every week during hunting season, disassemble all String's guns, clean, polish and oil them, assemble them back; lovingly maintaining String's firearms so they would not rust and deteriorate, all the while enjoying the storytelling time with String. Grandpa did this for years all for just one reason. String was his friend, and friends did for friends. How beautiful - a pure friendship.

All the more horrible to imagine the next morning, Grandpa had tried to call String to have breakfast together; troubled because he got no answer, Grandpa went to the Akeman farm and found his dear friends. . . lying as the killing bastards had left them. Grandpa never really got over it, and in fact, left Nashville for many years to live in Arkansas with his wife Ramona.

I first met Stringbean in 1954 at the Shrine Mosque in Springfield, Missouri on a package show with Carl Smith and Little Jimmy Dickens. He was friendly to everyone, and he really proved his spirit of human kindness when he befriended me on my first guest appearance on the Grand Ole Opry. In later years we worked a lot of shows together - one tour in particular sticks out in my memory as a special time with String: We were booked on a tour up through the Eastern States and he called and asked if I would travel with him in his car and do the driving so Estelle could stay home and tend to her garden. I gladly agreed, and we left the next day from his farm and headed east. While doing a show in Salisbury, Maryland I started feeling bad, and by that night I had a raging fever and a bad case of the Asian flu. Well, there wasn't much to do but keep going, we had shows to do and I was the only one who could drive. . . this went on for two days and two more shows; I was getting dehydrated from not being able to hold anything down; not even water, and weak from the fever. String and I were in the middle of the West Virginia mountains when we rounded a curve; there sat a flat bed truck full of watermelons. String held his hand up and said: "Chief, if you'll pull 'er over by that truck full of watermelons, I'll show you how to get rid of that old Asian Flu bug." I pulled over, and String bought the biggest watermelon that fellow had on the truck. He got me out of the car, sat me up under a shade tree, cut the melon with his pocket knife and proceeded to stuff every bit of that watermelon down me. . . I mean I had watermelon coming out my ears, but by golly, it worked. My fever broke; the liquid from the melon just worked it's magic. Two hours later I was feeling like a human being once more. String claimed it was an old mountain cure-all and I still swear by it today. I'm thinking 'bout bottling it, getting a horse and wagon, and going around the country selling it for flu healer. . . I could make a million. My taxes would be a million and a half and I would end up losing money. . . darn, it happens every time. . . good idea. . . bad return. . . you raise a good crop and the prices drop every time. It's the hillbilly way. It's like the old boy in Oklahoma who sold tornado insurance to mobile homes in that land known as tornado alley.. . .he sold a lot of policies, but the payoffs were hell. He was losing money, but man, was he ever doing volume.

Painting by Stan Hitchcock
1982

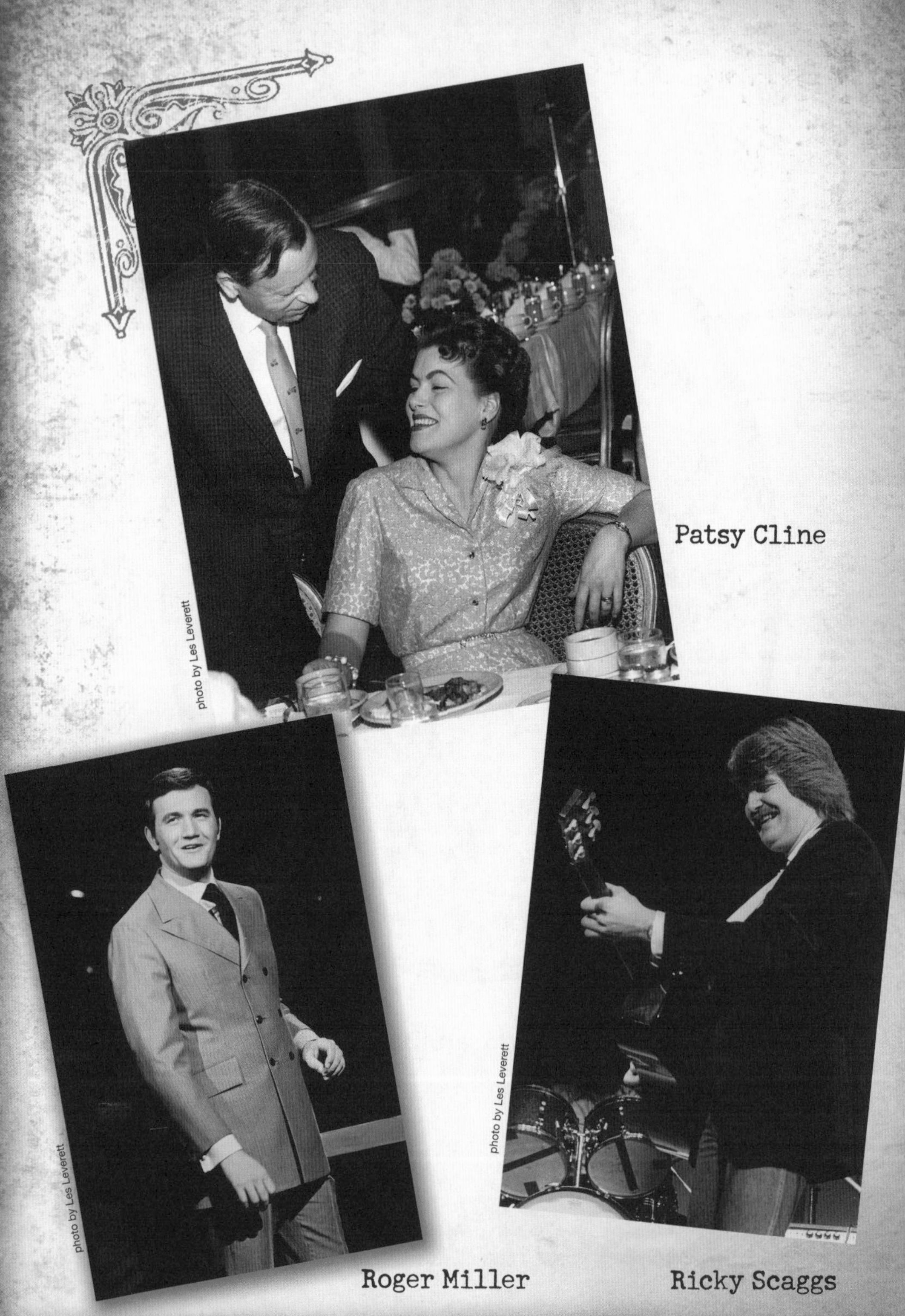

Patsy Cline

Roger Miller

Ricky Scaggs

chapter 37

The Shadow of Your Smile

. . .when you are gone, will color all my dreams and light the dawn

. . .Stan Hitchcock and Curly Chalker 1970

It was spring in 1969 and my band and I were playing cowboy bars in Idaho and other points west. It was my first trip to this particular part of the country and I was enjoying the experience. We had finished our last show in Lewiston, Idaho and were making our long journey back to Tennessee, when I stopped to call home and found out that my mother had died that morning.

The grief of losing your mother is a lifetime companion; it simmers there in the dark recesses of your memory to be rekindled time and time again by some song or phrase, the face of the stranger that resembles her, the favorite flower she always loved, a meal that she would cook especially for you; the childhood remembered that is so woven around her. There are kitchen smells that still hit me in memory central; pies baking, a ham in the oven, fresh bread, chili on the first cool day of autumn, or a pineapple up-side-down cake. Most of all, you remember that your Mother is probably the only one in the world who will ever love you without reason, totally and unconditionally.

I still remember how the music community of Nashville poured out their love and understanding during the period just after Mom's death; whether with an arm around the shoulder backstage at the Ryman, a written note, a phone call, or the flowers at the funeral; they just were there. . . and they cared.

It has always been like that in this business of entertainment. First of all; you are talking about people who live a rarefied lifestyle, who are openly emotional, who constantly chronicle the travails of mankind in their country songs, who must love and trust people just to exist in this life of music. When one of us is cut, we all bleed.

There have been so many pass since I arrived in the city in '62, but the other members of this strange tribe of pickers, singers, strutters, starvers, grinners, bookers, writers, publishers, managers, promoters, pushers, shovers, takers and givers, seem to be bound together with a deep and abiding love for each other that never fails to surface and spill over on those occasions when we all join together to say goodbye to one of our own. There are special memories that we take with us from these final going away parties; Red Foley singing Peace in the Valley at Hank Williams funeral, J. D. Sumner and the Stamps singing it again at Presley's wake, Ricky Skaggs beautiful singing at Keith Whitley's farewell, the great outpouring of love in the stories told at Roger Miller's celebration of life, the overwhelming spirit of love and respect at Minnie Pearl's funeral, and the passing of an era when we lost Ernest Tubb, Roy Acuff, Bill Monroe and Grandpa Jones. I shall never forget the look of love in Brenda Lee's eyes as she sang her goodbye to the man who guided her recording career, Mr. Owen Bradley, nor the depth of sadness at the passing of Tammy Wynette, after a lifetime of pain.

There have been some who were cut down in the prime that have been particularly hard to take; Mel Street, Bob Luman, Nat Stuckey, Conway Twitty, Keith Whitley, O B McClinton, Marty Robbins, George Morgan, Eddie Rabbitt, Patsy Cline, Cowboy Copas, Hawkshaw Hawkins, Randy Hughes, Jack Anglin, Jim Reeves, Dottie West, Tammy and, of course, Roger Miller.

It seems that when we lose one of our stars, whom has a special significance to all of us who have been touched by their music, we take it in a way that is intensely personal. Maybe they sang the song that was the song you dated to in high school, or got married to, or had some other personal attachment to that brought a loved one into a part of your life. Yes, these are our heroes and it is hard to give them up.

Sometimes the loss just makes no sense. When Keith Whitley died, after drinking straight alcohol until his heart stopped, I was just angry; I loved him and I couldn't reconcile him doing something like that. Or when Mel Street got up from the breakfast table, with all his family sitting there, climbed the stairs to the second story bedroom and shot himself to death: Wasted years that could have been so good, with family and friends that loved them: I still grieve for the senseless loss.

It was particularly pitiful when Dottie West died when her car broke down on the way to the Opry and she hitched a ride from an elderly neighbor that happened by; he wrecked while taking the Opry exit off Briley Parkway and Dottie was killed.

Conway, who knew something was not quite right within himself, but kept putting off going to the doctor until the day he left Branson, Missouri after a concert. About hundred miles up The Road, the aneurysm in the main artery in his stomach ruptured and he bled to death.

Bob Luman, who I took on a fishing trip just weeks before he died, kept complaining of being cold in the eighty-degree weather. Cold, 'cause he was bleeding inside and his body was slowly shutting down. Bob Luman was one of the best entertainers I have ever met and I just loved him like a brother. I thought he would live to be at least a hundred and twenty.

Eddie Rabbitt, one of the nicest men I ever met, was kind, calm, considerate, and full of talent. He finally lost his fight to lung cancer, but he fought it hard. The last time we were together, he came up to Branson, Missouri with me, and we shot a "Heart to Heart" show together - just the two of us with two flat top guitars and some funny stories to tell. He was my friend, and I miss him.

Just since I began writing this journal of country music and the early years, so much time has gone by; sometimes it feels like lost years. I guess it is just on my mind strong today as I sit here at my keyboard; the rain falling outside my window and running in little miniature rivers down to the creek in the bottom; the ghosts of my old friends strolling through my memory like old soldiers in a Veterans' Day parade, still walking proud and straight - just as I remember them.

A couple of years ago one of my musician friends called me and told me that one of my old compadres had died that morning, namely Curly Chalker; the best dang steel guitar player that ever slid a bar across strings, and asked me if I would I come and sing at the funeral. Many years ago, around 1970, I recorded a song called "The Shadow Of Your Smile"; an old pop standard with one of the prettiest melodies I have ever heard. The reason I recorded it was so that I could feature Curly playing the steel guitar turnaround, no small feat for a country steel guitar player; but Curly wasn't just any steel player--he was Curly Chalker, the best. I met Curly in the late sixties when he moved to Nashville from Las Vegas where he had a legendary show band in which other musicians would just come to watch in amazement as they played everything from western swing to far-out Jazz, and all the in-between. Curly came to Nashville to get into session work, but the producers in power were so intimidated by his talent, and his no-bullcrap attitude, that they froze him out of most of the big sessions. My bass player, Buck Evans, would go down to Printer's Alley and play with Curly as part of the Curly Chalker Trio when we weren't on The Road. Curly had put together the trio, which consisted of Curly, Buck, and Jimmy Stuart on drums. I would come by the club to listen and Curly got to asking me to get up and sit in on vocals. Then one night, he wondered if I knew the song, "The Shadow Of Your Smile". When I said no, he asked me to learn the song so we could do it on stage. Well, I learned the song and the first night we tried it on stage, he went into the jazz-swing turnaround and just played his ever-lovin' butt off: I was hooked.

A couple of years later when I was putting the material together for a new album, I decided to bring in Curly and feature him on that song. Tommy Allsup was my producer. He was a man who understood music and musicians and who loved Curly's playing also. Well, we had cut a couple of good songs and I felt about in the mood, so I sent most of the extra musicians out of the studio for a break but kept Jimmy Capps on gut-string guitar, Bob Moore on the acoustic bass, Buddy Harman using brushes on the snare and a mixed quartet of background voices, and brought Curly in. We dimmed the lights real low; Curly touched those strings with his magic hands and we started the song. I sang a verse and a chorus and then very quietly said, "Ladies and Gentlemen, may I present my very good friend, Mr. Curly Chalker." What followed was a special moment in our country music: Curly played a classic turnaround that every steel guitar player since who has ever heard it still just shakes his head in wonder. The record came out in an album and the label pulled the song for the backside of a single, but the song was there - and in the areas where it got play - it was a smash, all because of the steel part. We had one problem; none of the other musicians could play it, so I only got to perform it on The Road, once. . .

I was booked for a concert in St. Louis, Missouri in 1970 when "The Shadow Of Your Smile" reached number one on WIL Radio: the top country station in that whole region. Well, I was sweating it 'cause I knew folks would be wanting to hear the song and I knew we couldn't play it without Curly. The auditorium was packed, and we had set up on the front part of the stage, in front of the curtain; that's is how the promoter wanted it said Buck. I was sorta skeptical about this set-up; shoot, who ever heard of setting up in front of the curtain? We were introduced and came out to a great welcome from the crowd. We launched into our first song and the show was on. We did about three songs without stopping and then we cooled down and I started talking to the crowd, just as they started hollering for the "The Shadow Of Your Smile". I was just getting into the explanation about how it was impossible to play our number one song. . . when from behind the curtain came the sweetest sound; the steel guitar intro to the song. The curtain parted and there sat Curly behind that old guitar, grinning from ear to ear. We did the song three times before the crowd would let us be. . . it was a great moment. Buck had told Curly about our problem and he had flown in to do the show with us. . . just 'cause he wanted to. It is my fond memory of Curly, and one I will always cherish.

At the funeral I stood off to a room at the side, facing the casket, and sang "The Shadow of Your Smile" to Curly for the last time. I looked out across the crowd of pickers and we were all taken back to those special times when the music was all that mattered; when we were all young and the fire was still in our bellies. . . and Curly Chalker was the best dang steel guitar player that ever slid a bar across a string.

Every time it happens, when that call comes that another friend, compadre, fellow traveler, pardner, sweetheart, lover or just a "many others" has been lost, it diminishes the well that you never thought would run dry. . . that gushing spring of talent that was part of our youth. . . hell, these folks can't die. . . they're immortal. . . bigger than life. . . it was on their backs that this business of country music was built; their creative sweat oiled the gears that ran the machinery that fed the world the constant stream of material called entertainment, in whatever form. These are folks that I stayed up with all night, in dingy hotel rooms after the shows, pickin', roaring, laughing, caring, joking, listening and doing whatever it took to get another day under our belts and another mile down The Road. Memories, all.

Bob Luman

Stan, Johnny Seay,
and promoter on tour in Germany
1964

chapter 38

The Great Musical Ride of The Sixties Was Over, But. . .

Tell the World That We Tried, But we called it a day,
We took love for a ride. . . At Least Part Of The Way
Stan Hitchcock 1970, GRT Records (Bill Rice-Jerry Foster)

My recording career with Columbia's Epic Records came to a close in 1969 when the president of the company, Len Levy, left to take over the reins at GRT Records. He asked me to go with him, and since my contract was drawing to a close with Epic anyway, I felt it would be a good move. I loved Len Levy: he had been my mentor at Epic and a fine and honorable a man as I ever met - and a man that really knew the business of the recording world. GRT hired Tommy Allsup to head up the Nashville office and he became my producer.

Tommy Allsup has a great history in our business; from working with Bob Wills, Buddy Holly, Asleep at the Wheel and playing bass and guitar on gazillion records in Nashville, Texas, California and anywhere else they have a recording machine, he is a good friend and a man that knows how to handle artists, because he is one.

I loved to hear Tommy's stories about Bob Wills, who was quite a character while he was on his way to being a legend; with that big white hat and ever present cigar: a smile that could capture a whole crowd and a capacity for whiskey that is still bragged about in Texas and Oklahoma. Anyone that could come up with Faded Love and San Antonio Rose gets my vote any day. . . man, what music

Tommy got to produce a tribute album to Bob Wills while Bob was still alive and able to appreciate it. They brought Bob to the session in his wheel chair, rolled him in front of a mic and he was able, once more, to give his trademark Ah-Haaaa while the original members of his old band played the old songs once more, misty eyed and choked up, but playing it the way it was supposed to be played: Bob Wills and The Texas Playboys' style. Bob had another stroke and passed away just a few days later, closing out that chapter of musical history.

Tommy loved twin fiddles and a lot of my records from that period, under his production, featured two of the greatest fiddlers to ever pick up a bow, Buddy Spicher and Johnny Gimble. What great musicians, and what fine guys to work with. They just had a style of playing together that was unmistakable: when you heard it you knew it was Spicher and Gimble. Johnny finally got tired of the rat race and moved back to Texas, just outside of Austin, but he still plays as good as ever and is in demand as much as he wants to work.

Anyone who lived the life of a musician in the sixties will always say, "Yeah, buddy, those were the days alright; the days when the music business was like a family, when something new was always coming down the pike, and the excitement level was just unbelievable. Uh-huh son, those were the days." Well, if that sounds like something any old man would say when looking back to his youth, maybe that explains it, but ya know, I believe there really was something special going on in those early years. I sometimes dig through my record collection (yeah, records, you remember those little round black pieces of vinyl that had music on them. . .before CD's?) anyway, I listen to the music of the sixties and realize we really were making it up as we went along; playing it from the heart, inventing new licks, new ways to phrase a word, bending our voices different ways for emotional effect. They were good years, with good people leading the charge, and I feel privileged to have been a part of it. Yeah, I sure miss those days.

The great musical ride of the sixties was over, but what

memories it left those who had lived it, loved it and survived it. The next generation had a heck of an act to follow.

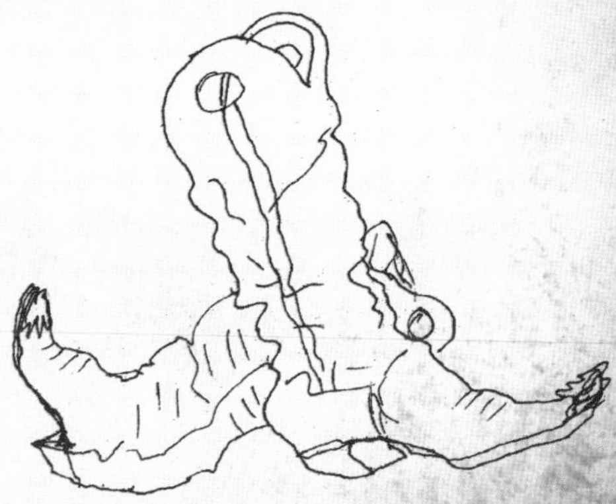

Illustration by Stan Hitchcock
"Boots"

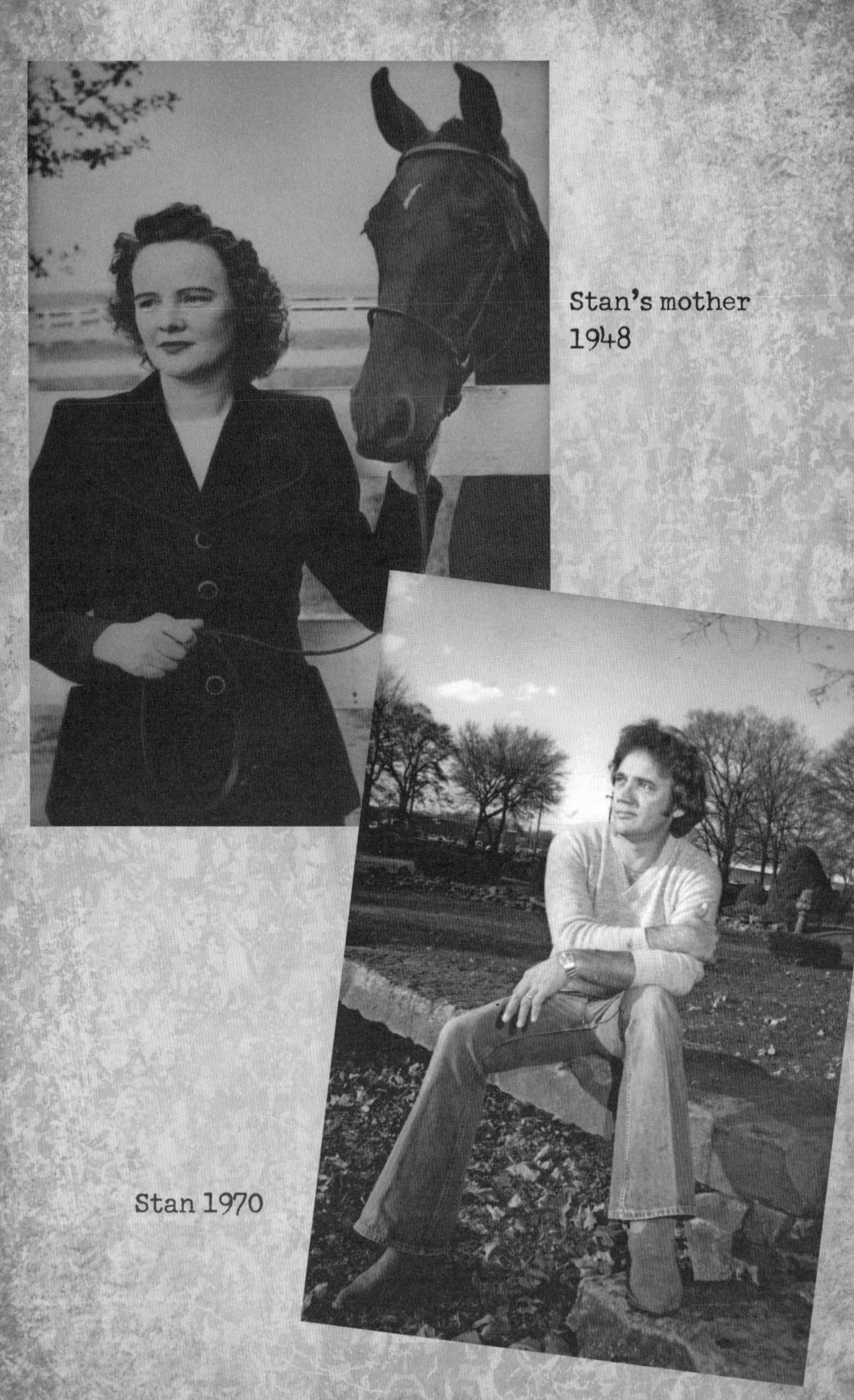

Stan's mother
1948

Stan 1970

SECTION III

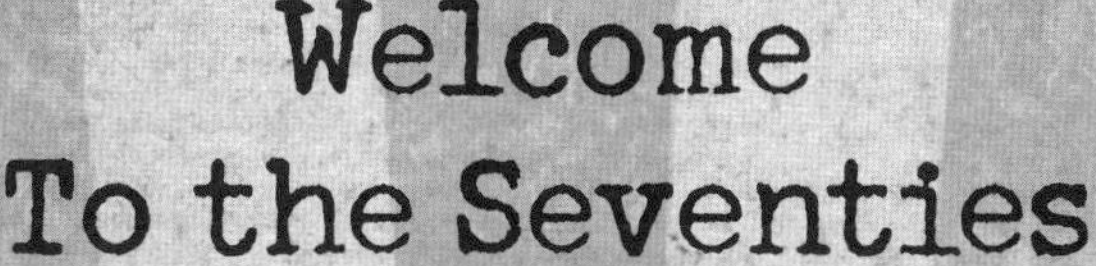

Welcome To the Seventies

Painting by Stan Hitchcock
"Sumner County, TN Backroad"

To pass to the 70's, please enter your personal code number now, put on a fresh pair of white socks. . . buy a pair of cheap cowboy boots. . . a hat with a pheasant feather band. . . practice up on your hip cowboy lingo. . . learn to ride a mechanical bull. . . and hang on to your Ray-Bans 'cause this could get rough.

The Bellamy Brothers
Heart to Heart
1994

chapter 39

Chewing Tobacco Breaks

The Language Barrier

IT'S OVER AND DONE WITH, TOO LATE TO WORRY
...no tears to cry no regrets
...Stan Hitchcock 1972

I always felt the 70's were sort of an anti-climax; after all, they had to follow the 60's. In fact, looking back now, I don't even like the 70's. There was a lot of turmoil in my life. I was starting to feel the results of too much, too much, too much: Too much of the Road, too much pressure from managers, agents and other people that try to run an entertainer, too much tension and unhappiness in my marriage, yep, too much of too much. But, nevertheless, it was here and we had to live in it.

Country music actually did pretty well in the first part of the 70's with Willie, Waylon and Tompall Glaser doing the Outlaw bit, Ronnie Milsap cutting great records, Haggard singing better than ever, Buck Owens and Roy Clark having great success with HeeHaw, and big touring shows were drawing big crowds on The Road; The Charley Daniels Band, Mel Tillis and the Statessiders, Porter and Dolly, Jack Greene and Jeannie Sealy, Jim Ed Brown and Helen Cornelius, Del Reeves, Marty Robbins. Kenny Rogers left rock and roll and cut some great records with Dottie West. Barbara Mandrell was starting to really tear them up, and I was out there with the rest of them, singing my little songs and doing my road thing.

The "Road thing" was kinda changing also. Country music was showing off in some real different places than it had in the past. In the 50's, Red Foley, Ernest Tubb, Minnie Pearl and a host of other Grand Ole Opry stars did the first ever appearance of a country music concert in Carnegie Hall, in New York City. We were always striving for a bigger audience; trying to move it on up, kinda like the Jeffersons on TV. In the 70's country really started going international, and maybe we were not quite ready. The Bellamly Brothers told me this story, and I'll pass it on to y'all. There was a big group of country stars booked on a show in Paris and The Bellamy's and Bobby Bare were two of the headliners. Charlie McCoy had put together the bunch of session pickers that made up the band, and the whole group arrived at Charles DeGaulle Airport on a cold rainy morning, after flying all night. They were supposed to have limousines for each star, or group, and the headliners were supposed to go to the nearby hotel for some rest while Charlie McCoy took the musicians in the band out to the auditorium for a sound check. Bobby Bare's limo didn't make it, and he was standing on the sidewalk getting a little red around the neck, pacing up and down, tired and grumpy, wanting to get to the hotel and get some rest. The Bellamy's were right behind Bobby, at the curb in their Limo and leaned out the window and hollered for Bobby to come ride with them. Bobby got in the front seat, with his ever-present styrofoam coffee cup which he used as a spit cup for his chewing tobacco, and the limo driver pulled off. Well, the boys could see their hotel from the airport, but the French Limo driver took off driving in the opposite direction. When it became obvious that they were not heading to the hotel, The Bellamy's started hollering at the driver, "No, no, hotel. . . hotel!!" The driver only accelerated a little more and shouted back, "No, No. . . thee-aa-ter!!" The driver reached up on the dash and grabbed a clipboard with papers on it and handed it to The Bellamy's, glancing over at Bobby Bare who was spitting in his cup, with great disdain - as only a true Frenchman can do. The Bellamy's looked at the papers on the clipboard and realized that they had gotten into the limo that was meant for Charlie McCoy and the Band - and Charlie had gotten their Limo. Trying to make the driver understand was proving impossible. . . he was hollering right back at them, and it was obvious he wasn't about to turn around for a bunch of long-haired, tobacco-chewing hillbilly Americans. Finally, Bobby had enough of this Frenchie, he scooted over next to the driver, stuck his face up next to his and said: "You understand English?" "No. . . No. . . No!!!" the driver hollered. Bobby brought the spit cup, full to the brim with second hand tobacco juice, held it right over the lap of the Frenchman's fancy limo driver uniform and said, in his Bobby Bare drawl, "Well, you sumbitch, you better get to hotel, NOW, or I'm gonna give you a tobacco juice bath you ain't never gonna forget!" Five minutes later they pulled up in front of the hotel. It was an amazing feat of communication and understanding between two widely diverse cultures. Bare should have been an ambassador, don't you think?

The Seventies was a time when Europe made hits out of some good ole boys in country music; Slim Whitman, Box Car Willie and George Hamilton all started having great success in Europe and selling tons of records. This wasn't American companies exporting country music to Europe: heck no, this was European companies selling our American country music, with artists that the record labels in the states wouldn't touch. They were selling their products with direct marketing, a process that American record labels have just never understood. Slim ended up with a whole bunch of money from royalties in Europe, and later America, while Box Car ended up in Branson, Missouri with his own theater--selling out every night. George Hamilton has a giant career in Europe and still draws huge crowds doing great shows, just as he always has. Good guys, all, and they finished first.

My contract had ended with Epic records; I had signed with GRT Records and had my first single out called "At Least Part Of The Way". The record company change wasn't the only ending for me the first part of the 70's: My syndicated television show, which by now was in around a hundred and fifty major markets, was suffering terribly from re-runs and the success of another show was killing mine.

The Production Company, 21st Century Productions - owned the CBS Affiliate in Nashville, WLAC-TV, and WLAC-TV, owned my show and distributed it around the country. In the late 60's the word came out of Hollywood that there was a television show in the works described as a country music Laugh-In. They were calling it HeeHaw.

Roy Smith, the head of 21st Century Productions, journeyed out to Hollywood, got a meeting with the HeeHaw folks, showed them a copy of my show as an example of the quality production they could do and landed the contract to be the production center for HeeHaw. It started out as a network show on CBS, and when they moved into the studios at WLAC-TV in Nashville it looked like a small country had invaded; they brought everything they owned with them. While this was good for the economy of Nashville, it was not good for the Stan Hitchcock Show; we couldn't get into the studio to shoot new shows. After a year of this and re-run city, the stations carrying my show were getting a little cross, they said: "Either send us some new shows, or forget it." The end result being the cancellation of my show across the country, and a real mad sponsor who wanted to continue. After years of producing shows myself, I could understand the problems the producers were having, but at the time I had a hard time with it. It's hard watching a hit show die on the vine.

Meanwhile, HeeHaw was creating quite a buzz on the CBS Network and providing a lot of work for lot of musicians and singers. Sam Luvello, the man that made it all happen at HeeHaw is a wonderful guy; he worked hard to bring the very best out of the show. The show made even bigger stars of Buck Owens and Roy Clark. and gave a whole new career to Grandpa Jones, Stringbean, Junior Samples, Kenny Price and Minnie Pearl. It was a fun show to work and I enjoyed appearing on it with my band, even though it was bittersweet not being able to continue my own show.

One television event that was good for me did come to be during this period however: in August 1971 I landed a nationwide network television commercial for Purina Dog Chow. Purina was sponsoring the country music show, "That Good Ole Nashville Music", and they were picking entertainers to do their network commercials. They contacted me and I agreed to do the spot. I suggested that they do it on location. I wanted to film my dog and me fishing: a situation we were both comfortable with. I have always hated shooting television in studios, trying to act natural when it's all fake lighting, scenery and camera angles. I convinced them to go to the Harpeth River, (you remember, the one that Pillow and I almost drowned him on), take the little aluminum fishing boat and shoot my dog, Flash, and me on the river. Well, you won't believe how involved a network commercial shoot can be; it's like shooting a movie. They bring in script writers, a crew of about seventy people, lights, film camera, boom, makeup, people to do nothing but wipe the sweat off the star, etc. And the best of all, they brought a Hollywood dog as a stand-in for my dog Flash, and an animal trainer and handler. Flash was a beautiful blonde cocker spaniel; the most docile little dog that I ever owned. He would do anything I wanted him to do, so I knew we wouldn't need the extra dog: wrong again, Rin- Tin-Tin.

They started swarming Flash and me, as only a Hollywood crew can do, patting, puffing, powdering, combing, fluffing, and generally irritating me and my poor dog with their attention. The plan was to shoot a long shot the dog and me in the boat as we were pulling up to the shore for lunch after a morning of fishing. The dog would then jump out of the boat, I would climb out with his little silver bowl (you know you always carry it where ever you go), pull out a bag of Purina Dog Chow and proceed to feed Flash on the gravel bar while talking about how I loved Purina. Well, it seemed like a good plan, so we got ready to try it. It was a beautiful day on the river and I decided this was a pretty neat way to make a living all right, shoot, just film a few commercials, do a little fishing and live the good life. I got Flash in the boat and he like to have had a fit (I forgot to tell you, I had kinda told the producers that me and Flash went fishing together in this boat all the time. . . well, actually I had thought about it a lot but never actually done it, and now I found out that Flash was deathly afraid of the boat, the water, and all these Hollywood folks: he was not a happy camper). As I pulled the boat out into the river, I turned it around to face the camera, and headed back in to shore. When the boat run up on the gravel, the Producer hollerd: "cut" just like in the movies, and the Hollywood animal handler reached out to grab Flash so he could move him to the next location where the camera would capture him eating. When he reached to grab Flash, the dog like to have tore his arm off - I mean a Doberman could not have done a better job: just a growling, biting, slashing mouth full of teeth all over that mans arm. I just barely got hold of Flash before he reached the jugular and ripped the guy's throat out, apologizing all the while to the high-priced animal handler. This fancy looking fella with his safari jacket and campaign hat on acted like he had never been bitten before, well shoot, him and Flash were even 'cause he had never bitten anyone before either! Maybe it was the preparation we went through to get Flash ready for his big Hollywood break. The producers had come out to my house to work on the script, and while they were there, they asked that I not feed Flash for twenty-four hours before the shoot, just to get him in the mood for good old Purina. Uh, that's another thing; I kinda told the producers that I fed Flash Purina all the time, ya know? Well, actually I thought about feeding him Purina, 'cause the Company had sent me a whole bunch of it awhile back, but old Flash was a meat and taters kind of dog. If it didn't come off my table then it couldn't have been edible. Flash was real particular about what he stuck his nose into - I mean, he didn't even hardly like to smell other dogs rear ends like most dogs do, yeah, real particular. But, I figured after starving him for twenty-four hours, he would gladly gobble up the old Dog Chow, just like on TV. Well, we got the Hollywood animal handler all band-aided up and decided to shoot the scene in which I pour the Dog Chow into the shiny metal bowl and Flash runs in and gobbles it up. A couple of the assistant dog handlers held Flash off camera as I looked at the camera and gave my pitch, then leaned over and poured a generous portion of Dog Chow into the bowl. On cue, the dog handlers let loose of Flash who galloped hungrily toward me with his tongue hanging out and slobbers already forming on the edge of his mouth - I mean the dog was serious hungry, shoot, the animal handlers arm didn't hardly fill him up at all. He ran up to the bowl, crammed his nose down in amongst the Dog Chow looking for the table scraps that he was sure were hidden there somewhere, when it dawned on Flash that the only thing this bowl had to offer was Dog Chow. He raised his head, gave me a look of total disgust, turned and stalked off. I tried to assure the Producer that Flash was just having a bad day and if I held his head down in amongst that Dog Chow long enough he was bound to eat, sooner or later. However, the Producer was an old hand at this sort of thing. He walked over to the production truck and dug out his briefcase, opened it up, and took out a couple of cans of potted meat. Walking back over to the dish of dog food, he removed the top layer, spread a double thick amount of the potted meat on top of the remaining dog food, sprinkled a little Purina on top of the potted meat, and said: "Try it again, folks". We repeated the shot and when Flash stuck his nose down in the dog food this time, he just kept going down till he hit that potted meat, and woofed it down like he hadn't eaten in twenty four hours. It was a great shot, and you could tell that Flash really loved that good old Purina Dog Chow. After that shot, I was supposed to pat the dog on top of the head, get up, grab my fishing pole and cast to the other side of the river where a deep pool of water lay in the shade of a big tree on the riverbank. The camera was positioned on a boom on the other side of the river shooting across the pool and catching me on the far bank. I had tied on a Rapalla top-water floating minnow on my six-pound test line ultra-light fishing rig and was ready for the shot. I patted the dog on the head, got up and got my pole. Talking to the camera all the time, I eased back the bail of the reel, hooked that finger around the line and made a perfect long cast to the other side of the river, just about a foot and a half from where the roots of that old tree entered the water. The lure settled perfectly, bobbed once and the water exploded with a three-pound small mouth bass that had just been laying there in that deep pool thinking about dinner. The camera was right on the lure when the fish explosion happened; it was an incredible shot. No one would ever believe it was real, but it was, hey would I lie to you about a fish? Shoot no, I might lie about my dog eating Dog Chow, but never about a fish. Ok, maybe it was just two and a half pounds: are you happy now? The commercial went on to be a success, I don't know if it sold any dog food, but it sure did buy me a farm.

Gardner Advertising Company
10 Broadway | St Louis Mo 63102 | (314) 444-2000

CLIENT: Ralston Purina Co.
PRODUCT: Dog Chow
FILM NO.: RPDC0130
TITLE: "Stan Fishing"

DATE: August, 1971
PRODUCER: Metromedia
JOB NO.: 24001-19021
LENGTH: :60

1. (Natural sfx under) STAN: Hi, I'd like you to meet my fishing buddy.

2. I call him the Phoenix Flash.

3. I named him after one of my records.

Stan Hitchcock & Eddie Rabbitt
Heart to Heart, 1993

chapter 40

The "Folk Hero" and The Godfather

HOW COULD SUCH A LITTLE TEARDROP...
...hold such a big hurt. (Written by Eddie Rabbitt)
Recorded by Stan Hitchcock... Epic Records 1969

In 1974 I was abruptly thrown into politics: me, a guy that hates politics and most politicians with a passion. I got a call from the Illinois Democratic Fund, the IDF, located in Chicago, Illinois. Country music had long proven itself a good vehicle for raising money for politicians: in fact it put Jimmy Davis in the Governor's Mansion of Louisiana and George Wallace was using country stars like Tammy Wynette to gather money for a run at the president of the United States job. Roy Acuff even thought about being Governor of Tennessee once. The IDF wanted me to produce a series of country music concerts across Illinois to raise funds for the then Governor of Illinois, Dan Walker. Governer Dan had gotten elected by walking across the width and breadth of the state, shaking hands and howdying all the good folks and just being a good ole boy that the common folks could relate to.

I made the trip to Chicago, met with the IDF folks and took on the job of putting together five shows across Illinois including Moline, Carbondale, Peoria, Chicago, and Belleville. Booked for the shows were Tanya Tucker, Del Reeves, Jack Greene, Jeannie Seely,

Mickey Gilley, Jim Ed Brown, The Cates Sisters, Jean Shepard, The Sego Brothers and Naomi and Jake Hess. I produced the show, emceed, performed and traveled to every radio station in the state that played country music, to promote it. I set up offices in the state capitol of Springfield, right across the street from the Capitol building, and started putting it all together. An old country music pro by the name of Bill Starnes was hired to promote and publicize the shows; he was the son of Jack Starnes from Beaumont, Texas - founder of Starday Records (along with Pappy Daily). Bill was a real character. He had made a great impression on the leaders of IDF, just like he always did because he had the gift. . . the gift of selling himself. Bill had a checkered history, an impressive resume, and was probably a genuine genius–and--he was a wild man.

Bill Starnes had managed Ray Price, George Jones, and worked with Lefty Frizzell as well as dozens of lesser knowns. And he lived the life of a country song by being a convicted felon, a real live bank robber. Bill's dad, Jack, was a business man in Beaumont and had gotten into the entertainment business while booking acts into a night club that he and his wife owned. Forming Starday Records with Pappy Daily, he was the catalyst for George Jones' and Lefty Frizzell's careers, so Bill had grown up in the business. When he was nineteen years old he got mad at his Dad, so he walked into the Bank in Beaumont, where his Dad did business, and calmly held it up: he walked out with twenty-thousand dollars and about two hours later gave himself up. He told me he only did it to embarrass his Dad. . . but what he got out of it was a few years in the Federal Pen. Nevertheless, Bill was a good friend and he always treated me right, so that is what I judged him on.

While putting the shows together, I spent a lot of time with Governor Dan Walker and his family across the street at the Mansion, and became very impressed with his down to earth manner and good nature. He told me the story of how he had walked across Illinois meeting the people in his campaign and how close he felt to them. I sat down one night in my Hotel room and started writing a song about his famous walk, and titled it "A Winner Walking Home". About a week later I was at a reception for the Governor and all the IDF big wigs were there to meet with me about the upcoming concerts. It was after the reception; we were all in one of those smoky back rooms that politicians seem to favor, I got my guitar out and started singing my song for the Governor: all the boys got real excited. Judging by their excitement, I gathered that they had big plans for the Governor on a national scale. The Fund Director of the IDF, David Cleverdon asked me if it would be possible to record the song and promote it as a commercial release, and what the cost would be. I gave them the figure of fifteen-thousand to record, manufacture and distribute the record. They huddled over in the corner for the rest of the evening, and told me they would let me know in a couple of days about making the record. Two days later I got a call at my Hotel in Springfield and the secretary to the Fund Director of the IDF asked if I could be in Chicago the next day. I reckoned I could, so the meeting was set.

I drove into Chicago the next day and made my way downtown to the high rise office building that housed the offices of the Illinois Democratic Fund. The office was right in the middle of downtown Chicago, directly across the street from the offices of Mayor Daly. While having a cup of coffee in the Fund Director's office, we talked about his plan for my song. The Democratic party was very interested in promoting Governer Dan Walker on the national scene as a possible candidate for president the next election, and they wanted to portray him as a folk hero. Well, that's what my song did all right. I made up a pretty good story song, "A Winner Walking Home".

Well, yeah, it's kinda smaltzy, maybe even a little bit corny. But hey, I've already told you what my opinion of politics and politicians is, it's just another gig, man, don't sweat it. The IDF Director was a pretty nice guy, and I believe he really believed in his man, but he was real concerned that the press not get hold of the story that the IDF was behind my recording the song, it had to look like all my doing. He told me to go downstairs to the entrance of the building and wait outside on the street and someone would come along and pick me up. I didn't stop to wonder how they would recognize me, (in my black Levi's and custom made boots, and hillbilly singer shirt). I followed his instructions and stepped out the front door of the office building and immediately noticed a 1948 Lincoln Continental limousine parked at the curb in a no parking zone. As I stepped out the front door, a very dignified black uniformed driver stepped around the car and approached me. Another man, about six-foot-six stood by the side of the car scanning the people walking by. The driver came up and said, "Mr. Hitchcock, if you will follow me sir." He walked back to the car and opened the back passenger door and I crawled in. The minute my country butt hit those leather seats I knew I was in some kinda strange situation. There was an older man sitting on the far side of the car, looking straight ahead - he never even blinked an eye at my entrance into his museum piece of a car - just quietly signaled the driver to drive around the block. As we circled the block he asked, again without ever looking at me, "You say it takes fifteen-thousand dollars to do this record?" "Yessir, that's right," I replied. He reached down between his feet and picked up a briefcase and placed it on my lap, at the same time signaling the driver that the meeting was over. As we are pulling up in front of the office building again, I nervously studied the old mans profile: stick just a little more cotton in those jaws and man you would have Marlon Brando as the Godfather, for sure!

The old man never said another word and he had never looked at me the whole time I was in the car, but hey, what would I talk to him about anyway? I got back up to the office of the IDF, went into the Director's office and we opened the briefcase. Neatly stacked in old bills was exactly fifteen-thousand dollars. The Director closed up the briefcase, handed it to me and said, "Hmmmm, this must belong to you, I sure never saw it before." Politics has some strange bedfellows doesn't it?

I recorded the song and distributed it to radio stations around the country; it got a lot of play and created a lot of interest in the media, after all no one had ever released a political campaign song as a commercial record before. Newsweek Magazine did a story on it as did dozens of newspapers, and I just did it because I thought Governor Dan was a folk hero--uh-huh, that's right, and all in all I'm glad I got to work with him. After all, how else is a hillbilly gonna get to ride around Chicago with the Godfather!!!

Paintings by
Stan Hitchcock

Stan Hitchcock & Jerry Jeff Walker
Austin, TX 1992
In his home

chapter 41

Songwriter Heroes

I KNEW A MAN BOJANGLES. . .

Jerry Jeff Walker. . .

Songwriter. . . Entertainer. . . American Hero

As I've told you before in this rambling dissertation on how to be a card carryin' hillbilly; my heroes are the folks who create the music: Those special people who take empty words and music notes and string them together with beauty. One of my favorite songwriters is transplanted Texas legend, Jerry Jeff Walker. Jerry Jeff is originally from New York State, but you couldn't have tied him there when he left High School in the 60's and hitch-hiked south - he didn't care where, just south. After spending a few days in Florida, he joined up with some other vagabonds and headed for New Orleans. Jerry has never gotten over New Orleans, from that first night he found it; as he arrived in the French Quarter, he thought there must be some special holiday celebration going on. . .but no, it was just a regular night in the Quarter. It didn't take Jerry long to acclimate to this crowd of rowdies, gypsies, musicians, slight of hand artists, con men, con women, drifters and settlers that made up the street scene of the Quarter in the 60's and 70's. One night he was walking along, feelin', carrying his guitar to his favorite spot to do a little street entertaining when some buttoned up College boys stopped him and pointing their finger at the free spirit with the guitar they admonished Jerry with: "Boy, you can't spend the rest of your life livin' like this!" To which Jerry calmly replied, "You just stay right there and watch me." He has - and it's been good to him. He and I both wonder if those boys are still waiting, and watching.

Jerry Jeff told me how he came to write Mr. Bojangles, and it goes like this: "I was walking along down by one of the open air Cafe's in the Quarter when I spotted this beautiful girl, sitting there having a glass of wine. I immediately walked over and told her that she was so beautiful that I could be in love with her. . . she huffed up, put her hands on her hips and said, "Now you stop that, you're just acting foolish!" I looked over at one of the next tables and saw this young couple sitting there holding hands. I walked over and asked them to take up for me as I told this girl I loved her, 'cause it was obvious that they were in love. The Restaurant Manager was pulling on my shoulder; saying I had to stop it. . . it got all out of hand, and I ended up waving at the girl from the patrol car as they were hauling me away: she was still huffin'. Well, they locked me in this cell with this old black man and when I told him what had happened, he just laughed and said, "Ah, youth." That was Bojangles. He was a street dancer with a drinking problem, (probably an occupational hazard in his line of endeavor). It was a holiday weekend, like the fourth of July or something and I was locked up with him all through that long weekend. He knew it was my first time in jail so he said, "We can just sit here and stare at the floor, or we can tell some stories, pass the time away." I didn't have any stories yet, so he told all of his. Sometime later I got to needing a character for a song and I thought; that old man, Bojangles, he'd be perfect - and turns out, he was."

I've spent some great times with Jerry Jeff - some of them down in Austin, some on the Road. I consider him one of the wisest men I know--and a man who knows how to be a good friend. He and his wife Susan live the good life, dividing their time between their home next to the Governor's Mansion in Austin, a beautiful town house in the Quarter in New Orleans, and a beautiful new beach home down in Belize. Not a bad life for a former street singer, gypsy-living balladeer.

Mel Tillis and the Half a Million Dollar Boots

Mel Tillis had never written a song when he made his first trip to Nashville in 1957. He came to Music City to be a singing star: They told him they didn't need no stutterin' singers; that if he cut a record it would have to be as big around as a truck tire. "Well," he says, "I took that insult and asked them what did they need, and they said songs--copyrights--so I said, OK, and then went back to Florida and tried to write one." Mel wrote a song and he and his manager at the time, A. R. "Buck" Honest John Petty, went over to Tampa to see Ray Price who was doing a concert there. Mel got back stage and sang the song to Ray. He kinda liked it, so Mel let him take a copy of it back to Nashville to maybe record it. The next weekend Ray was singing it backstage at the Opry and Webb Pierce walked by and heard it and said, "What is that song? I kinda like it." Ray said some kid that couldn't talk gave it to him down in Florida. Pierce said, "Let me have it Ray, you don't need it, you've had the number one song for the past year [Crazy Arms]." Ray gave the song to Webb, except Mel hadn't give Ray the whole song, just a verse and chorus. Webb took the song and had Wayne Walker, a staff writer at his publishing company, write another verse and then went into Columbia Studios and recorded it.

Weeks later, Mel and his mother were at home in Florida listening to the Eddie Hill Show on WSM radio out of Nashville when Webb Pierce's new hit record came on: "I ain't never, no darlin', seen nobody like you, never, have I ever seen nobody like you. . ." Mel jumped up and said, "That's my song Mama! At least I think it's my song. . . I never heard that other verse but I know the first verse and the melody's mine. . . WE'RE GONNA BE RICH MAMA! WE'RE GONNA BE RICH!!!" A week later he moved to Nashville to write other songs like "Burning Memories". "Detroit City", and the masterpiece, "Ruby, Don't Take Your Love To Town". Mel is one of the genuine good guys, and his success is well deserved.

Mel ended up buying the publishing company that Webb Pierce, Carl Smith and Jim Denny started. He wrote for them for years and finally made enough money to buy the company. In the early years when he was struggling, he had to give away parts of his songs to Webb Pierce when he recorded them. One time, Mel was at the publishing company on Music Row and had just finished writing a song when Webb Pierce came in. Webb had on a pair of boots that were the prettiest things that Mel had ever seen; they had stars on them - lightning bolts: man, they were pretty, and Mel just had to have them. He told Webb he had just finished a song and Webb said to go ahead and sing it for him. When Mel got through Webb said, "I kinda like that Lad, I kinda like that". Mel said well, he'd give Webb half of it for those boots. Webb said, "That's a deal, I'll bring them in tomorrow." So Mel ended up with Webb's pretty boots and Webb made a half a million dollars on the song, "Oh Lord I'm tired, tired of living this old way."

The publishing company that Webb, Carl and Jim Denny started and Mel ended up buying is called Cedarwood Publishing, but they missed out on one big writer; and it's a good story.

"I'll tell you what boy, you go get your hair cut, and I'll listen to your songs."

Songwriting for Haircut

In the late 1970's a young man graduated from his East Tennessee High School and immediately headed down Interstate 40 for Nashville with a pocket full of songs, an old beat up guitar and a beautiful head of hair that hung all the way down his back. He was eighteen years old and his name is Dean Dillon. He hitched into town and made his way to Music Row not knowing anyone, and having no idea how to get his songs to the right people. He saw a sign on the front of a building across the street from Capitol Records that sounded pretty good, "Cedarwood Publishing Company." He made his way across 16th Avenue South and walked in the front door of the office building. He was trying to explain to the secretary that he would like someone to listen to his songs when a man stuck his head around the corner and said, "My name's Bill Denny (Jim's son), come on back to my office, I'll listen to your songs." Well this was it man, only been in town thirty minutes and here comes his big break. Whew, man, gotta calm down. . . don't want to blow it. As soon as they got through the door of Bill's office, the phone rang and Bill stayed on the phone for what seemed like thirty minutes, while Dean just sat there with a knot as big as Texas in his stomach. Finally Bill hung up the phone and turned to Dean with these famous words, "I'll tell you what boy, you go get your hair cut, and I'll listen to your songs." A crushed Dean Dillon walked back out into the sunshine with the first of many cuts and wounds to the pride that is the norm in a business where you wear your heart on your sleeve. Several years later Dean was working at Opryland Park when they decided to showcase this young talent (at the park) for the big wigs on Music Row. Dean Dillon got up on stage and just knocked them all out, like he always does, singing one great song after another that he had written. When he finished, he stepped off stage and stood face to face with an excited Bill Denny, who had no remembrance of ever seeing this kid, (because Dean had to get his hair cut for the work in the Park). Bill Denny grabbed Dean's arm and exclaimed, "Man, that's great, how soon can you get me those songs?" Dean looked him straight in the eye and said, "When you get your hair cut." Since then, Dean Dillon has written twelve (count them Bill) George Strait songs that have gone to the number one spot, and has sold millions of records, along with a whole bunch of other hits by different artists. This is the story as Dean tells it to me, and it shows the wide chasm that has always separated the suits from the talent in the music business. Bill Denny says he has no recollection of this happening, and I don't blame him for not wanting to remember. The power brokers in Nashville have always feared the times when the artists would get control, after all, pickers can't do business: they have to be managed, uh-huh, tell that to Garth Brooks in the 90's when suddenly control shifts and the whole of Music Row shakes in it's boots as he calls the shots at Capitol Records. A few years down the road it would really get out of hand when some of these same artists would go to Branson, Missouri, my old growing up area, starting their own theaters, running their own business enterprises, and having absolute control over their destiny.

In the 70's, Branson was just easin' along: The Baldknobbers and the Presleys opening up shows and the tourists starting to go there for the Ozark experience. In 1977 I started heading up a show for a friend of mine named Warren Stokes In Springfield, Missouri - about 36 miles from Branson. I did that for a year while I was scopin' out the Branson market. There were three or four shows there at that time, so in 1978 I entered into a partnership agreement with a developer in the Branson area to build and operate a music theater.

At the same time, I worked a deal with another company to start a syndicated television show from Branson. In 1978 we went on the air with "The Stan Hitchcock Show - From The Ozarks", which was syndicated in about 80 markets nationwide. The theater did pretty well, although it was ahead of the boom; but the developer got in trouble on some of his construction loans and the theater had to be sold. I believed that Branson would surge, but I did not foresee the huge boom that later took place. It is a town that folks love and where the artists can finally control their careers.

The whole time I was back in the Ozarks, and every time one of my friends would come to my theater and do a show for me, I wanted to leave with them on their bus and head back to Tennessee, man, I missed those Tennessee hills. I was really wound up inside, and I felt like I would fly into a thousand pieces.

Dean Dillon
Heart to Heart
1994

Stan Promo 1972

"Along a Summer Country Road..."
painting by Stan Hitchcock

chapter 42

Precious Memories - How They Linger...

MEANWHILE, BACK ON THE FARM...

It was a beautiful fall day in September 1978 as I pulled my car through the gate at the old Hitchcock farm, deep in the Ozark Mountains. I'd been a long-time gone from these hills and I came searching for some good memories; maybe a memento or two of the carefree farm-kid that I had been, so many years and miles ago.

When I left these hills to go to Nashville in the late summer of 1962, I hardly took the time to even look back; I was in a hurry 'cause I had a song to sing and the world had an ear to listen and I couldn't wait to get started.

Coming back seventeen years later, everything had changed in my life, and I was having a hard time getting a handle on just what I was all about. My Mother had died the spring of '69, Dad had gotten remarried and moved to town, my own marriage was on the rocks and would soon end in divorce, and traveling The Road to sing that song had flat wore my body out. I was tired, depressed, hurt, and pretty well convinced that the world didn't care to hear my song anyway.

I got out of the car, shut the gate, and drove on up to the house; all the while thinking how bad I missed Mama and wishing I could talk it over with her; after all we had some unfinished business to discuss.

When I left for Nashville, pretty sure the world was my oyster and all I had to do was shuck it, my Mom was really torn up about it. "Son, that music business will kill you; you'll end up drinking and running around, and Lord knows what all, and you'll end up with a broken heart." Well, it was all these years later and dang if she hadn't been 'bout right, and I wished I could tell her so.

When Mom had passed away they like to have never found me on The Road, playing a string of one-night stands across the far western states. I just got there in time for the funeral: there was so much I needed to say to her, but just never had the time, and now I had come back looking for the pieces of me that I had lost somewhere along the way.

After Dad got married again, he boxed up most of Mom's stuff, stored it in the old farm house, and moved to town. This was the first time I had been back since then, and I really didn't know what I was looking' for, I just knew I had to be there.

The old house was about gone, windows boarded up, roof about caved in, and you definitely got the feeling that the old place had died of a broken heart when the family left. There is a presence about old, abandoned houses that is almost like the human feeling of homesickness; so many memories, so many good times. . . all gone; all gone.

I got the front door open and started exploring through some of the boxes. . . some of Mom's dishes. . . here's some pictures of us kids growing up. . . a whole box of hats. . . yeah, Mom loved hats. . . cooking utensils. . . boxes of shoes. . . a whole flea market of one person's life. But, this wasn't Mom, this was just stuff. . . somehow, I had expected more.

I gathered up my flashlight and the few mementos I had found, and decided to venture back to the real world; shake this melancholy feeling that was weighing me down, when I noticed the closet under the stairs, which I hadn't gotten around to searching. I opened the door, shined my light up onto the shelves and saw the corner of a book sticking out from the top shelf. I reached up, lifted it down, blew the dust off, and immediately recognized that I held in my hands the single item that most connected me to the memory of my Mother: Her Old Bible!

Every day of my life as a child, I remember Mom taking time each day to read and study her Bible. There was hardly a page in that Old King James that didn't have notes written in her handwriting of lessons she had learned from her studies.

We, as a family, would all sit down in the living room in front of the fireplace, and Dad or Mom would read to us from this Bible teaching us what we should know about how to live your life the right way. Oh, oh, oh, chill bumps and butterflies in my stomach. This was heavy stuff, friends.

With fingers that weren't too steady, and eyes that were starting to blur, I opened the cover: and there on the inside first page, pinned with an old rusty straight pin, was a letter. . . addressed to me. It was a letter from my Mother, written just weeks before she died, and it was written, not only about me, but from my own perspective. Here, let me share it with you:

Well, Mom's kneeling down again
And I can hear her cry,
"Oh Lord, don't let my boy go away
to that big city, he wants to try.
Down here in these hills and hollers,
You made them with your hand.
Someone else is a'wantin' my son,
and Lord, I don't understand."

As I walked down the well house lane
I hated the day I was born
And out of these hills I'll go,
somehow, I'll find a way
That night when I came in for supper

and sat on my old wooden stool
Mom had washed all my ragged clothes
and shined my old scuffed shoes

I didn't know Mom was feelin' so bad
and I really loved her so
So when she went, I left too,
where she prayed I'd never go
But I'm back in these hills and hollers now
sitting in Mom's old chair
Now I know why she loved these hills
I know what made her care.

When it was meetin' time in the valley
off to the neighbors she would go
on each door she would knock
"It's meeting time you know"
Such singing, you have never heard
clappin' their hands that way
If you'd ask them why,
they'd shake their head
without a word to say.

Yes, I've come home again to stay
it's been just like you said it would
I made fame, fortune, heartache too
surely I'd change it if I could
These hills and hollers are beautiful now
these folks are good and kind
Oh Lord, please tell my Mom, I've changed
Her boy, up there, some day she'll find.

To My Dear Son, Stanley Edward, From your Mom As God Inspired me to Write When He awakened me one night, December 3, 1968

Well friends, when you get a letter from the grave, ten years after the fact, and it tells you just the way your life has gone, it tends to clean out your tear ducts; and it will straighten up you life, in a hurry.

It still amazes me that Mom knew I would find that letter. She knew she would be dead, but still able to teach me a thing or two, and she left me a road map, her old family Bible: it would lead me back home. Praise the Lord for good mamas, even the ones who have sons that grow up to be cowboys and sing them old songs, but that is another story, and we'll get to that soon enough.

You know, looking back down that old trail that I've been on for so long, it has been pretty bumpy at times, there sure have been a lot of detours, and I've even run off The Road a few times, but taking it all in and sifting through it: It's been a helluva ride.

Sam, Big Stan, Ruby, Danny, Stan
1953

Little Jimmy Dickens

Jerry Sullivan and Family

Stan and Eddie Raven

Hank Thompson

SECTION IV

The Later Nashville Years 1980's

The Crossroads

Illustration by Stan Hitchcock

Stan and Ronnie Reno at Wynnewood
in 1986

chapter 43

Musician - Turned Televisionary

"Hi Stan, this is Nyhl. Let's start up a Television Network... you can be the Countrymusicologist...

I'll be the mogul." Conversation between Nyhl Henson and Stan Hitchcock in 1983 that led to the start up of CMT.

Looking over at my old Gibson guitar in the stand in the corner of my office I remember how painful it was when I made the change from musician to businessman. I had been singing almost my entire life and suddenly I was putting it away to embark on an adventure in television that had never been tried before. I could not imagine just what an adventure it would turn out to be but in essence, the Eighties were great, no doubt the best decade of my whole life--up to that time anyway. I had the opportunity to start up a world-wide cable television network that would help change the whole demographic of the typical country music fan and open doors of opportunity for dozens of new artists. Billboard Magazine called the network: "The definitive country music interview show". But the most important thing that this opportunity brought to me was to change my personal life from a terrible unhappiness to a life of joy and fulfillment that I never dreamed I would find.

It's amazing how simple comments can lead to serious thought; serious thought can lead to direct action; and direct action can cause massive consequences that have a major impact. This is how the cable television network, Country Music Television (CMT) came to be.

I had moved back to Nashville and was working with some developers on a project in Hendersonville, just north of Nashville, called Music Village USA. It was a theme park for country music and I had helped them design a theater and had mounted a daily stage show while acting as the entertainment director. I had met a man named Nyhl Henson who was in town consulting Group W on the viability of starting a television network featuring country lifestyles, sports and music, which they were starting in partnership with the Gaylord Entertainment Group. Nyhl had a background in cable television from working with Warner Communications, Qube, cable television experiment, which spawned such networks as MTV and Nickelodeon. He was a rock and roll kid from the 60's who had very little knowledge of country music, so he kept coming to me for information and advice on the entertainment scene in Nashville. He had been in college at Carbondale, Illinois when I came through in the 70's promoting Gov. Dan Walker. He even remembered the "Winner Walkin' Home" recording, (which was more than I could say for myself - I had tried to forget it). We became fast friends and I ended up introducing him to the developers at Music Village USA. When his contract with Group W ran out, he took a consultant position with us.

I had been watching with fascination the startup and early success of MTV as they introduced the world to music video. Nyhl had several friends at the MTV headquarters, and together we started researching the possibility of forming a group of investment people to start a video programming network that would feature country music. I made a trip to New York and spent a couple days at the MTV headquarters and uplink facility, bringing myself up to speed on this music video business. I was sure that if it worked that well in rock-and-roll that it would do the same for country. We started searching out investment partners and doing all our home-work on the idea of a country music video network.

While we were going about our business of figuring out the ways we might get a network started; one dropped right into our lap.

There was a company called Telestar located in Albuquerque, New Mexico that had put together a penny stock offering and formed a cable venture called CMTV. They had come to Nashville and cut a programming deal with a man called "Big Daddy" Daniels who had a small production company in Hendersonville specializing in producing low budget television shows for tax shelters. "Big Daddy" had a stock-pile of low cost videos and utilized them to get enough programming to go on the air with in 1983, launching just one day before The Nashville Network. They were on-the-air all right, but trouble is, no one hardly even knew about it, and just about then their partnership blew all to heck. Telestar, "Big Daddy", and the investment group of penny stock traders put together by Blinder Robertson just flew all apart and "Big Daddy" left town real quick. I have no idea what the problem was, but the first Nyhl and I heard about it was when Telestar's president, Mr. Joseph Corrozzi, came to meet with us at Music Village USA; saying that he had heard we were interested in starting a video network and would we be interested in buying the Network CMTV before they shut it down. Well, the only thing that they had that we were interested in was their one million subscribers and the name. So the investment group I had been working with at Music Village USA, consisting of Gilbert Biggers and Hall Hardaway, agreed to put three million dollars into the deal if Nyhl and I would run it. The complete assets of CMTV at that time were one million subscribers (they claimed two million, but our audit turned up one million), three 3/4 inch Sony videocassette players, a very tired transmitter, a switcher, a satellite disk (only slightly larger than the ones you use in your backyard), a lease on the Telestar satellite transponder, a box of 3/4 inch videocassettes that contained some of the worst videos I have ever seen, (hey, that's my opinion - I'm not a fan of tax-shelter videos), and the name Country Music Television, CMTV, (which we found out came with a lawsuit). Well, you got to start somewhere, I reckon.

Our deal was that Telstar would carry the note for the three million and furnished the satellite transponder space for fifty-thousand dollars a month lease. We quickly built a playback facility above the Music Village Theater, hired some tape operators and an engineer, and we were in business. Well, we were in business all right, but we had nothing to play. We also found out, after we took it over, that MTV had a lawsuit against the company over the name CMTV. We solved that one real quick when I changed the name to CMT. All of the major record companies, the ones that produce and provide the music videos for video networks, had refused to give videos to the previous operators because of what they considered to be poor quality programming. I quickly called a special meeting of all the representatives of the record labels at the theater at Music Village and explained that we had bought the name of Country Music Television and were changing the name from CMTV to CMT: We were serious about doing this the right way and that we believed we could have an impact on the country music business.

All of the record folks knew me from my years in the business and took on good faith my promise that we were going to make a real network out of this, and that I truly believed it could help spread the popularity of country music. They pledged their support and told me to come by and start gathering up all their music videos. Well, I'll tell you folks, it came as quite a shock to find that there was only thirty (30) music videos that were worth playing in the whole country music world; (I cheated by playing some John Cougar Mellencamp, Georgia Sattellites, and a couple of other pop and rock acts that had some good, middle of The Road videos). Thirty videos to program a twenty-four hour a day video channel: Wow, this ought to be fun. I immediately began a campaign to prove to the record companies that somebody out there in television land was watching, and it could make a difference in slow record sales if they would just get busy and produce some good videos.

At first it was like pulling teeth, because I was dealing with people who were SOUND experts, and they really didn't understand the impact that PICTURES and SOUND could have. Shoot, those music videos cost money to produce, and record company big wigs sure don't like to spend that extra money, particularly when they can't prove that the video is selling records. My argument to that has always been; videos are not supposed to sell records, they sell the artists: by giving him or her a face and a personality that is recognizable when that TV viewer goes into a record store to buy some music. It speeds up the process of artist development by years. Back when I started in the 60's, an artist had to travel around the country for years, doing personal appearances and calling on radio stations, trying to put a face and personality with the voice they heard on their radio. Music video changed that process, forever. Marty Stuart is a good example: He had been around for years, knocking people out with personal appearances but having little luck with radio and record sales - until he put out a music video called "Hillbilly Rock". The general public finally got to see this dynamic personality singing his song and the folks loved it! I world premiered it, putting it in heavy rotation on CMT, and Marty made a career that is still going strong. Some more of my CMT breakouts are Travis Tritt, Clint Black, Kathy Mattea, Reba, George Strait, James House, Billy Joe Royal, (when he went country). . . and don't forget Garth.

The artists were the first to get it. I never will forget at the end of the first year of our operation 1984; we had been struggling along, playing a lot of the same videos much too often - but at least playing good ones, when I got a call from Waylon Jennings. He said: "Stan, I just want you to know that I was out on The Road doing concerts; after the show I was signing autographs and people were coming up and saying, 'Hey Waylon, we been seeing your video on CMT, and we really like it.' Man, folks are watching: you keep it up." The next thing you know, other artists were having the same thing happen, and of course they came right back home and went to the record companies and told them about this reaction.

In mid-1984 I filed for divorce and in October it was final. My sixteen year old son, Stan the II and I moved to a little hillside farm that I had bought up on the Cumberland Plateau about seventy miles from Nashville. When I walked out of that house for the last time, carrying my guitar and a few clothes, I heard the door open and close behind me; he was running up beside me saying, "Dad, you can't leave without me. . . I'm going with you." And He was always my bud, from his early years, three and four years old, sitting on a stool on stage at the Opry while I went out and sang my little songs, he was always with me - where ever I happened to be at the time. I just left it all behind; the cars, the furniture, all the things you gather in an eighteen year marriage, and it felt like the end of the road. I called my Dad back in the Ozarks and he told me, "Son, it's not over, it just feels that way. . . God's got something real good for you down the road, just wait and see." It sure didn't feel like it at the time.

"Along Bledsoe Creek"
Painting by Stan Hitchcock
1982

chapter 4

Girl in the Blue Dress

"Denise! The FedEx man is here with a diamond ring!"

- 1985

The first week of December, 1984 I flew out to Anaheim, California to meet Nyhl and attend the Western Cable Television Show. This is the big annual gathering of cable biggies, medium sizers, and wannabe's. It was the first time that CMT had attended and had our own booth space on the convention floor. That year I had talked Conway Twitty into coming out and being in our booth to kinda stir up some excitement. The Show was held at the Anaheim Convention Center, adjacent to the Anaheim Hilton--right across the street from Disneyland. It was quite a convention because cable television was booming, and the cable affiliates were starting to notice us a little.

The Anaheim Hilton will always be a special place to me; that is where I met the woman that I had been looking for all my life. I didn't know it at the time, but it was what God had in store for me: a healing and a blessing. I was staying at the Anaheim Hilton on the seventh floor and as I walked out of my room one evening to go down to a reception that one of the Networks was having, I noticed a woman coming out of a room just down the hall from me. I turned and walked on to the elevator: my mind on a million matters, and not paying any attention. I entered the elevator without looking back and punched the ground floor. The elevator closed right in the face of the lady coming behind me, but it was too late to stop it, even though I did try. I went on down to the lobby, saw Nyhl and his wife Sue waiting for me, walked over and started talking. Meanwhile, the woman who missed my elevator caught another one and was just now stepping out into the lobby. Wow, I'm sorry I missed her in the elevator I thought, as she walked toward us with a beautiful smile. "Nyhl, Sue how good to see you!" They were all hugging and patting one another as I stood there and waited to be introduced. "Stan, this is Denise". Sue did the honors as I shook her hand and apologized for not holding the elevator. We stood there and chatted for a few moments, and then all had to head off to different special events. Denise was wearing a blue dress and I thought how beautiful she was as I hurried off to my meeting, vowing to follow up on this introduction and try to get to know her better. Talking later to Nyhl and Sue I found out that Denise was a vice president of a cable television PR firm and had an impressive history in the industry. She had worked with Nyhl in the Warner Qube Project in Columbus, Ohio, which was a highly respected experiment in interactive television and way before it's time. She had been in cable franchising also, and moved to California to help franchise the Los Angeles area for United Cable.

About three months later, a friend that worked with us at CMT, Mike Abney, was in California for some meetings and ran into Denise. She knew Mike, and knew that he worked with me, and she gave him her business card to bring back to me in Nashville. On the back was written, "The Girl In The Blue Dress." I was delighted when he gave me the card, and sat right down and called her. I told her I was coming out to Los Angeles soon, for some meetings, and we should get together, an idea she agreed with, then we said goodbye. In April of 1985 I checked into the Beverly Hills Hotel, made my way up to my room and called Denise at her office telling her I was in town: How about some supper tonight? That evening I slicked up some, (put on clean Levi's, and shined my boots), and went downstairs to meet Denise. I must have looked quite the hillbilly come to town in my black Levi's, black silk shirt and Pink (yeah, that's right PINK--you got a problem with that?) raw silk sport jacket, and my yellow Tony Lama's, shined up and looking good. If you have ever been inside the Beverly Hills Hotel, it's all decorated in green and pink, so I looked like I was camouflaged, special for the hotel. I stepped off the elevator and there stood the woman that I would spend the rest of my days with: Denise Thornburg. Wow, what a woman she is too. Sure, she's beautiful, but that is not what strikes you first about Denise, it's a certain glow that she seems to carry. . . a glow of goodness that is so evident that everyone who meets her senses it. I may be a hillbilly, but son, I can spot a thoroughbred when I see one, and when I stepped off that elevator in the Beverly Hills Hotel, lookin' gaudy in my hillbilly finery - and with a wounded heart that needed healing, my life changed: forever. Miss Denise was fixing to make me whole, and prove that everyone really does have a soul mate; it just takes some of us a little longer to find 'em.

What followed was a whirl-wind romance, (no, I'm not gonna give you the details of it all. What? you think I'm crazy?) After the weekend in Beverly Hills, there was another week-long convention a month later in Las Vegas for the National Cable Television Convention, (how nice that they schedule these industry events to coincide with my romance). At the end of the week in Vegas, I proposed, she accepted, I went back to Nashville, bought an engagement ring and had it FedEx'd to Hollywood, where her office was located. We were married in September of 1985 on stage at Music Village USA with all my music buddies coming and wishing us well: it was a glorious event.

We bought a log house in Sumner County with a little patch of land to keep a few horses and we had a life. . . some would say, 'bout dang time. I adopted a scripture as my daily creed: BUT THOSE WHO WAIT ON THE LORD, SHALL RENEW THEIR STRENGTH, THEY SHALL MOUNT UP WITH WINGS LIKE EAGLES, THEY SHALL RUN AND NOT BE WEARY, THEY SHALL WALK AND NOT FAINT. Isaiah 40:31, New King James Version. Most of the unhappiness in my life has been caused by my inability to wait. . . I am driven to run ahead; hey, I can do it by myself, no sweat, uh-huh. . . OK, how come you just fell on your butt then? Because, we are all basically selfish and self-centered; wanting to do it our way, like Elvis sang about, but if we will wait and be patient, really seeking the way the Lord would have us go, well then, we can be eagles: the sky's the limit. I had a real bad track record in my personal life but I was learning to wait on the Lord.

The Wedding!!!
1985

Maddoleine, Lori, Stan Jr.,
Denise, Stan, Joli, Marilyn, Big Stan

Stan, Mark Collie and Marty Stuart
Heart to Heart
1994

chapter 45

Pickin' Up Steam - That Steam Roller Rolled Right Over Me...

HITTING THE BIG TIME...1985

Meanwhile, CMT was picking up steam, starting to attract attention in the world of cable television and slowly growing as we improved the programming. The start of the second year, 1985, I started getting on the screen and asking folks to write to me and tell me what they liked and didn't like. I said, "Y'all write me, or call me at CMT, after all, this is your network and we want to play what you want to watch." Not very sophisticated audience research I guess, but man, the mail just started coming in. . . and I did exactly what I said I would do: I played what they wanted to watch. CMT was starting to touch people's lives and I was loving it.

In 1985 we had hired a fiery red-head from Texas named Rene Ray to go out across the country and sell CMT to the cable operators, and she hit the ground running. Rene loves country music so it was a joy for her to sell it. Slowly, ever so slowly, we started growing our subscriber numbers. . . two million. . . three million. . . four million. . . man, when we hit five million it was a real great feeling, and party time around headquarters. We were the only game going where you could see country videos. The Nashville Network programmed a couple of shows with videos and VJ's, but they never really took music video serious. It was good years to grow.

The investment group of Gilbert Biggers and Hall Hardaway were intensely loyal and courageous folks who had no knowledge of cable television and never intended to be long-term investors. They stepped up to the plate when it was necessary, and there would have never been a CMT without them. They asked Nyhl and myself to try to bring in a strategic partner, someone who had knowledge of the entertainment industry and could help take the network forward. Nyhl knew a guy in Colorado named James William Guercio, a semi-legendary record producer and ranch-owner who had put together the group Chicago, worked with the Beach Boys, owned Caribou Recording Studio and at one time had been a producer at CBS Records. Nyhl gave Guercio a call and he agreed to come in and meet with us, soon. Looked like we were on a roll. . . yeah, look out it don't roll right over you, son.

Early in the winter of '86, around February or so, James William Guercio came in to meet with us. Nyhl did the wining and dining bit and then brought him out to CMT's offices at Music Village, introducing him to me for an overview of the programming concept and my vision for going forward with the Network. Guercio is a small statured man, about five foot six or so, wears expensive ranchers garb, including a gray Stetson, and has a very charming personality - when he wants to turn it on. Well, he wanted to turn it on that day, and he charmed the heck out of me. We talked for hours about the creative process of cable television, about my years on The Road as a country entertainer, and about his as an old rock and roller. We hit it off good. Looking back on that first meeting now, after the years of really getting to know him, Guercio was playing me just like a fiddle: no one could stroke any better than Guercio - he had it down to an art form. He had come from pretty simple roots; growing up in a rough section of Chicago, was a child prodigy musically, got into the rock and roll thing as a teen-ager, and traveling with some of the early R&B groups. He really started making money at music in the 60's and 70's. He is a millionaire, several times over, and he didn't get that way by being the easy going guy that he wanted you to think he was: Underneath it all ran a cold streak, hard as a rock, as just about every group that ever worked with him found out. Being a trusting country boy, I played right into his hands, as I would find out the hard way just a few years down the line.

Guercio made a deal to take over the three million note from Biggers and Hardaway, put a quarter of a million dollars into the CMT operating fund, becoming our main investor in the Network, along with Telestar, a bunch of small penny stock investors and our management group. When Guercio took over the note from the Music Village investors, we made the decision to move the operation to downtown Nashville, right on Music Row. I found an old two-story house that had been made into an office complex on 18th Avenue South, and we moved from our Hendersonville location. The Music Village days were behind us: they were good years, and we had good friends that worked together getting us off the ground.

Billy Joe Shaver & Stan Hitchcock
Heart to Heart, 1988

chapter 46

Billy Joe's Lost Fingers and Bouncin' Betty's

"I been to Georgia on a fast train,
honey, I wasn't born no yesterday"
- Billie Joe Shaver

In 1986 I started a show called "Stan Hitchcock's HEART TO HEART". I felt the need for a show that would break up the steady stream of videos, and one that would be a vehicle that would show the real human side of the artists. The artists were all friends of mine so it was just friends sharing some songs, stories, and picking a couple of flat tops. It was so simple and real that people immediately took to it and started watching religiously. The mail was just starting to pour in, and I could feel it beginning to work.

I have some great memories of those early CMT and "Heart to Heart" days, some real good times spent with friends.

I was sitting under a shade tree just outside of Nashville one hot summer day in 1987, fingers kinda running over the strings of my old flat top guitar, talking to my friend Billy Joe Shaver about songs, about lost romance, about how The Road will wear you out, about. . . "Billy, how the heck did you lose your fingers, son?" Billy Joe looked down at his right hand, stretched it out in front of him and studied the two short stubs that are all that remain of his two middle fingers. "I got in an accident in a sawmill where I worked. I remember how I realized when it happened, God, I know what I'm supposed to be doin'. . . when they got cut off, I got down and gathered my fingers together and took them over to the doctor's office to see if they could put them back on. Doctor looked at 'me and said: 'Naw, man, they all mangled up from gettin' hung in the chain.' I remember there was a colored nurse there and she wanted them. . . I asked her what in the world did she want 'em for? And she said: 'Aw, I'm gonna put 'em in a jar', so my fingers are probably still sittin' up on a shelf somewhere down in Texas. . . floatin' around in a jar of vinegar, or something. After I got my fingers cut off I started playing the guitar and writing real hard, 'cause I knew that was what I was supposed to be doing." Yeah buddy, I reckon you did Billy Joe. "Old Chunk Of Coal" for John Anderson, "Honky Tonk Heroes", and a whole album full of songs that Waylon recorded, and another one of my favorite's, "I Been To Georgia On A Fast Train".

Sittin' there, kinda ruminating on Billy Joe's lost fingers, I made a remark about how he and I had seen a lot of strange things happen in this business of music, and ended the thought with, "And Billy Joe, we didn't come to town on a truck load of watermelons, no sir, we been around some." Billy Joe glanced up at me and said, "Nope, it was a truck full of cantaloupes." I could see he was serious and asked him what he was talking about, and here came another story: "Well, I had left Texas with about five dollars. I got as far as Memphis when I ran out of money and a ride. I was hitchhikin' on to Nashville when a man driving a truck full of cantaloupes stopped and gave me a ride; I had to sit in the back with all those melons. When I got to Nashville, I started knocking on doors on Music Row, trying to talk to people about my songs and they all kept looking at each other saying, "'what's that smell?'" I smelled like a cantaloupe patch for a month after that."

Billy Joe Shaver is a man who has lived some and survived to tell us about it in his music. I love him 'cause he's real, and what you see is what you get with Billy Joe. That's what is so fascinating about this world of creative people, yes, they have a special talent but inside they are just real folk, with real stories to tell.

One day, sometime in 1986, I was in the RCA Records offices on Music Row in Nashville talking with Randy Owen of Alabama;

just remembering good times, past experiences and where we came from. Randy was saying,

"Right out of college, in the July heat, I was in Myrtle Beach, South Carolina which was the proving ground for our group, Jeff Cook, Teddy Gentry, John Vartanian and myself, who later became the band "Alabama". There was a place in Myrtle Beach called 'The Bowrey', which I thought was totally unique when we found it and still later when we left it. It was a bar that probably seated, at the most, three hundred people: seat-to-seat. There was no dancing, and if you were caught dancing you were immediately escorted to the front door. Let's see, there were waiters instead of waitresses, 'cause you had to be tough, there was 'Don't Cry Joe', the singing, dancing bartender, 'Bouncin' Betty', a three-hundred pound go-go dancer; there was another girl I remember who was seven foot tall and also a go-go dancer, and still another girl named April/May who danced from the ceiling on chains. We were called "Wild Country" at the time and we played for tips. These ladies, and some other girls that we could talk into it, collected our tips in a P Pot: it was actually a real chamber pot that we passed around; people would put in dimes, nickels, quarters, they even threw in some joints, ya know, people thinking we might want to participate. They put in just everything you could imagine, from coupons to bottles of Canadian beer they'd smuggled in from Canada: it was just amazing what they would put in. We had a lot of letters and notes like, 'I'm in room 901': now, think about it, there's nine million motel rooms in Myrtle Beach. . . but above all the craziness, the people in charge let us play whatever we wanted - just as long as we played something."

Randy stared off in space, out the window of the Music Row offices, remembering, and smiling. He continued,

"I told myself that by the time I was thirty years old, if something very definite wasn't happening, in the group Alabama or whatever group I was playing with, the name, whatever. . . if something wasn't happening, I would go back to college, get my masters, possibly teach junior college and live on my farm raising cattle. That's what I wanted to do, but something happened just in the nick of time. . ."

"Yeah, Randy, I don't believe you're gonna get to do that, son, "

I said with a laugh.

Randy kinda grinned, and then turned serious, "Yeah, but I think it's important that people in the music business have other things to do. . . I mean, you know, I've had a great career, but if something happens to that, I believe there's lots of other things I can do. I don't think you should punish yourself or the public when it gets to where only fifty people come out to see you play, it's just like a baseball pitcher, there comes a time when that fast ball just don't come in there no more. . . I'm prepared for the future: if it's not happening then I'll just go back to Alabama, stay on my farm and raise cows."

It has been great to watch the group Alabama grow and prosper. . . and stay the good guys that I remember them to be. Like the time in the 70's when I played a theme park down in a gulch in Alabama, just outside of Ft. Payne, and you had to take a cable car down to the concert area. When I arrived, carrying my old Gibson and ready to do a show, I found the house band that was to back me up - called "Wild Country". Good guys then, good guys now, and the music goes on.

The first time I met Garth Brooks, his record label called me and asked me to meet Garth and listen to his songs. Garth had just been signed to Capitol Records by my friend Jim Fogelsong, one of the finest men this music business has ever been privileged enough to call its own. He didn't have a video out yet, but they wanted me to meet him. I invited Garth out to our little log cabin house in Sumner County and he arrived with his wife Sandy, his guitar and his dog. Garth had been working at a cowboy boot store in Nashville, writing his songs and waiting for his big break. When he drove up in his old pickup and got out, we shook hands, got our guitars out, sat on the patio and he started singing me his songs. I liked him immediately because he was real. He didn't come on strong at all, just natural and easy, singing one song after another that he had been writing, and telling me about growing up in Oklahoma. We spent a couple of hours together and they left, leaving me behind as a new recruit for Garth Brooks' music.

My son, Scott Austin T. Hitchcock, was born on September 25th, 1986, and I was there to receive him into my arms, squalling and bawling, bloody and wet from the birth, and a champion from day one. To really appreciate this event you have to remember that my generation of fathers waited in the waiting room, nervously pacing the floor until the Doctor came out through the swinging doors and told you what had just been born to you. Man, have things changed in the past thirty years. Denise is of the younger, modern generation of women who, several years ago, got together and said, hey, if I got to go through this passing a watermelon, then by dang the Daddy can be there to help!! I told her later, after I had recovered, that if men of my generation had known what it was really all about there would not be the overpopulation problem that there is now. But, there is nothing like that feeling of being the one the Doctor hands the baby to first, and then being the one to lay him on his mothers belly for their first meeting. Scotty looked me in the eye, just like he knew me, from the first minute. For months I had been playing my guitar and singing to him in his momma's belly, and I believe he knew my voice. Being a new Daddy at fifty was different than being one at nineteen, as I had been with my daughter Marilyn. In fact, if you remember, I wasn't even in the country for that birth: I was in Japan. But Marilyn was there when her brother Scott was born, the oldest and the youngest meeting for the first time.

I was talking to my friend Sammi Smith the other day; she knew me back in my younger days, when I was fathering my first children. I told her that I had started over and had a new young son, and was doing it all different this time. She said, "What have you learned?" I said, "To just be there for every occasion." All through my early career I was chasing that dream so hard that I managed to miss every important occasion that came up; birthdays, ballgames, graduations, parties, tooth pullings, first steps: not because I didn't want to be there, because I dang sure did, but because I was out touring the world, singing my songs, trying to make a living and raise a family on my music. I don't miss nothin' now. My priorities have definitely changed. Denise, Scotty and the rest of our precious family are my world, and after all these years, I've learned where my treasures are - and they are not inside my old guitar.

photo by Les Leverett

Keith Whitley

chapter 47

Will the Circle Be Unbroken

by and by, Lord, by and by. . .
Old traditional hymn

I first met Keith Whitley in the early years when he came in to do the Opry with Ralph Stanley. Keith and Ricky Skaggs were both young bucks working with the old master blue-grasser, and they had a great sound. Keith had gone on to his own career, signed with RCA Records in the early 80's and sung his ever-lovin' butt off on everything he did. Keith took to coming over and visiting me at CMT and I just loved him like a brother. His first video was "Miami, My Amy" and we played the fire out of it on the channel.

One day he called and said, "Hey, I want to do Heart to Heart with you." A couple of days later his manager, Jack McFadden called up and said, "Keith says you'all gonna do Heart to Heart. When you gonna do it?" We were not in production for the show then, but I planned on doing it soon as we got back. Meanwhile, Keith's popularity just blossomed, and he put out a string of great records and videos. He was definitely a video boomer, just a natural for the tube. I got so much mail for his videos: it was unbelievable. By 1987 I had started a weekly video chart and playlist that we sent to all the record labels. It was reprinted in Billboard Magazine too. It was the first video chart in existence and it brought a lot of attention to country music videos. I also started a weekly countdown show that would play on Saturday night in prime time TV featuring the top ten videos of the week. In 1987 I become the very first music video programmer to list the songwriter, publisher, and video producer at the end of each video. I believe in celebrating the creators, and I'm proud that listing the credits is still being done today. We now had seven million, five hundred thousand subscribers, and we were into the latter half of 1987.

In October of 1987 I called Keith Whitley and said, "Hey, let's go down to the Ryman Auditorium and do a Heart to Heart." We set the date and I called Opryland to get permission to go into the old Opry House. The Ryman had not been reconditioned then and had been closed up for a while, but they let us come in. The camera caught Keith and myself walking down the street outside the Ryman and followed us inside. We leaned against one of the old wooden church pews and just re-lived a lot of the good times we both remembered in that old building. Keith was still shining from his wedding to Lori Morgan and they had born a son, whom he was mighty proud of. It was a wonderful Heart to Heart, one of the favorite times I have ever spent with one of my friends on the tube. At the end of the show he told me about a new album he was working on. He said that looking at that old Ryman stage reminded him of all his heroes that had stood on that stage; Hank, Bill Monroe, and Lefty. He said, "Lefty was always my hero and I always wanted to cut one of his songs, but I never have until this new album. Mary Martin, at RCA, called me and said she liked the old Lefty Frizzell song, "I Never Go Around Mirrors", but she wished it had another verse, 'cause it only had one verse and a chorus. Well, of course Lefty is dead, but he co-wrote the song with Whitey Shafer, so I thought it was worth a shot. I called Whitey up and he agreed to write another verse. When he called me back a couple of days later and read me the new verse, well, I just cried on the phone it was so pretty. The day of the recording session, and I know this is going to sound strange to some people, I went out to the cemetery where Lefty is buried, found his tombstone and I stood beside it and recited the new verse. A couple of hours later I recorded it in the studio; Lefty's brother Allen Frizzell sang harmony on it and sounded just like Lefty, man, I've got chill bumps now just talking about it." As Keith was telling his story, my mind was going back in time, and I remembered another time, and another group of friends, and the same song.

It was a special night, in the early 70's, there had been a big package show at the Auditorium in Atlanta, after which a bunch of the folks gathered in my motel room just to come down after the performance high. I was sitting on the lumpy bed in the corner watching and listening as Lefty Frizzell picked my guitar and sang a song he had just written with Whitey Shafer called "I Never Go Around Mirrors". Over in the other corner of the room Bobby Bare was sitting, deep in thought, staring through the cigarette smoke that filled the room in lazy layers, like clouds on a dark summer sky. Leaning against the wall, over by the door, Jack Greene was deeply lost in the song, and stretched out on the other bed, Jeannie Sealy was listening, with her eyes closed, scarcely breathing. It was a special moment and I thought, "Hitchcock, this is good, isn't it?" Indeed it was good--taking the music the way it was intended, straight from the source, raw, uncut, real. Just a short time later, Lefty died in Nashville: wrung out, used up, and burnt down, with nothing left to give. He had sung it all up, and gone on. That song, "I Never Go Around Mirrors", was one of his last recordings. Little did I know it would also be one of Keith's last recordings.

Lefty Frizzell

Stan and Michael Johnson during the CMT years
1988

chapter 48

A Banner Year for CMT

*Feuding, fussin' and a fightin'
all around the boardroom*
CMT 1988

Early in 1988, around February I reckon, Denise and I found out we were going to have another baby. When she came home and told me, it was one of the happiest days I can ever remember. I had no idea life could be this good.

1988 was a banner year for CMT, we moved up to eight million subscribers and we also gained a new investor. Telstar had sold a bunch of their properties to a man in New York by the name of Robert F. X. Sillerman, one of the pieces was their interest in CMT. Sillerman is a huge conglomerate of communication and entertainment properties now, but then he was mostly radio stations. Our board of directors was now a three-man board, Guercio, Sillerman and myself. I was senior vice president in charge of the Nashville operation: there was no president, and Guercio and Sillerman were the co-chairmen of the corporation. I completely ran the Network, with no interference whatsoever from the other two members who were content to come into town about once a quarter for board meetings. One reason they didn't hamper me was this: They hated one another. Yeah buddy, ain't that a hoot? Two bigger egos have never lived: they fought each other on every hand, lawyers going back and forth. I had to break up huge arguments at the board meetings, both of them coming to me to try to put me in the middle, but somehow I stayed above the fray.

One fray I couldn't stay above was the tension between Nyhl and Guercio. It had been building almost from the time that Guercio signed on as an investor, had culminated in early 1988 with the removal of Nyhl Henson as an officer and member of the board, and ended up in a subsequent lawsuit that was raging between the two. I have studied the history of it all and dang if I know how it all started. I was so busy running the network and Nyhl was in California, Guercio in Colorado. I tried my best to keep out of it, but of course, it took its toll. In mid-1988 I was diagnosed with hypertension (high blood pressure) and I've always believed it was brought about by the fighting and tension between the Nyhl, Guercio, and Sillerman. You got to understand that the business was doing great, value being added to the investment every day with new subscribers coming on. Television Ratings looked fantastic, and the Network was really taking country music to a vast new audience: all without ignoring the wonderful audience that had been with country music through the early years. I was now getting about a thousand to fifteen hundred letters a week from the fan base of faithful viewers that we had behind us. The way the pie was split up was Guercio and Sillerman had about forty percent each and the rest was scattered among the smaller investors. Guercio had CMT repay the initial two hundred and fifty thousand he'd initially put in, (with interest), so now all he had at risk was the three million dollar note to Biggers and Hardaway. Sillerman actually had put about a million and a half in cold cash into CMT for operating costs in addition to whatever he had paid Telstar for the stock. Meanwhile, I was starting to operate this network from cash flow and my crew of about fifteen employees was doing a heck of a job of running a network in spite of the intense fighting among the other principals.

Illustration by Stan Hitchcock
1982

Stan Hitchcock & Ferlin Husky 2005
Singing "Wings of a Dove" at
Missouri Country Music Hall of Fame Induction

chapter 49

A Room at the Top of the Stairs - Hardly Used

Ferlin Husky Recording 1960

"Where No One Stands Alone"
Stan's favorite song
- written by Mosie Lister

In September of 1988 my son Dennis Walker T. Hitchcock, called DW by his family almost from the first day, was born. It was a more difficult birth than Scotty's and they had a little trouble getting him to start breathing on his own, but finally I heard that wonderful cry of a baby announcing himself to the world. We took him home to his brother Scott and his big brother Stan the 2nd. His big sister, Marilyn, had helped bring him into the world, right beside me in the delivery room. It was a wonderful time.

DW was a perfect baby; beautiful, bright eyed, with a grin that would just melt your heart. We couldn't wait to take him to Wisconsin to see his Grandparents, Duane and Marcella Thornburg, and his Aunty Em and Uncle Mark. Two days before Thanksgiving we loaded up the van with Scott, Stan the II, Dennis Walker, Denise and myself and headed off for Prairie du Chien, Wisconsin, where the Thornburgs live. All the family was going to be home to see the new baby. When we got there the house was just bursting with love and pride and we looked forward to a wonderful visit.

Thanksgiving Day dawned cold and clear and the whole house smelled of the wonderful smells of Thanksgiving dinner. Denise and I spent the morning playing with DW and sharing him with the whole family like the treasure he was. Finally, just before dinner, DW went to sleep on my shoulder and I carried him in and laid him in the crib in the bedroom, went back downstairs and we all had Thanksgiving dinner. After the meal I went back upstairs to check on DW. As I walked over to his crib I noticed he was laying unusually still, I picked him up: he wasn't breathing.

I only remember bits and pieces of the next few days: there is a black hole there and it comes from the hole in my heart. Dennis Walker T. Hitchcock died during Thanksgiving dinner on Thanksgiving Day in 1988. We buried him in the Thornburg family cemetery that looks out over the Mississippi River.

We left Prairie du Chien and just started driving, aimlessly, I don't remember now how we got there, but we ended up in Hot Springs, Arkansas; a place where we had often gone to get away. My office called the Arlington Hotel in Hot Springs and told them we were coming and what the situation was, so when we got there they just took us in, gave us a suite of rooms and took care of us for a week until we could get enough of our minds back to even function. I will always love them for that.

The hardest thing we had to face was going back to our house without our baby. Peggy Hall, our friend and DW's godmother, went in, packed up all his little things and put them away, and we came back home.

SIDS, Sudden Infant Death Syndrome, is the cruelest nightmare a parent can face, because there is no way to reason it or explain it. You cannot get over the WHY. I barely remember standing outside the hospital in Prairie du Chien screaming at the sky, "WHY. . . WHY!" But, there is no why: just an emptiness that never goes away. Our baby cannot be dead, he's not even sick, but, he is dead, no why, just is.

I couldn't go back to the office for a long time, I don't know how long now, maybe a month. . .maybe longer. But when I went back, finally, and was sitting there trying to function, the phone would ring and it would be Keith Whitley, somewhere out on the road pulling into some pay phone to call me at CMT. "Stan, I just want you to know I'm thinking about you and I love you man." My friend Skip Ewing did the same, and my buddy Ronnie Reno checked on me every day, along with Ray Pillow and a lot of others. Friends just do for friends. . . that's the way it is.

Six months later, on May 9th, 1989, I was sitting in my office at CMT reading my viewer mail and the phone rang. I picked it up and it was Jack McFadden, Keith Whitley's manager and one of my best friends. He was crying, and it was hard to understand him - but then I understood, "He's dead Stan, Keith is dead." Keith Whitley, who I didn't even know had a problem, who everyone thought had the world by the tail; this kind-hearted friend who cared for everyone else and worried about their problems, had died of an alcohol overdose. He had been found that morning at home alone while Lori was touring on The Road. I felt all the grief wash over me once again as I wept for my lost friend.

1989 is still kinda like a blur, I can't explain it, but it is. I guess CMT kinda ran itself a lot of the time, and still it was growing and it was successful. I just don't remember much of it.

People grieve in different ways: Denise joined a SIDS support group, but I couldn't go tell strangers my story and listen to theirs. I just wanted to be left alone and blot it out. As much as it hurt me, it must have been twice as bad for Denise: a mother's grief is just unbearable, and only a mother can understand.

There are several of my friends in the music business that have lost children: Jan Howard, a son in the Viet Nam war; Ferlin Husky, a son; Bobby Bare, a daughter; Willie Nelson, a son; Johnny Carver, a son; my friend, the late, Gail Talley, who was married to the great record producer Jerry Kennedy lost a son, and wrote me a precious letter when DW died that I will always cherish; Helen Cornelius, a son; Ernest Tubb lost a baby; Cal Smith lost a son in a tragic car accident; George Strait lost a daughter; and Eddie Rabbitt lost a child to a rare disease. He would call and talk to me, helping me through the black days. With all my heart I love these people and I know they understand.

Stan, Denise and Scott
1996

chapter 50

A Crossroad or a Dead End?

WELL BOYS AND GIRLS, LET'S GET THIS STUFF LOADED UP. . . and head on back to Nashville. . . I've just been sold out.
- Stan Hitchcock to his television crew, The Peach Festival, Gaffney, South Carolina. August 1990.

1990 was a banner year for CMT, we reached the ten million subscriber mark and an independent audience survey, reported in R & R magazine confirmed that we had finally broken the demographic barrier that country music and it's industry had always aspired to reach. In the eighteen to thirty-four year old viewer demographic, country music television (CMT) was beating the socks off of The Nashville Network, and now the recording industry was aware of it. All the years of trying to convince people that what we were doing was making a difference, was now proven with research data, and proving to be very strong. R & R magazine was a highly respected trade journal, avidly read by all the record Industry and the radio industry. I was very proud of what my team had accomplished; we had done it with almost no major funding, scratching it out as best we could, but letting the music and the artistry guide us, and letting the love of the music be our driving force. It really was for the music, folks, and that's a fact.

The tension between Guercio and Sillerman was almost unbearable in the year of 1990. I went to New York early in the winter of '90 and spent three days with Sillerman, trying to get some kind of peace, and then went out to Colorado and spent three days at the Caribou Ranch with Guercio talking and soothing, trying to be a peacemaker, but to no avail.

In March of 1990 I told Guercio that I believed we should make a strategic alliance with Group W, and The Gaylord folks in an effort to try to take the Network forward in this new decade. I arranged a meeting with Bud Wendell, the head of Gaylord, and proposed that we try to form an alliance that would let Group W market both of our networks to the cable industry. Gaylord could put some investment money into CMT and take some equity that would grow with the network. We could operate them with our separate management and it would be good for the whole music industry.

Bud Wendell is a nice man and he listened with interest as I gave my pitch; we parted with the promise to both think about the deal.

I called Guercio and told him I believed it was something that, in the long term, could be worked out. Then I went back to running the Network.

I was starting a new series called The CMT Roadshow: a series of concerts that would be held in major theme parks and at festivals across the country. The first one was in May at Busch Gardens in Virginia. I booked Charlie Daniels Band, Restless Heart, Wild Rose, and Ronnie Reno and the Reno Brothers. It was a big success: Busch Gardens paid for all the expenses, including the television production expense for the promotion on the network, and CMT got original programming for an hour special.

In June I took a production crew out to Santa Maria, California and shot a special on the Gary Leffew Bull Riding School. This was a beautiful event which we captured with our television camera, despite the fact that one of our camera operators got knocked down and stomped by a mad bull, he still kept the camera going - and got a great shot.

I had a call from Jim Cudd, the man in charge of the Peach Festival in Gaffney, South Carolina, and we made a deal to bring The Roadshow over there with The Reno Brothers, Shenendoah and Garth Brooks.

Guercio was acting kinda funny and I couldn't figure it out. We had a board of directors meeting in July and the topic kept coming up about how much ownership of the network I had been given, by verbal agreement with the investors, for my so called "sweat equity" of being responsible for the success of the network. The amount was solidly stated and agreed upon in the board meeting, just as it had been before, and we got on with other business.

What I didn't know was that Guercio was secretly meeting behind closed doors with lawyers, brokers, Gaylord and Group W making plans to sell the network. He had sent me in to break the ice, got a favorable report and went after it.

Hey, that's the way the big boys play; I know it better than anyone, but it doesn't make it any easier to swallow when you're on the receiving end of the castor oil. I had no idea that the deal was being made until that night in Gaffney. Guercio and Sillerman are extremely wealthy men, and I helped make them even wealthier, but I had to scrap for my little portion - let me tell you.

I drove back to Nashville and went right to the lawyer's office where Guercio was waiting in a conference room. He got right to the point, and all the friendship, good feelings and charm were gone. They were selling CMT to Gaylord and Group W and they needed my signature for the agreement. I'll never forget Guercio looking me in the eye and asking how much equity I thought I had. I repeated the amount that we had always agreed on and he said, "Do you have anything in writing on that?" I said that the corporate records would reflect our agreement. They called a board meeting and with Sillerman, teleconferencing on the phone, the three man board voted, and wouldn't you know it--the vote carried majority in favor of the sale. I had one thing to say to Guercio and Sillerman at the end of that last board meeting, "Fellas, you are making a big mistake, in eight or ten years this network could be worth a hundred million dollars and you could own most of it." They both kinda chuckled at my optimism and ended the board meeting.

The lawyers came in and the pressure was on. Now, Stan, sign this paper. No, I don't believe so. I'm going home. I'm tired; I've just lost a network that I've given six hard years to. . . No, I'm not gonna sign anything now. I'm outa here. This started the intense pressure from the lawyers, and Guercio to sign the agreement and take their little offering: like they were really doing me a favor. The buzz was all over the Row about the pending sale and the stalemate between myself and Guercio. I'll have to say that Sillerman never said a word or put any pressure on me at all--it all came from Guercio--he was playing hard ball.

I resigned from the board of directors of CMT, resigned as the operating head of the network, and got my lawyer involved. Rush Hicks, my attorney, is a savvy music guy and he was a jewel. The thing is, I was walking wounded: I didn't have the resources to fight Guercio and I had already seen how cold he could be in his fight with Nyhl Henson.

Denise and I prayed about the direction we should go; we decided it wasn't worth a ten year fight and wasted years of resentment to pursue what we knew was our right. Our lawyer made our demands and we just sat out at the old log cabin and waited.

Finally, in November, my lawyer called and said, "OK, it's done. Guercio has accepted your terms, and I'm going by the lawyers office and pick up your check." It was a small victory, but at least it let us get on with our life. I learned a lot about people from that transaction, and the different needs that drive them to do the things that they do to other people.

All the trade publications spelled out the sale: Thirty-six million dollars for the sale of the network that we had worked so hard to birth. Guercio walked away a mighty proud man, but shoot, he was proud before that. He was really proud about the extra one million dollars he and Sillerman received as network consultants, although as far as I know they never got to consult anyone. But what did they care? They had just sold a network in which they had almost nothing invested for the big amount of thirty-six million, yeah buddy, what a deal.

Gaylord took possession of CMT in January 1991 and they did a great job of carrying the network forward. I have nothing but praise for the value they added to the assets and the subscriber growth they achieved. CMT is a world force in our country music and I'm proud of it.

I had to chuckle the other day when eight years later CMT sold to CBS for somewhere between three hundred and five hundred million dollars. Now friends, THAT'S a deal.

Painting by Stan Hitchcock
1982

Stan and Denise's home
"Desha Creek Farm" 2006
Sumner County, Tennessee

chapter 51

They Shall Mount Up with Wings Like Eagles. . . Isiah 40:31

STEP UP TO THE MIKE AND SING SON, THEY WANT TO HEAR SOME MORE. . .
Roy Acuff to Stan Hitchcock. . .
The Opry Encore that almost was. . . 1962

December 29th, 1990. Denise and I were in Prairie du Chien, Wisconsin and we were walking along the street talking and trying to figure out what comes next in our lives. We both were kinda scarred up and scabbed over from the past two years, but we were learning to trust more in God's leading and he was bringing us along pretty good. I was walking along with my head down, running it all over and over, like a television re-run, when Denise said softly, "You have to start another network, it's what you do Stan. People love the programming that you give them because you care, and they know it. There are a lot of good things happening out there in the heartland of America; things that will encourage people as well as entertain them. You have to start another network--but not just another video channel like CMT you've already done that. The next one needs to be different." I gazed out across the Mississippi river bottom, my eyes lifting to the high bluffs on the western side, where, just barely, way in the distance, I could make out an eagle riding on the wind off the bluffs, soaring over the heartland.

Well, that's another story and it may take a while

to tell it, old friend. Meanwhile, hey, I appreciate you taking the time to go the distance with me. It would have been a long road without ya'll to travel it with me. Let's get together sometime and listen to some good Country music and tell a story or two. I reckon you've heard most of mine--it's your turn next time.

The first singer/songwriter was David, way back in the Old Testament. He wrote in Psalms: "Yea, though I walk in the valley of the shadow, I will fear no evil. . . Thy Rod and Thy Staff they comfort me. Surely goodness and mercy shall follow me all the days of my life, and I will dwell in the House of the Lord. Forever."

Thank you God, for that promise; I'm in the forever part now.

Partners in BlueHighways Television
Ronnie Reno and Stan
sitting on those same steps at Wynnewood
20 years later in 2006

EPILOGUE

OK, OK, IT'S THAT TIME IN THE BOOK WHERE YOU GET TO UPDATE THE READERS! STAND BY. . . QUIET ON THE SET, CUE STAN. . . STAN. . . HEY, WHERE'S STAN? OH, I SEE, HE'S DRIFTED OFF AND IS ASLEEP OVER BY THE BIG OAK TREE BY THE CREEK. . .

CAMERA ZOOMS IN TO 2006 AND THE HILLBILLY, NOW MUCH OLDER IF NOT WISER, BRINGS YOU, THE READER, UP TO DATE.

Stan, Denise and family today

Since I started writing this book, my life has gone on; my wife Denise and I, and a small group of our friends have started a new television network called BlueHighways TV. We have moved to a small farm in Sumner County, Tennessee not far from the Cumberland River, on a small stream called Deshea Creek that runs right in front of our old farm house. The old farm house was built in 1920 and it has the old fashioned front porch running all the way across the front. It holds the three rocking chairs and the old porch swing, just like Grandma's house had when I was a kid. God has blessed us so much with family and friends and we are eternally grateful for His mercy and love.

I got up this morning with the sunrise, brewed a pot of real coffee (with an extra scoop, for that fighting edge), walked down to the creek that runs in front of our old farm house, and reflected on the beauty that God has created for us to enjoy. I went back in the house and got dressed in a fresh laundered pair of Levi's which seem to fit the worn seat of my rusty old '57 Chevy Pickup just about right as I drive the two lane backroads to my office located in a small town in the Tennessee mountains.

This is how I choose to live and it may account for the driving force that makes me so determined to provide some good programming and entertainment for the friends and neighbors around the country. BlueHighways creates this good programming and entertainment by traveling on the backroads of America to find the traditional lifestyles, music, art and culture still flourishing in the heart of the American people.

I am a product of the 50's and 60's, born and raised in the very center of the United States, with small towns, family farms, old country churches and neighbors helping neighbors. These are flag waving, God fearing people whose truth and beauty grow side by side with mountains, valleys, prairies and waterways - and they make up the interior and heart of this great country.

Well, it may sound a little old fashioned and out of step, but we want to be marching to the sound of a different drummer 'cause the music and programming played all across the spectrum of television right now is mighty hard for us to dance to. When I was growing up the old road maps, all the backroads and small towns, were always inked in blue; and since my passion has always been exploring the backroads that wend through the heart of America, we named our network BlueHighways TV.

I come from people that are the "regular folk" of America. We may not be "cutting edge" or followers of the latest trends, but we are a people of resilience and fortitude. We believe that a job worth doing is worth doing well. We're tough and we stick to it - and we're tougher than whet leather - 'cause you have to be tough to survive on a rocky hillside farm and raise a family, or to work in the factories of mid-America.

I'm "regular folk", conditioned to survive in hard times and give thanks in good times. I'm a believer in keeping your word, even when it hurts; loving your neighbor even when their dog barks all night; making your home a gathering place for the teen age friends of your community and watching out for them just like your own children; of cooking for your friends after church on Sunday; and of wading the spring fed creek in the summertime looking for that world class Smallmouth Bass that you just know lives in that next blue hole under the shade of that big oak tree.

I believe that prayer works, faith is a motivator, and ultimately hard work gets it done. I'm "regular folk", the "grassroots" of America, Scandinavian blood from Minneapolis; Scot Irish from Appalachia and the Ozark Mountains; German from Guttenburg, Iowa and the hill country of Texas; Hispanic from California; and Blacks from the Mississippi Delta and the Chicago tenements. I'm the melting pot and the bread basket; and I'm the first to volunteer for the rough jobs and unpopular wars that keep this nation free.

Yes, just "regular folk" that makes up the quilt work of cultures that call that great stretch of land from New York and Los Angeles home. It is this great mass of "regular folk" that is being ignored by present day television. We are small business owners; we own our property and it is paid for; or it was until we took out another mortgage to send the kids to college. We don't ask a whole lot of our government except to be left alone in pursuit of our independence and freedom. We are cable, dish or direct TV users and we keep hoping that someone out there in television heaven will send us some programming that speaks to us; the "regular folk". We are loyal and support good family programming.

I have been involved in the creation process of television since 1962, first as a performer on the, "The Stan Hitchcock Show" and then with (CMT), developing and running that Network from 1984 to 1991. Later, I founded and operated Americana Television Network (ATN) from 1992 to 1995 when it was sold to Liberty Media.

Through this lengthy process of learning and defining just what the "regular folk" wanted to see out there in television land, I developed the concept that we follow today: "Good, grassroots, down to earth, back to basics, genuine and uplifting programming that speaks to folks of integrity and commitment." We "encourage as well as entertain." We are unashamedly "patriotic and spiritual".

We believe that good music "soothes the soul, and gives comfort in the hard times." We believe in the "folk art" of America as an expression of the creative spirit, so alive and vibrant. We love the "folk storytelling" that has preserved the lifestyle of our pioneer ancestors in Appalachia and the American West. We believe that there are "good things happening in America" that deserve to be told and celebrated. We have the hard rock determination to bring to the "regular folk", television that is good and solid in its content, beautiful to behold, and speaks to them in the language of family, neighbor and friend.

Stan, Moe Bandy
and Band
Heart to Heart 1994

Stan doing a show in
Washington DC
for the Congressional
Club at the
Smithsonian 1969

Stan and Red Steagall
Heart to Heart 1994

SECTION V

Some of My Songs

Memories of a Life That Used to Be

Illustration by Stan Hitchcock

I remember when I was about twelve years old, going into the drug store of the little town of Pleasant Hope, Missouri. It was so exciting when I would find that month's copy of "Country Song Roundup", which had the words to all the country music songs - along with pictures of the artists. I couldn't wait to get back to the house, grab my guitar and start singing those songs: following the words and maybe making up a melody to go with it. Shoot, it didn't matter whether I knew the song or not: I was making music!

Still today, the creators of those words and music are my heroes. They sparked my life-long love affair with music. Through the years of my music career I have had the joy of putting some words together and expressing my feelings in song. It's no big deal, but it does give an insight into my musical soul. I've included a few of my songs for your consideration; and even though it's hard to dance to words on paper, give it a try anyway. I would like to think someone, somewhere has my book laying open on the mantle or coffee table, and they are dancing to my songs.

"Have You Got A Heart"
by Stan Hitchcock

Have you got a heart?
Do you have a soul?
What about your life. . .
Is it out of control?
Are you alone and aching..
You don't know what to do.
Well, I've got a friend
for you.

Have you got a heart?
Do I see a tear?

What about your mind..
Is it full of fear?
And are you needing someone
To put your trust into?
Well, I've got a friend
and He loves you.
Chorus:
He will take your heart.
He will cleanse your soul.
He'll straighten out your life.. . .
Just give Him control.

And you will be free,
Your soul will be at rest.
A Life that's full of joy,
Yes, you will be blessed.

He will heal the ache inside you,
You'll never be alone.
'Cause you've got a friend,
Yes, you've got a friend.
You've got a friend. . .
His name Is
Jesus.

Stan Hitchcock

I wrote this from such a personal perspective of healing and faith. To attempt to live without a personal, daily walk with God is just beyond my comprehension. I wouldn't last a day without His loving guidance.

"Guitar, My Old Friend"

Stan Hitchcock and Ronnie Reno

Well, guitar, here I am old friend,
back to sing some blues, again,
ain't it funny, I always come
right back to you.
This heart has been a fool once more,
stood and watched her walk out that door,
Well, guitar, it's just you and me,
tonight.

Most all my life you've been around,
you've watched me go up and down,
but this time, I'm 'bout as low as I can go
So, guitar, let me hold you tight
help me make it through another night
guitar, no one else would understand

Chorus:
For we've traveled so far,
chasin' that elusive star,
But, niether one of us
ever dreamed it would end
like this.

So, guitar, let me hold you tight,
help me make it through another night
ain't it funny, I always come
right back to you

Yes, old friend,
I always come
right back
to you.
© HitPro Music
1984

A song that Reno and I wrote about our guitars, back in the years when a guitar was about all I had left. Ronnie Reno has been my friend and brother-in-music for so many years and through so many experiences that it is hard to imagine how I made it before I knew him.

"My Ozark Mountain Valley Home"

Stan Hitchcock

Acuff-Rose Publishing, 1972

Sunrise through the mountains
has always been a special time
of day for me
Early breezes blowing
bob white quail 'a calling
In the meadows free.
Cattle standing round the barn
waiting for my Daddy
to come and feed,
While ole traveler's barking
by the creek
starting out another day
with something treed.

Chorus:
In my Ozark Mountain Valley Home
memories of a life that used to be
My Ozark Mountain Valley Home
those boyhood days
are calling out to me
Waking up each morning
to the smell of biscuits cooking
on an old wood stove
Mama calling up the stairway
come and get it quick, son
'fore it all gets cold.
Sitting half asleep
on a milking stool
thinking of those places
so far away
Never dreaming that in later years
I'd be dreaming of this valley
wishing I had stayed
Chorus:
My Ozark Mountain Valley Home
Memories of a life that used to be
My Ozark Mountain Valley Home
Those boyhood days are calling out to me

"Cause sunrise through the Mountains
has always been a special time
of day for me.

(a song I dreamed, one homesick night, in 1972, and got up and wrote it down, as fast as I could write, words and melody.)

For a complete list of Music, and Television product
for family entertainment, write to us at:

HITCHCOCK ENTERPRISES, INC.
111 Shivel Drive
HENDERSONVILLE, TENNESSEE 37075
PHONE: 615-264-3292
www.HitchcockCountry.com

photo by Les Leverett

We will gladly send you a catalog of our "Heart to Heart" library, containing great music and stories from the finest musicians and singers that ever threw a guitar around their shoulder, stepped up to a mike and opened their heart and souls with a song.

photos from Heart to Heart

Leroy Van Dyke
1993

Sammi Smith
1994

Bill Anderson
1994

Red Foley

Fruit Jar Drinkers

photo by Les Leverett

1964

photo by Brenda McClearen

2006

Music up, stage lights down,
single spot on singer, big finish...

...to be continued.